More praise for
NOTES FROM A SMALL ISLAND

"A valentine to 'this small, enchanted island' . . . a journey into the British psyche and the heartland of its inhabitants . . . Bryson extrapolates from his experiences a deeper understanding of what makes Britain tick . . . He honors a hallowed English tradition: poking fun."

—*Newsday*

"A splendid travelogue . . . that is part valedictory journey and part love letter to Britain and the British."

—*The Sunday Telegraph* (London)

"Immensely entertaining . . . Bryson's trenchant, witty, and detailed observations on a variety of towns and villages will delight Anglophiles."

—*Publishers Weekly*

"An engaging, once-over-lightly account . . . Bryson is a good companion, and an observant one, with a bemused eye for the zany."

—*The New York Times Book Review*

"Sparkling . . . memorable . . . a singular and engaging travel book . . . Readers should be charmed, amused and enlightened."

—*Arizona Daily Star*

"An enchanting book . . . The narrative flows like a mournful last walk through a much-loved home . . . When Bryson goes for the kill he is unstoppable."

—*The Independent* (London)

Also by Bill Bryson

A DICTIONARY OF TROUBLESOME WORDS
THE LOST CONTINENT
THE MOTHER TONGUE
NEITHER HERE NOR THERE
MADE IN AMERICA

BILL BRYSON

Notes from a Small Island

HARPER **PERENNIAL**

HARPER **PERENNIAL**

This book was originally published in Great Britain in 1995 by Doubleday, a division of Transworld Publishers Ltd.

A hardcover edition of this book was published in 1996 by William Morrow and Company, Inc.

HarperCollins books may be purchased for educational, business, or sales promotional use. For information please write: Special Markets Department, Harper-Collins Publishers, 10 East 53rd Street, New York, NY 10022.

First Avon edition published 1997.

First Bard edition published 1998.

Reprinted in Perennial 2001.

Map illustration by David Cook

The Library of Congress has catalogued the hardcover edition as follows:
Bryson, Bill
  Notes from a small island / Bill Bryson.
    p. cm.
  ISBN 0-688-14725-9
  1. England—Civilization—20th century.   2. England—Description and travel.   3. Bryson, Bill—Journeys—England. I. Title.
DA566.4.B79 1996   95-43437
914.104'859—dc20   CIP

ISBN-10: 0-380-72750-1 (pbk.)
ISBN-13: 978-0-380-72750-6 (pbk.)

07 08 09 RRD 50 49 48 47 46 45 44 43 42 41

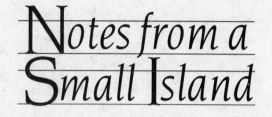

Notes from a Small Island

chapter
I

There are certain idiosyncratic notions that you quietly come to accept when you live for a long time in Britain. One is that British summers used to be longer and sunnier. Another is that the England soccer team shouldn't have any trouble with Norway. A third is the idea that Britain is a big place. This last is easily the most intractable.

If you mention in the pub that you intend to drive from, say, Surrey to Cornwall, a distance that most Americans would happily go to get a taco, your companions will puff their cheeks, look knowingly at each other, and blow out air as if to say, "Well, now, *that's* a bit of a tall order," and then they'll launch into a lively and protracted discussion of whether it's better to take the A30 to Stockbridge and then the A303 to Ilchester, or the A361 to Glastonbury via Shepton Mallet. Within minutes the conversation will plunge off into a level of detail that leaves you, as a foreigner, swiveling your head in quiet wonderment.

"You know that lay-by outside Warminster, the one with the grit box with the broken handle?" one of them will say. "*You* know, just past the turnoff for Little Puking but before the B6029 mini-roundabout."

At this point, you find you are the only person in the group not nodding vigorously.

"Well, about a quarter of a mile past there, not the first left turning but the second one, there's a lane between two hedgerows—they're mostly hawthorn but with a little hazel mixed in. Well, if you follow that road past the reservoir and under the railway bridge, and take a sharp right at the Buggered Ploughman—"

"Nice little pub," somebody will interject—usually, for some reason, a guy in a bulky cardigan. "They do a decent pint of Old Toe-jam."

"—and follow the dirt track through the army firing range and round the back of the cement works, it drops down onto the B3689 Ram's Dropping bypass. It saves a good three or four minutes and cuts out the rail crossing at Great Shagging."

"Unless, of course, you're coming from Crewkerne," someone else will add knowledgeably. "Now, if you're coming from Crewkerne . . ."

Give two or more men in a pub the names of any two places in Britain and they can happily fill hours. Wherever it is you want to go, the consensus is generally that it's just about possible as long as you scrupulously avoid Okehampton, the North Circular in London, and the Severn Bridge westbound between the hours of 3 P.M. on Friday and 10 A.M. on Monday, except bank holidays when you shouldn't go anywhere at all. "Me, I don't even walk to the corner shop on bank holidays," some little guy on the margins will chirp up proudly, as if by staying at home in Clapham he has for years cannily avoided a notorious bottleneck at Scotch Corner.

Eventually, when the intricacies of B-roads, contraflow black-spots, and good places to get a bacon sandwich have been discussed so thoroughly that your ears have begun to seep blood, one member of the party will turn to you and idly ask over a sip of beer when you were thinking of setting off. When this happens, you must never answer truthfully and say, in that kind of dopey way of yours, "Oh, I don't know, about ten, I suppose," because they'll all be off again.

"Ten o'clock?" one of them will say and try to back his head off his shoulders. "As in ten o'clock A.M.?" He'll make a face. "Well, it's entirely up to you, *of course,* but personally if *I* was planning to be in Cornwall by three o'clock tomorrow, I'd have left yesterday."

"*Yesterday?*" someone else will say, chortling softly at this misplaced optimism. "I think you're forgetting, Colin, that it's half term for schools in North Wiltshire and West Somerset this week. It'll be murder between Swindon and Warminster. No, you want to have left a week last Tuesday."

"And there's the Great West Steam Rally and Tractor Pull at Little Dribbling this weekend," somebody from across the room will add, strolling over to join you because it's always pleasant to bring bad motoring news. "There'll be three hundred and seventy-five thousand cars all converging on the Little Chef roundabout at Upton Dupton. We once spent eleven days in a tailback there, and that was just to get out of the car park. No, you want to have left when you were still in your mother's womb, or preferably while you were spermatozoa, and even then you won't find a parking space beyond Bodmin."

Once, when I was younger, I took all these alarming warnings to heart. I went home, reset the alarm clock, roused the family at four to protests and general consternation, and had everyone bundled into the car and on the road by five. As a result, we were in Newquay in time for breakfast and had to wait around for seven hours before the holiday park would let us have one of its wretched chalets. And the worst of it was that I'd only agreed to go there because I thought the town was called Nookie and I wanted to stock up on postcards.

The fact is that the British have a totally private sense of distance. This is most visibly seen in the shared pretense that Britain is a lonely island in the middle of an empty green sea. Of course, the British are all aware, in an abstract sort of way, that there is a substantial landmass called Europe nearby and that from time to time it is necessary to go over there to give old Jerry a drubbing or have a holiday in the sun, but it's not nearby in any meaningful sense in the way that, say, Disney World is. If your concept of world geography was shaped entirely by the content of British newspapers and television, you would conclude that America must be about where Ireland is, that France and Germany lie roughly alongside the Azores, that Australia occupies a hot zone somewhere in the region of the Middle East, and that pretty much all the other sovereign states are either mythical (e.g., Burundi, El Salvador, Mongolia, and Bhutan) or can only be reached by spaceship. Consider the acres of news space in Britain devoted to marginal American figures like Oliver North, Lorena Bobbitt, and O. J. Simpson, and compare that with *all* the news reported in any year from Scandinavia, Austria, Switzerland, Greece, Portugal, and Spain and you will see what I mean. It's crazy really. If there is a political crisis in Italy or a nuclear spill in Karlsruhe, it gets maybe eight inches on an inside page. But if some woman in Shitkicker, West Virginia, cuts off her husband's dick and flings it out the window in a fit of pique, it's second lead on the *Nine O'clock News* and *The Sunday Times* is mobilizing its investigative unit. You figure it.

I can remember, when I first moved to Bournemouth, on England's south coast, fiddling with the car radio and being astounded at how many of the stations it picked up were in French, then consulting an atlas and being no less astounded to realize that I was closer to Cherbourg than I was to London. I mentioned this at work the next day and most of my colleagues refused to believe it. Even when I showed them on a map, they frowned doubtfully and said things like "Well, yes, it may be closer in a strict *physical* sense," as if I were splitting hairs and that really a whole new concept of distance was required once you waded into the English Channel—and of course to that extent they were right. Even now, I am frequently dumbfounded to realize that you can get on an airplane in London and in less time than it takes to get the foil lid off the little container of milk for your coffee and its contents distributed all over yourself and the man next to you (and it's amazing, isn't it, how much milk one of those little tubs holds?), you're in Paris or Brussels and everyone looks like Yves Montand and Jeanne Moreau.

All this is a roundabout way of explaining how it was that I came to be standing, one bright, clear autumn afternoon in my forty-fourth year, on a dirty beach at Calais, staring across the English Channel to an outcrop on the horizon that was clearly and sunnily the White Cliffs of Dover, and experiencing something of the same sense of wonder.

I had come to Calais because I was about to embark on a grand tour of Britain and wanted to reenter the country as I had first seen it, from the sea. After nearly twenty years in England, my wife and I had taken the decision to move back to America for a while, to give the children the chance of experiencing life in another country and my wife the chance to shop until 10 P.M. seven nights a week. I had recently read that 3.7 million Americans, according to a Gallup poll, believed that they had been abducted by aliens at one time or another, so it was clear that my people needed me. But I had insisted on having one last look at Britain—a kind of valedictory tour around the green and kindly island that had for two decades been my home.

I knew, in a theoretical sort of way, that England was only a spit over twenty miles off, but I couldn't quite believe that I could stand here, on this sunny French beach, and actually see it. I was so incredulous, in fact, that I sought confirmation from a man trudging past in reflective mood.

"*Excusez-moi, monsieur*," I inquired in my best French. "*C'est Angleterre* over there?"

He looked up from his thoughts to where I was pointing, gave a deeply gloomy nod as if to say, "Alas, yes," and trudged on.

"Well, fancy," I murmured and almost immediately fell into one of those reveries that are traditionally depicted on television by bringing up the music and making the screen go wavy.

I was remembering my first sight of England more than twenty years before. It was a foggy March night in 1973 when I arrived in Dover on the midnight ferry from Calais, having walked and hitch-hiked from Luxembourg, where I had disembarked three days earlier from an Icelandic Airlines jet from New York. It was my first time away from home, my first experience of being truly alone, and I was still in that strangely exhilarating state in which wonderment, confusion, and trepidation all fight for primacy.

For twenty minutes, the Dover terminal area was aswarm with activity as cars and trucks poured forth, customs people did their duties, and everyone made for the London road. Then abruptly all was silence and I wandered through sleeping, low-lit streets threaded with fog, just like in a Bulldog Drummond movie. It was rather wonderful, in a mildly confusing, vaguely trepidatious way, having an English town all to myself.

The one disconcerting thing was that all the hotels and guest-houses appeared to be shut for the night. I walked as far as the rail station, thinking I'd catch a train to London, but the station, too, was dark and shuttered. I was standing wondering what to do when I noticed the gray light of a television filling an upstairs window of a guesthouse across the road. *Hooray,* I thought, *someone awake,* and hastened across, planning humble apologies to the kindly owner for the lateness of my arrival, and imagined a cheery conversation that concluded with the proprietress (played by Margaret Rutherford) bustling me to the kitchen table against my feebly hollow protests about inconveniencing her—"Now I won't hear another word. You just sit yourself down, young man. Why, you must be positively ravenous after that long trip, you poor thing"—and provisioning me with a sandwich of thick-cut roast beef, a little potato salad, and perhaps a bottle or two of beer.

The sidewalk to the guesthouse was pitch-dark, and in my eagerness and unfamiliarity with British doorways I tripped on a step, crashing face-first into the door and sending half a dozen empty milk bottles clattering to a noisy oblivion. Almost immediately the upstairs window opened.

"Who's that?" came a sharp voice

I stepped back, rubbing my nose, and peered up at a silhouette with hair curlers. The person looked nothing like Margaret Rutherford.

"Hello, I'm looking for a room," I said.

"We're shut."

"Oh." But what about my supper?

"Try the Churchill. On the front."

"On the front of what?" I asked, but the window was already banging closed.

The Churchill was sumptuous and well lit and appeared ready to receive visitors. Through a window I could see people in suits in a bar, looking elegant and suave, like characters in a Noël Coward play. I hesitated in the shadows. I was socially and sartorially ill suited for such an establishment and anyway it was clearly beyond my meager budget. Only the previous day, I had handed over an exceptionally plump wad of colorful francs to a beady-eyed Picardy hotelier in payment for one night in a lumpy bed and a plate of mysterious *chasseur* containing the bones of assorted small animals, much of which had to be secreted away in a large napkin, and had determined thenceforth to be more cautious with expenditures. So

I turned reluctantly from the Churchill's beckoning warmth and trudged off into the darkness.

Farther along Marine Parade stood a shelter, open to the elements but roofed, and I decided that this was as good as I was going to get. With my backpack for a pillow, I lay down and drew my jacket tight around me. The bench was slatted and hard and studded with big roundheaded bolts that made reclining in comfort an impossibility—doubtless their intention. I lay for a long time listening to the sea washing over the beach below, and eventually dropped off to a long night of mumbled dreams in which I found myself being pursued over Arctic ice floes by a beady-eyed Frenchman with a slingshot, a bag of bolts, and an uncanny aim, who thwacked me repeatedly in the buttocks and legs for stealing a linen napkin full of seepy food and leaving it at the back of a dresser drawer in my hotel room. I awoke with a gasp about three, stiff all over and quivering from cold. The fog had gone. The air was now still and clear, and the sky was bright with stars. A beacon from the lighthouse at the far end of the breakwater swept endlessly over the sea. It was all most fetching, but I was far too cold to appreciate it. I dug shiveringly through my backpack and extracted every potentially warming item I could find—a flannel shirt, two sweaters, an extra pair of jeans. I used some woolen socks as mittens and put a pair of flannel boxer shorts on my head as a kind of desperate headwarmer, then sank heavily back onto the bench and waited stoically for death's sweet kiss. Instead, I fell asleep.

I was awakened again by an abrupt bellow of foghorn, which nearly knocked me from my narrow perch, and sat up feeling wretched but fractionally less cold. The world was bathed in that milky predawn light that seems to come from nowhere. Gulls wheeled and cried over the water. Beyond them, past the stone breakwater, a ferry, vast and well lit, slid regally out to sea. I sat there for some time, a young man with more on his mind than in it. Another booming moan from the ship's foghorn passed over the water, reexciting the irksome gulls. I took off my sock mittens and looked at my watch. It was 5:55 A.M. I looked at the receding ferry and wondered where anybody would be going at that hour. Where would *I* go at that hour? I picked up my backpack and shuffled off along the seafront, to get some circulation going.

Near the Churchill, now itself peacefully sleeping, I came across an old guy walking a little dog. The dog was frantically trying to pee on every vertical surface and in consequence wasn't so much walking as being dragged along on three legs. The man nodded a good morning as I drew level. "Might turn out nice," he announced, gazing hopefully at a sky that looked like a pile of wet towels. I asked him if there was a restaurant anywhere that might be open. He knew of a place not far away and directed me to it. "Best transport caff in Kent," he said.

"Transport calf?" I repeated uncertainly, and retreated a couple of paces as I'd noticed his dog was straining desperately to moisten my leg.

"Very popular with the lorry drivers. They always know the best places, don't they?" He smiled amiably, then lowered his voice a fraction and leaned toward me as if about to share a confidence. "You might want to take them pants off your head before you go in."

I clutched my head—"Oh!"—and removed the forgotten boxer shorts with a blush. I began to form an explanation, but the man was scanning the sky again.

"Definitely brightening up," he decided, and dragged his dog off in search of new uprights. I watched them go, then turned and walked off down the promenade as it began to spit with rain.

The café was outstanding—lively and steamy and deliciously warm. I had a platter of eggs, beans, fried bread, bacon, and sausage, with a side plate of bread and greasy marge, and two cups of tea, all for 22p. Afterward, feeling a new man, I emerged with a toothpick and a burp, and sauntered happily through the streets, watching Dover come to life. It must be said that Dover was not vastly improved by daylight, but I liked it. I liked its small scale and cozy air, and the way everyone said "Good morning!" and "Hello!" and "Dreadful weather—but it might brighten up!" to everyone else, and the sense that this was just one more in a very long series of fundamentally cheerful, well-ordered, pleasantly uneventful days. No one in the whole of Dover would have any particular reason to remember March 21, 1973, except for me and a handful of children born that day and possibly one old guy with a dog who had encountered a young fellow with underpants on his head.

I didn't know how early one could decently begin asking for a room in England, so I thought I would leave it till midmorning. With time on my hands, I made a thorough search for a guesthouse that looked attractive and quiet, but friendly and not too expensive, and at the stroke of ten o'clock presented myself on the doorstep of the one I had carefully selected, taking care not to discompose the milk bottles. It was a small hotel that was really a guesthouse, indeed was really a boardinghouse.

I don't remember its name, but I well recall the proprietress, a formidable creature of late middle years called Mrs. Gubbins, who showed me to a room, then gave me a tour of the facilities and outlined the many complicated rules for residing there—when breakfast was served, how to turn on the heater for the bath, which hours of the day I would have to vacate the premises and during which brief period a bath was permitted (these seemed, oddly, to coincide), how much notice I should give if I intended to receive a phone call or remain out after 10 P.M., how to flush the loo and use the loo brush, which materials were permitted in the bedroom wastebasket and which had to be carefully conveyed to the outside dustbin, where and how to wipe my feet at each point of entry, how to operate the three-bar electric fire in my bedroom and when that would be permitted (essentially, during an Ice Age). This was all bewilderingly new to me. Where I came from, you got a room in a motel, spent ten hours making a lavish and possibly irredeemable mess of it, and left early the next morning. This was like joining the army.

"The minimum stay," Mrs. Gubbins went on, "is five nights at one pound a night, including full English breakfast."

"Five nights?" I said in a small gasp. I'd only intended to stay the one. What on earth was I going to do with myself in Dover for five days?

Mrs. Gubbins arched an eyebrow. "Were you hoping to stay longer?"

"No," I said. "*No*. As a matter of—"

"Good, because we have a party of Scottish pensioners coming for the weekend and it would have been awkward. Actually, quite impossible." She surveyed me critically, as she might a carpet stain, and considered if there was anything else she could do to make my life wretched. There was. "I'm going out shortly, so may I ask that you vacate your room within quarter of an hour?"

I was confused again. "I'm sorry, you want me to leave? I've just got here."

"As per the house rules. You may return at four." She made to depart but then turned back. "Oh, and do be so good, would you, as to remove your counterpane each night. We've had some unfortunate occurrences with stains. If you do damage the counterpane, I will have to charge you. You do understand, of course."

I nodded dumbly. And with that she was gone. I stood there, feeling lost and weary and far from home. I'd spent a hysterically uncomfortable night out of doors. My muscles ached, I was dented all over from sleeping on boltheads, and my skin was lightly oiled with the dirt of two nations. I had sustained myself to this point with the thought that soon I would be immersed in a hot, soothing bath, followed by about fourteen hours of deep, peaceful, wallowing sleep, on plump pillows under a downy comforter.

As I stood there absorbing the realization that my nightmare, far from drawing to a close, was only just beginning, the door opened and Mrs. Gubbins was striding across the room to the fluorescent light above the sink. She had shown me the correct method for turning it on—"There's no need to yank it. A gentle tug is sufficient"—and evidently remembered that she had left it burning. She turned it off now with what seemed to me a sharp yank, then gave me and the room a final suspicious once-over, and departed again.

When I was sure she was quite gone, I quietly locked the door, drew shut the curtains, and had a pee in the sink. I dug a book from my backpack, then stood for a long minute by the door surveying the tidy, unfamiliar contents of my lonely room.

"And just what the hell is a counterpane?" I wondered in a small, unhappy voice and quietly took my leave.

What a different place Britain was in the spring of 1973. The pound was worth £2.46, nearly a dollar more than now. Average weekly take-home pay was just over £30. A packet of potato chips was 5p, a soft drink 8p, lipstick 45p, chocolate biscuits 12p, an iron £4.50, an electric kettle £7, a black-and-white TV £60, a color TV £300, the average meal out £1. A scheduled airline ticket from New York to London cost £87.45 in winter, £124.95 in summer. You could have eight days in the Canary Islands on a Cook's Golden Wings Holiday for £65, or fifteen days from £93. I know all this because before this trip I looked up the issue of *The Times* for March 20, 1973, the day I arrived in Dover, and it contained a full-page advertisement from the government outlining how much most of these things cost and how they would be affected by a zippy new tax

called VAT, which was to be introduced a week or so later. The gist
of the advertisement was that while some things would go up in price
with VAT, some things would also go down. (Ha!) I also recollect
from my own dwindling cerebral resources that it cost 4p to send a
postcard to America by air, 13p for a pint of beer, and 30p for a
Penguin paperback. The decimalization of English currency had just
passed its second anniversary, but people were still converting in
their heads—"Good lord, why that's nearly six shillings!"—and you
had to know that a sixpence coin was really worth 2½p and that
guinea signified £1.05.

A surprising number of headlines from that week could as easily
appear today: FRENCH AIR TRAFFIC CONTROLLERS STRIKE,
WHITE PAPER CALLS FOR ULSTER POWER SHARING, NUCLEAR
RESEARCH LABORATORY TO BE CLOSED, STORMS DISRUPT RAIL
SERVICES, and that old standby of cricket reports, ENGLAND COL-
LAPSE (this time against Pakistan). But the most arresting thing
about the headlines from that dimly remembered week in 1973
was how much industrial unrest there was about: STRIKE THREAT
AT BRITISH GAS CORPORATION, 2,000 CIVIL SERVANTS STRIKE,
NO LONDON EDITION OF *DAILY MIRROR*, 10,000 LAID OFF AFTER
CHRYSLER MEN WALK OUT, UNIONS PLAN CRIPPLING ACTION
FOR MAY DAY, 12,000 PUPILS GET DAY OFF AS TEACHERS
STRIKE—all this from a single week. This was to be the year of
the OPEC crisis and the effective toppling of the Heath government (though there wouldn't be a general election until the following January). Before the year was out, there would be gasoline
rationing and half-mile queues at filling stations all over the country. Inflation would spiral up to 28 percent. There would be acute
shortages of toilet paper, sugar, electricity, and coal, among much
else. Half the nation would be on strike and the rest would be on
three-day weeks. People would shop for Christmas presents in department stores lit by candles and watch in dismay as their television screens went blank after *News at Ten* by order of the

government. It was the year that Britain entered the European Common Market and—it scarcely seems credible now—went to war with
Iceland over cod (albeit in a mercifully wimpy, put-down-those-
whitefish-or-we-might-just-shoot-across-your-bow sort of way).

It would be, in short, one of the most extraordinary years in
modern British history. Of course, I didn't know this on that drizzly March morning in Dover. I didn't know anything really, which
is a strangely wonderful position to be in. Everything that lay before me was new and mysterious and exciting in a way you can't
imagine. England was full of words I'd never heard before—
streaky bacon, short back and sides, Belisha beacon, serviettes,
high tea, ice cream cornet.* I didn't know how to pronounce *scone*
or *pasty* or *Towcester* or *Slough*, I had never heard of Tesco's,
Perthshire or Denbighshire, council houses, Morecambe and Wise,
railway cuttings, Christmas crackers, bank holidays, seaside rock,
milk floats, trunk calls, Scotch eggs, Morris Minors, or Poppy
Day. For all I knew, when a car had an L-plate on the back of
it, it indicated that it was being driven by a leper. I was positively
radiant with ignorance. The simplest transactions were a mystery
to me. I saw a man in a newsagent's ask for "twenty Number Six"
and receive cigarettes, and presumed for a long time afterward that
everything was ordered by number in a newsagent's, like in a Chinese takeaway. I sat for half an hour in a pub before I realized
that you had to fetch your own order, then tried the same thing
in a tearoom and was told to sit down.

The tearoom lady called me love. All the shop ladies called me
love and most of the men called me mate. I hadn't been here twelve
hours and already they loved me. And everyone ate the way I did.
This was truly exciting. For years I'd been the despair of my mother

*Respectively, a type of bacon, a style of haircut, a warning light at pedestrian crossings,
napkins, a fancy name for dinner, and what we would call an ice cream cone. For the rest,
here and throughout the book, you will find a helpful glossary beginning on page 319.

because as a left-hander I politely but resolutely declined to eat the American way—grasping the fork in your left hand to steady the food while cutting, then transferring it to your right hand to lift the food to your mouth. It seemed ridiculously cumbersome, and here suddenly was a whole country that ate the way I did. And people drove on the left! This was paradise. Before the day was half over, I knew that this was where I wanted to be.

I spent a long day wandering aimlessly and happily along residential streets and shopping streets, eavesdropping on conversations at bus stops and street corners, looking with interest in the windows of greengrocers and butchers and fishmongers, reading fly-posters and planning applications, quietly absorbing. I climbed up to the castle to admire the view and watch the shuttling ferries, had a respectful look at the white cliffs and Old Town Gaol, and in the late afternoon on an impulse went to a movie, attracted by the prospect of warmth and dryness, and by a poster depicting an array of scantily clad young ladies in seductive mood.

"Circle or stalls?" said the ticket lady.

"No, *Suburban Wife Swap*," I answered in a confused and furtive voice.

Inside, another new world opened for me. I saw my first cinema advertisement, my first trailers presented in a British accent, and my first British Board of Film Censors certificate ("This movie has been passed as suitable for adults by Lord Harlech, who enjoyed it very much"), and discovered, to my small delight, that smoking was permitted in British cinemas and to hell with the fire risks. The film itself provided a rich fund of social and lexical information, as well as the welcome opportunity to rest my steaming feet and see a lot of attractive young women disporting in the altogether. Among the many terms new to me were *dirty weekend, loo, au pair, semidetached house, shirt-lifter*, and *swift shag against the cooker*, all of which have proved variously useful since. During the interval—another exciting new development for me—I had my first Kia-Ora (a kind of warm, orange-flavored linctus that you would have to be British to find refreshing), purchased from a monumentally bored young lady who had the remarkable ability to pull selected items from her illuminated tray and make change without ever removing her gaze from an imaginary spot in the middle distance. Afterward I dined at a small Italian restaurant recommended by the premovie adverts and returned contentedly to the guesthouse as night stole over Dover. It was altogether a thoroughly satisfying and illuminating day.

I had intended to turn in early, but on the way to my room I noticed a door marked RESIDENTS LOUNGE and out of curiosity put my head in. It was a large parlor, with easy chairs and a settee, all with starched antimacassars; a bookcase with a modest selection of jigsaw puzzles and paperback books; an occasional table with some well-thumbed magazines; and a large color television. I switched on the TV and looked through the magazines while I waited for it to warm up. They were all women's magazines, but they weren't like the magazines my mother and sister read. The articles in my mother's and sister's magazines were always about sex and personal gratification. They had titles like "Eat Your Way to Multiple Orgasms," "Office Sex—How to Get It," "Tahiti: The Hot New Place for Sex," and "Those Shrinking Rain Forests—Are They Any Good for Sex?" The British magazines addressed more modest aspirations. They had titles like "Knit Your Own Twin Set," "Money-Saving Button Offer," "Make This Super Knitted Soap-Saver," and "Summer's Here—It's Time for Mayonnaise!"

As the TV warmed to life, another resident came in, carrying a bowl of steaming water and a towel. He said "Oh!" in surprise when he saw me and took a seat by the window. He was thin and red-faced and filled the room with a smell of liniment. He looked like someone with unhealthy sexual ambitions, the sort of person your P.E. teacher warned that you would turn into if you masturbated too extravagantly (someone, in short, like your P.E. teacher). I couldn't be sure, but I would almost have sworn that I had seen him buying a packet of fruit gums at *Suburban Wife Swap* that afternoon. He looked stealthily at me, possibly thinking something along the same lines, then covered his head with the towel and lowered his face to the bowl, where it remained for much of the rest of the evening.

A few minutes later a baldheaded, middle-aged guy—a shoe salesman, I would have guessed—came in, said "Hullo!" to me and "Evening, Richard" to the toweled head, and took a seat beside me. Shortly after that we were joined by an older man with a walking stick, a dicky leg, and a gruff manner. He looked darkly at us all, nodded the most tinily precise of acknowledgments, and fell heavily into his seat, where he spent the next twenty minutes maneuvering his leg this way and that, as if positioning a heavy piece of furniture. I gathered that these people were all long-term residents.

A sitcom called *My Neighbour Is a Darky* came on. I suppose that wasn't its actual title, but that was the gist of it—that there was something richly comic in the notion of having black people living next door. It was full of lines like "Good lord, Gran, there's a colored chappie in your cupboard!" and "Well, I couldn't see him in the *dark*, could I?" It was hopelessly moronic. The baldheaded guy beside me laughed until he was wiping tears from his eyes, and from under the towel there came occasional snorts of amusement, but the man with the dicky leg, I noticed, never laughed. He simply stared at me, as if trying to remember what dark event from his past I was associated with. Every time I looked over, his eyes were fixed on me. It was unnerving.

A starburst briefly filled the screen, indicating an interval of adverts, which the baldheaded man used to quiz me in a friendly but confusingly disconnected way as to who I was and how I had fallen into their lives. He was delighted to find that I was American. "I've always wanted to see America," he said. "Tell me, do you have Woolworth's there?"

"Well, actually, Woolworth's is American."

"You don't say!" he said. "Did you hear that, Colonel? Woolworth's is American." The Colonel—he of the dicky leg and scowling mien—seemed unmoved by this intelligence. "And what about cornflakes?"

"I beg your pardon?"

"Do you have cornflakes in America?"

"Well, actually they're American, too."

"Never!"

I smiled weakly, and begged my legs to stand me up and take me out of there, but my lower body seemed oddly inert.

"Fancy! So what brings you to Britain then if you have cornflakes already?"

I looked at him to see if the question was serious, then embarked reluctantly and falteringly on a brief résumé of my life to that point, but after a moment I realized that the program had restarted and he wasn't even pretending to listen, so I tailed off, and instead spent the whole of Part Two absorbing the heat of the Colonel's glare.

When the program finished, I was about to hoist myself from the chair and bid this happy trio a warm adieu when the door opened and Mrs. Gubbins came in with a tray of tea things and a plate of biscuits of the sort that I believe are called teatime variety, and everyone stirred friskily to life, rubbing their hands keenly and saying, "Ooh, lovely." To this day, I remain impressed by the ability of Britons of all ages and social backgrounds to get genuinely excited by the prospect of a hot beverage.

"And how was *World of Birds* tonight, Colonel?" asked Mrs. Gubbins as she handed the Colonel a cup of tea and a biscuit.

"Couldn't say," said the Colonel archly. "The television"—he smacked me in the side of the head with a meaningful look—"was tuned to another channel." Mrs. Gubbins gave me a sharp look, too, in sympathy. I think they were sleeping together.

"*World of Birds* is the Colonel's favorite," she said to me in a tone that went some distance past hate, and handed me a cup of tea with a hard whitish biscuit.

I mewed some pitiful apology.

"It was puffins tonight," blurted the red-faced fellow, looking very pleased with himself.

Mrs. Gubbins stared at him for a moment as if surprised to find that he had the power of speech. "Puffins!" she said and gave me a still more withering expression that asked how anyone could be so lacking in fundamental human decency. "The Colonel adores puffins. Don't you, Arthur?" She was definitely sleeping with him.

"I do rather," said the Colonel, biting unhappily into a chocolate bourbon.

In shame, I sipped my tea and nibbled at my biscuit. I had never had tea with milk in it before or a cookie of such rocklike cheerlessness. It tasted like something you would give a canary to strengthen its beak. After a minute the baldheaded guy leaned close to me and in a confiding whisper said, "You mustn't mind the Colonel. He hasn't been the same since he lost his leg."

"Well, I hope for his sake he soon finds it," I replied, hazarding a little sarcasm. The baldheaded guy guffawed at this and for one terrifying moment I thought he was going to share my little quip with the Colonel and Mrs. Gubbins, but instead he thrust a meaty hand at me and introduced himself. I don't remember his name now, but it was one of those names that only English people have—Colin Crapspray or Bertram Pantyshield or something similarly improbable. I gave a crooked smile, thinking he must be pulling my leg, and said, "You're kidding."

"Not at all," he replied coldly. "Why, do you find it amusing?"

"It's just that it's kind of . . . unusual."

"Well, *you* may think so," he said and turned his attention to the Colonel and Mrs. Gubbins, and I realized that I was now, and would doubtless forever remain, friendless in Dover.

Over the next two days, Mrs. Gubbins persecuted me mercilessly, while the others, I suspected, scouted evidence for her. She reproached me for not turning the light off in my room when I went out, for not putting the lid down on the toilet when I'd finished, for taking the Colonel's hot water—I'd no idea he had his own until he started rattling the doorknob and making aggrieved noises in the corridor—for ordering the full English breakfast two days running and then leaving the fried tomato both times.

"I see you've left the fried tomato again," she said on the second occasion. I didn't know quite what to say to this as it was incontestably true, so I simply furrowed my brow and joined her in staring at the offending item. I had actually been wondering for two days what it was.

"May I request," she said in a voice heavy with pain and years of irritation, "that in future, if you don't require a fried tomato with your breakfast, you would be good enough to tell me?"

Abashed, I watched her go. "I thought it was a blood clot!" I wanted to yell after her, but of course I said nothing and merely skulked from the room to the triumphant beams of my fellow residents.

After that, I stayed out of the house as much as I could. I went to the library and looked up *counterpane* in a dictionary so that I might at least escape censure on that score. (I was astonished to find out that it was a bedspread; for three days I'd been fiddling with the window.) Within the house, I tried to remain silent and inconspicuous. I even turned over quietly in my creaking bed. But no matter how hard I tried, I seemed fated to annoy. On the third afternoon as I crept in, Mrs. Gubbins confronted me in the hallway with an empty cigarette packet, and demanded to know if it was I who had thrust it in the privet hedge. I began to understand why innocent people sign extravagant confessions in police stations. That evening, I forgot to turn off the water heater after a quick and stealthy bath and compounded the error by leaving strands of hair in the plughole. The next morning came the final humiliation. Mrs. Gubbins marched me wordlessly to the toilet and showed me a little turd that had not flushed away. We agreed that I should leave after breakfast.

I caught a fast train to London, and had not been back to Dover since.

chapter
2

and now here I was in Calais, about to revisit Dover for the first time in twenty-three years. Tomorrow I would catch an early ferry and begin the serious business of investigating Britain, examining the country's public face and private parts, as it were, but today I was carefree and unattached. I had nothing to do but please myself.

Calais is an interesting place that exists solely for the purpose of giving English people in track suits somewhere to go for the day. Because it was heavily bombed in the war, it fell into the hands of postwar town planners and in consequence looks like something left over from a 1957 Exposition du Cément. An alarming number of structures, particularly around the cheerless Place d'Armes, the central square, seem to have been modeled on supermarket packaging, primarily packets of Jacob's Cream Crackers. A few even extend across roads—always a sign of 1950s planners smitten with the novel possibilities of concrete. One of the main buildings in the center, it almost goes without saying, is a Holiday Inn/cornflakes box.

But I didn't mind. The sun was shining in a kindly Indian summer way and this was France and I was in that happy frame of mind that always comes with the start of a long trip and the giddy prospect of spending weeks and weeks doing nothing much and calling it work.

I was disappointed to note that nobody on the streets of Calais looked like Yves Montand or Jeanne Moreau or even the delightful Philippe Noiret. This was because they were all Britons dressed in sportswear. They all looked as if they should have whistles around their necks and be carrying a soccer ball. Instead, they were lugging heavy carrier bags of clinking bottles and noisome cheeses and wondering why they had bought the cheese and what they were going to do with themselves until it was time to catch the four o'clock ferry home. You could hear them bickering in small, unhappy voices as they passed. "Sixty francs for a packet of bloody goat's cheese? Well, she won't thank you for *that*." They all looked as if they ached for a nice cup of tea and some real food. It occurred to me that you could make a small fortune with a hamburger stand. You could call it Burgers of Calais.

It must be said that apart from shopping and bickering quietly, there isn't a great deal to do in Calais. There's the well-known Rodin statue outside the Hôtel de Ville and a single museum, the Musée des Beaux-Arts et de la Dentelle ("The Museum of Beautiful Art and of the Teeth," if my French hasn't abandoned me), but the museum was closed and the Hôtel de Ville was a long hike—and anyway the Rodin statue is on every postcard. I ended up, like everyone else, nosing around the souvenir shops, of which Calais has a certain amplitude.

For reasons that I have never understood, the French have a particular genius when it comes to tacky religious keepsakes, and in a gloomy shop on a corner of the Place d'Armes, I found one I liked: a plastic model of the Virgin Mary standing with beckoning arms in a kind of grotto fashioned from seashells, miniature starfish, lacy sprigs of dried seaweed, and a polished lobster claw. Glued to the back of the Madonna's head was a halo made from a plastic curtain ring, and on the lobster claw the model's gifted creator had painted an oddly festive-looking *"Calais!"* in neat script. I hesitated because it cost a lot of money, but when the lady of the shop showed me that it also plugged in and lit up like a fun-fair ride at Blackpool, the only question in my mind was whether one would be enough. *"C'est très jolie,"* she said in a kind of astonished hush when she realized that I was prepared to pay real money for it, and bustled off to get it wrapped and paid for before I came to my senses and cried, "Say, where am I? And what, pray, is *this* tacky piece of Franco-*merde* I see before me?"

"C'est très jolie," she kept repeating soothingly, as if afraid of disturbing my wakeful slumber. I think it may have been some time since she had sold a Virgin Mary with Seashells Occasional Light. In any case, as the shop door shut behind me, I distinctly heard a whoop of joy.

Afterward, to celebrate, I called in for a coffee at a popular café on the rue de Gaston Papin et Autres Dignitaires Obscures. Indoors, Calais seemed much more agreeably Gallic. People greeted each other with two-cheek kisses and wreathed themselves in blue smoke from Gauloises and Gitanes. An elegant woman in black across the room looked uncannily like Jeanne Moreau having a quick smoke and a Pernod before playing a funeral scene in a movie called *La Vie Drearieuse*. I wrote a postcard home and enjoyed my coffee, then passed the hours before dusk waving in a friendly but futile way at the bustling waiter in the hope of coaxing him back to my table to settle my modest account.

I dined cheaply and astonishingly well at a little place across the road—there is this to be said for the French: They can make fries—drank two bottles of Stella Artois in a café where I was served by a Philippe Noiret look-alike in a slaughterhouse apron, and retired early to my modest hotel room, where I played with my seashell Madonna for a time, then got into bed and passed the night listening to cars crashing in the street below.

In the morning, I breakfasted early, settled my bill with Gérard Depardieu—now, there was a surprise—and stepped out to another promising day. Clutching an inadequate little map that came with my ferry ticket, I set off in search of the ferry terminus. On the map it looked to be quite nearby, practically in the town center, but in reality it was a good two miles away at the far end of a bewildering wasteland of oil refineries, derelict factories, and acres of open ground strewn with old girders and piles of jagged concrete. I found myself squeezing through holes in chain-link fences and picking my way between rusting railway carriages with broken windows. I don't know how other people get to the ferry at Calais, but I had the distinct feeling that no one had ever done it this way before. And all the while I walked, I was uncomfortably aware—actually in a whimpering panic—that departure time was drawing nigh and that the ferry terminal, though always visible, never actually seemed to get any closer.

Eventually, after dodging across a busy divided highway and clambering up an embankment, I arrived breathless and late and looking like someone who'd just survived a mining disaster, and was hustled aboard a shuttle bus by an officious woman with a serious case of dysmenorrhea. On the way, I took stock of my possessions and discovered with quiet dismay that my beloved and costly Madonna had lost her halo and was shedding seashells.

I boarded the ship perspiring freely and with a certain disquiet. I'm not a good sailor, I freely admit. I get sick on peddle boats. Nor was I helped by the fact that this was one of those Ro-Ro ferries (short for "roll on, roll over") and that I was entrusting my life to a company that had a significantly less than flawless record when it came to remembering to shut the bow doors, the nautical equivalent of forgetting to take off your shoes before getting into the bath.

The boat was chockablock with people, all of them English. I spent the first quarter of an hour wandering around wondering how they had gotten there without getting filthy, inserted myself briefly into the track-suited mayhem that was the duty-free shop and as quickly found my way out again, strolled around the cafeteria with a tray looking at the astonishingly costly fare and then put the tray back (there was a queue for this), searched for a seat among hordes of dementedly lively children, and finally found my way out onto the breezy deck where 274 people with blue lips and dancing hair were trying to convince themselves that because the sun was shining they couldn't possibly be cold. The wind whipped our anoraks with a sound like gunshots, scooted small children along the deck, and, to everyone's private gratification, tipped a plastic cup of tea onto a fat lady's lap.

Before long, the White Cliffs of Dover rose from the sea and began creeping toward us and in no time at all, it seemed, we were sailing into Dover Harbour and clumsily nuzzling up to the dock. As a disembodied voice instructed foot passengers to assemble at the starboard egress point on Deck ZX-2 by the Sunshine Lounge—as if that meant anything to anybody—we all embarked on long, befuddled, highly individual explorations of the ship: up and down stairways, through the cafeteria and club class lounge, in and out of storerooms, through a kitchen full of toiling lascars, back through the cafeteria from another angle, and finally—without knowing quite how—out into the welcoming, watery sunshine of England.

I was eager to see Dover again after all these years. I strode into the town center along Marine Parade and with a small cry of pleasure spied the shelter I'd slept in those many years ago. It was covered in about eleven more layers of bile-green paint but otherwise unchanged. The view out to sea was likewise unchanged, though the water was bluer and more glittery than when I'd last seen it. But everything else looked different. Where I recalled there being a row of elegant Georgian houses there was now a vast and unbecoming brick apartment block. Townwall Street, the main through road to the west, was wider and more menacing with traffic than I remembered, and there was now a pedestrian underpass to the central business district, which itself was unrecognizable.

The main shopping street had been pedestrianized and the Market Square had been turned into a kind of piazza with patterned paving and the usual array of cast-iron trimmings. The whole town center seemed uncomfortably squeezed by busy, wide relief roads of which I had no recollection, and there was now a big tourist edifice called the White Cliffs Experience, where, I presume from the name, you can discover what it feels like to be 800-million-year-old chalk. I didn't recognize anything. The trouble with English towns is that they are so indistinguishable one from another. They all have a Boots the Chemist and W. H. Smith bookshop and Marks & Spencer department store. You could be anywhere really.

I plodded distractedly through the streets, unhappy that a place so central to my memories was so unfamiliar. Then, on my third grumbling pass through the central area, on a lane I would swear I had never walked before, I came across the cinema, still recognizable as the home of *Suburban Wife Swap* despite a heavy patina of arty refurbishment, and everything suddenly became clear. Now that I had a fixed point of reference, I knew precisely where I was. I strode purposefully five hundred yards north and then west—now I could almost have done it blindfolded—and found myself square in front of Mrs. Gubbins's establishment. It was still a hotel and looked substantially unchanged, as far as I could remember, except for the addition of some paved parking space in the front garden and a plastic sign announcing color TVs and en suite bathrooms. I thought about knocking at the door, but there didn't seem much point. The dragonlike Mrs. Gubbins must be long since gone—retired or dead or perhaps resident in one of the many nursing homes that crowd the south coast. She couldn't possibly have coped with the modern age of British guesthouses, with their en suite bathrooms and coffeemaking facilities and people having pizzas delivered to their rooms.

If she is in a nursing home, which would certainly be my first choice, I do hope the staff has the compassion and good sense to scold her frequently for dribbling on the toilet seat, leaving her breakfast unfinished, and being generally helpless and tiresome. It would do so much to make her feel at home.

Cheered by this thought, and content to put Dover behind me, I strolled up the Folkestone road to the rail station and bought a ticket on the next train to London.

chapter
3

G oodness me, but isn't London big? It seems to start about twenty minutes after you leave Dover and just goes on and on, mile after mile of endless gray suburbs with their wandering rows of squat brick houses that always look more or less identical from a train, as if they've been squeezed out of a very large version of one of those machines they use to make sausages. How, I always wonder, do all the millions of occupants find their way back to the right front doors each night in such a complex and anonymous sprawl?

I'm sure I couldn't. London remains a vast and exhilarating mystery to me. I lived and worked in or around it for eight years, watched the local news on television, read the evening papers, ranged extensively through its streets to attend weddings and retirement parties or go on harebrained quests for bargains in far-flung salvage yards, and still I find that there are great fragments of it that I have not just never visited but never heard of. It constantly amazes me to read the *Evening Standard* or chat with an acquaintance and encounter some reference to a district that has escaped my notice for twenty-one years. "We've just bought a little place in Fag End, near Tung-

sten Heath," somebody will say and I'll think, I've never even heard
of that. How can this possibly be?

I had stuck into my battered knapsack a copy of *London A–Z*, a
popular atlas of the city streets, and came across it now while searching unsuccessfully for half a Mars bar I was sure was in there. Pluck-
ing it out, I idly leafed through its busy pages, as ever amazed and
quietly excited to find it peppered with districts, villages, sometimes
small swallowed cities whose names, I would swear, had not been
there the last time I looked—Dudden Hill, Plashet, Snaresbrook,
Fulwell Cross, Elthorne Heights, Higham Hill, Lessness Heath,
Beacontree Heath, Bell Green, Vale of Health. *Vale of Health?* How
could I have missed that? And the thing is, I know that the next
time I look there will be other, different names—Hamshanks, East
Stuttering, Radon Heath, Bollocks.

The *A–Z* really is quite the most absorbing tome. It scrupulously
fixes and identifies every cricket ground and sewage works, every
forgotten cemetery and wandering suburban close, and packs the
densest names onto the tiniest, most obscure spaces. I flipped to the
index and, for want of anything better to do, lost myself there. I
calculated that there are 45,687 street names in London (give or
take), including no fewer than 21 Gloucester Roads (as well as a
generous slew of Gloucester Crescents, Squares, Avenues, and
Closes), 111 Station Roads or similar, 35 Cavendishes, 66 Or-
chards, 74 Victorias, 159 Churches, 25 Avenue Roads, 35 The Avenues, and other multiples without number. There are, however,
surprisingly few really interesting sounding places—Cold Blow
Lane, Glimpsing Green, Hamshades Close, Cactus Walk, Nutter
Lane, and The Butts more or less exhausted the list of names that
could be called arresting. I read once that in Elizabethan times there
was a Gropecunt Lane somewhere in the city, but evidently no
longer. I spent half an hour amusing myself in this way, pleased to
be entering a metropolis of such dazzling and unknowable com-
plexity, and had the bonus pleasure, when I returned the book to

the bag, of finding the half-eaten Mars bar, its leading edge covered in a small festival of lint, which didn't do a great deal for the flavor but did add some useful bulk.

Victoria Station was swarming with the usual complement of lost-looking tourists, lurking touts, and passed-out drunks. On my way out, three separate people inquired whether I had any spare change—"No, but thank you for asking!"—which wouldn't have happened twenty years ago. Then, not only were panhandlers something of a novelty in London, but they always had a good story about having lost a wallet and now desperately needing £2 to get to Maidstone to donate bone marrow to a kid sister or something. Now they just flatly ask for money, which is quicker but less interesting.

I took a cab to Hazlitt's Hotel on Frith Street. I like Hazlitt's because it's intentionally obscure—it doesn't have a sign or a plaque or anything at all to betray its purpose—which puts you in a rare position of strength with your cab driver. Let me say right now that London cab drivers are without question the finest in the world. They are trustworthy, safe and honest, generally friendly and always polite. They keep their vehicles spotless inside and out, and they will put themselves to the most extraordinary inconvenience to drop you at the front entrance of your destination. There are really only a couple of odd things about them. One is that they cannot drive more than two hundred feet in a straight line. I've never understood this, but no matter where you are or what the driving conditions, every two hundred feet a little bell goes off in their heads and they abruptly lunge down a side street. And when you get to your hotel or railway station or wherever it is you are going, they like to drive you all the way around it so that you can see it from all angles before alighting.

The other distinctive thing about them, and the reason I like to go to Hazlitt's, is that they cannot bear to admit that they don't know the location of something they feel they ought to know, like a hotel, which I think is rather sweet. To become a London cab driver you have to master something called The Knowledge—in effect, learn every street, hospital, hotel, police station, cricket ground, cemetery, and other notable landmark in this amazingly vast and confusing city. It takes years and the cabbies are justifiably proud of their achievement. It would kill them to admit that there could exist in central London a hotel that they have never heard of. So what the cabbie does is probe. He drives in no particular direction for a block or two, then glances at you in the mirror and in an overcasual voice says, "Hazlitt's—that's the one on Curzon Street, innit, guv? Opposite the Blue Lion?" But the instant he sees a knowing smile of demurral forming on your lips, he hastily says, "No, hang on a minute, I'm thinking of the *Hazelbury*. Yeah, the Hazelbury. You want *Hazlitt's*, right?" He'll drive on a bit in a fairly random direction. "That's this side of Shepherd's Bush, innit?" he'll suggest speculatively.

When you tell him that it's on Frith Street, he says, "Yeah, that's the one. Course it is. I know it—modern place, lots of glass."

"Actually, it's an eighteenth-century brick building."

"Course it is. I know it." And he immediately executes a dramatic U-turn, causing a passing cyclist to steer into a lamppost (but that's all right because he has on cycle clips and one of those geeky slipstream helmets that all but invite you to knock him over). "Yeah, you had me thinking of the *Hazelbury*," the driver adds, chuckling as if to say it's a lucky thing he sorted that one out for you, and then lunges down a little side street off the Strand called Running Sore Lane or Sphincter Passage, which, like so much else in London, you had never noticed was there before.

Hazlitt's is a nice hotel, but the thing I like about it is that it doesn't act like a hotel. It's been there for years, and the employees are friendly—always a novelty in a big-city hotel—but they do manage to give the *slight* impression that they haven't been doing this for very long. Tell them that you have a reservation and want to check in and they get a kind of panicked look and begin a perplexed search through drawers for registration cards and room keys. It's really quite charming. And the delightful girls who clean the rooms—which, let me say, are always spotless and exceedingly comfortable—seldom seem to have what might be called a total command of English, so that when you ask them for a bar of soap or something, you see that they are watching your mouth closely and then, pretty generally, they return after a bit with a hopeful look bearing a potted plant or a commode or something that is manifestly not soap. It's a wonderful place. I wouldn't go anywhere else.

It's called Hazlitt's because it was the home of the famous essayist, and all the bedrooms are named after his chums or women he shagged there or something. I confess that my mental note card for the old boy is a trifle sketchy. It reads:

> *Hazlitt (sp?), William (?), English (poss. Scottish?) essayist. Lived: Before 1900. Most famous work: Don't know. Quips, epigrams, bons mots: Don't know. Other useful information: His house is now a hotel.*

As always, I made a mental note to read up on Hazlitt sometime to correct this gap in my knowledge and, as always, immediately forgot it. Instead, I dropped my rucksack on the bed, extracted a small notebook and a pen, and hit the streets in a spirit of inquiry and boyish keenness.

I do find London exciting. Much as I hate to agree with that tedious old git Samuel Johnson, and despite the pompous imbecility of his famous remark that when a man is tired of London he is tired of life (an observation exceeded in fatuousness only by "Let a smile be your umbrella"), I can't dispute it. After seven years of living in the country in the sort of place where a dead cow draws a crowd, London can seem a bit dazzling.

I can never understand why Londoners fail to see that they live in the most wonderful city in the world. It is, if you ask me, far more beautiful and interesting than Paris and more lively than anywhere but New York—and even New York can't touch it in lots of important ways. It has more history, finer parks, a livelier and more varied press, better theaters, more numerous orchestras and museums, leafier squares, safer streets, and more courteous inhabitants than any other large city in the world.

And it has more congenial small things—incidental civilities, you might call them—than any other city I know: cheery red mailboxes, drivers who actually stop for you at pedestrian crossings, lovely forgotten churches with wonderful names like St. Andrew by the Wardrobe and St. Giles Cripplegate, sudden pockets of quiet like Lincoln's Inn and Red Lion Square, interesting statues of obscure Victorians in togas, pubs, black cabs, double-decker buses, helpful policemen, polite notices, people who will stop to help you when you fall down or drop your shopping, benches everywhere. What other great city would trouble to put blue plaques on houses to let you know what famous person once lived there, or warn you to look left or right before stepping off the curb? I'll tell you. None.

Take away Heathrow Airport, the weather, and any building that the architect Richard Seifert ever laid a bony finger to, and it would be nearly perfect. Oh, and while we're at it, we might also stop British Museum employees from cluttering the forecourt with their cars and instead make it into a kind of garden, and also get rid of those horrible portable crush barriers outside Buckingham Palace because they look so straggly and cheap—not at all in keeping with the dignity of her poor besieged Majesty within. And, of course, put the Natural History Museum back to the way it was before they started dicking around with it (in particular, they must restore the display case showing insects infesting household products from the 1950s); and remove the entrance charges from all museums at once; and bring back Lyons Corner Houses but this time with food you'd like to eat; and finally, but most crucially, make the board of directors of British Telecom go out and personally track down every last red phone box that they sold off to be used as shower stalls and garden sheds in far-flung corners of the globe, make them put them all back, and then sack them—no, kill them. Then truly will London be glorious again.

This was the first time in years I'd been in London without having anything in particular to do and I felt a small thrill at finding myself abroad and unrequired in such a great, teeming urban organism. I wandered through Soho and Leicester Square, spent a little time in the bookshops on Charing Cross Road rearranging books to my advantage, sauntered aimlessly through Bloomsbury and the precincts of the University of London, and finally over to Gray's Inn Road to the old *Times* building, now the offices of a company I had never heard of, and felt a pang of nostalgia such as can be known only by those who remember the days of hot metal typesetting and noisy composing rooms and the quiet joy of being paid a handsome wage for a twenty-five-hour working week.

When I started at *The Times* in 1981, overmanning and slack output were prodigious to say the least. On the Company News desk where I worked as a subeditor, or copy editor, the five-man team would wander in about 2:30 and spend most of the afternoon reading the evening papers and drinking tea while waiting for the reporters to surmount the daily challenge of finding their way back to their desks after a three-hour lunch involving several bottles of jolly decent Châteauneuf-du-Pape. Once ensconced at their desks, the reporters would compose their expenses, complete hunched and whispered phone calls to their brokers with regard to a little tip they'd picked up over the crème brûlée, and finally produce a page or so of copy before retiring parched to the Blue Lion pub across the road. At about half past five, we subeditors would make some little marks on a few pieces of paper for an hour or so, then slip our arms into our coats and go home. It seemed very agreeably unlike work. At the end of the first month, one of my colleagues showed me how to record imaginary expenditures on an expense account sheet and take it up to the third floor, where it could be exchanged at a little window for about £100 in cash—more money, literally, than I had ever held before. We got six weeks' holiday, three weeks' paternity leave upon the valid production of a child, and a month's sabbatical every four years. What a wonderful world Fleet Street then was, and how thrilled I was to be part of it.

Alas, nothing that good can ever last. A few months later, Rupert Murdoch took over *The Times* and within days the building was full of mysterious tanned Australians in white short-sleeved shirts, who lurked in the background with clipboards and looked like they were measuring people for coffins. There is a story, which I suspect may actually be true, that one of these functionaries wandered into a room on the fourth floor full of people who hadn't done anything in years and, when they proved unable to account for themselves in a convincing manner, sacked them all at a stroke, except for one fortunate fellow who had popped out to the betting shop. When he returned, it was to an empty room, and he spent the next two years sitting alone, wondering vaguely what had become of his colleagues.

In our department the drive for efficiency was less traumatic. The desk I worked on was subsumed into a larger Business News desk, which meant I had to work nights and something more closely approximating eight-hour days, and we also had our expenses cruelly lopped. But the worst of it was that I was brought into regular contact with Vince of the wire room.

Vince was notorious. He would easily have been the world's most terrifying human had he but been human. I don't know quite what he was, other than it was five feet six inches of wiry malevolence in a grubby T-shirt. Reliable rumor had it that he had not been born, but burst fully formed from his mother's belly and then skittered off to the sewers. Among Vince's few simple and generally neglected tasks was the nightly delivery to us of the Wall Street report. Each night I would have to go and try to coax it from him. He was generally to be found in the humming, unattended mayhem of the wire room lounging in a leather chair liberated from an executive office upstairs, with his blood-tipped Doc Martens plonked on the desk before him beside, and sometimes actually in, a large open box of pizza.

Every night I would knock hesitantly at the open door, and politely ask if he had seen the Wall Street report, pointing out that it was now a quarter past eleven and we should have had it at half past ten. Perhaps he could look for it among the reams of unwatched paper tumbling out of his many machines?

"I don't know wevver you noticed," Vince would say, "but I'm eating pizza."

Everybody had a different approach with Vince. Some tried to get threatening. Some tried bribery. Some tried warm friendship. I begged.

"Please, Vince, can't you just get it for me, please? It won't take a sec and it would make my life so much easier."

"Fuck off."

"Please, Vince. I have a wife and family, and they're threatening to sack me because the Wall Street report is always late."

"Fuck off."

"Well, then, how about if you just tell me where it is and I get it myself?"

"You can't touch nuffink in here, you know that." The wire room was the domain of a union mysteriously named NATSOPA. One of the ways NATSOPA maintained its viselike grip on the lower echelons of the newspaper industry was by keeping technological secrets to itself, like how to tear paper off a machine. Vince, as I recall, had gone on a six-week course to Eastbourne. It left him exhausted. Journalists weren't even allowed over the threshold.

Eventually, when my entreaties had declined into a kind of helpless bleating, Vince would sigh heavily, jam a wedge of pizza into his face, and come over to the door. He would stick his face right into mine for a full half minute. This was always the most unnerving part. His breath smelled primeval. His eyes were shiny and ratlike. "You're fucking *annoying* me," he would say in a low growl, flecking my face with bits of wet pizza, and then he would either get the Wall Street report or he would retire to his desk in a dark mood. There was never any telling which.

Once, on a particularly difficult night, I reported Vince's insubordination to David Hopkinson, the night editor, who was himself a formidable figure when he chose to be. Harrumphing, he went off to sort things out and actually *entered* the wire room— a staggeringly audacious flouting of the rules of demarcation. When he emerged a few minutes later, looking flushed and wiping bits of pizza from his chin, he seemed a different man altogether. In a quiet voice he informed me that Vince would bring along the Wall Street report shortly but that perhaps it was best not to disturb him further just at present. Eventually I discovered that the simplest thing to do was get the closing prices out of the first edition of the *Financial Times*.

To say that Fleet Street in the 1980s was out of control barely hints at the scale of matters. The National Graphical Association, the printers' union, decided how many people were needed on each paper (hundreds and hundreds) and how many were to be laid off during a recession (none), and billed the management accordingly. Managements didn't have the power to hire and fire their own print workers, indeed generally didn't even know how many print workers they employed. I have before me a headline from December 1985 saying, AUDITORS FIND 300 EXTRA PRINTING STAFF AT *TELE-GRAPH*. That is to say, *The Daily Telegraph* was paying salaries to three hundred people who didn't actually work there. Printers were paid under an ancient piece-rate system so Byzantine that every composing room on Fleet Street had a piece-rate book the size of a telephone directory. On top of plump salaries, printers received special bonus payments—sometimes calculated to the eighth decimal place of a penny—for handling type of irregular sizes, for dealing with heavily edited copy, for setting words in a language other than English, for the white space at the ends of lines. If work was done out of house—for instance, advertising copy that was set outside the building—they were compensated for not doing it. At the end of each week, a senior NGA man would tot up all these extras, add a little something for a handy category called "extra trouble occasioned," and pass the bill to the management. In consequence, many senior printers, with skills no more advanced than you would expect to find in any back-street print shop, enjoyed incomes in the top 2 percent of British earnings. It was crazy and clearly unsustainable.

The end came with unexpected suddenness. In secret, Rupert Murdoch and his minions prepared new editorial and production facilities on reclaimed wasteland at Wapping, in London's East End. On January 24, 1986, the management of *The Times* abruptly sacked 5,250 members of the most truculent unions. On the evening of that day, the editorial staff was called into an upstairs conference room where Charlie Wilson, the editor, climbed onto a desk and announced the changes. Wilson was a terrifying Scotsman and a Murdoch man through and through. He said to us, "We're sending ye tae Wapping, ye soft English nancies, and if ye wairk very, very hard and if ye doonae git on ma tits, then mebbe I'll not cut off yer knackers and put them in ma Christmas pudding. D'ye have any problems with tha'?" Or words to that effect.

As four hundred skittish journalists tumbled from the room, jabbering excitedly and trying to come to terms with the realization that they were about to be immersed in the biggest drama of their working lives, I stood alone and basking in the glow of a single joyous thought: I would never have to work with Vince again.

chapter
4

i hadn't been back to Wapping since I'd left there in the summer of 1986 and was eager to see it again. I had arranged to meet an old friend and colleague, so I went now to Chancery Lane and caught an Underground train. I do like the Underground. There's something surreal about plunging into the bowels of the earth to catch a train. It's a little world of its own down there, with its own strange winds and weather systems, its own eerie noises and oily smells. Even when you've descended so far into the earth that you've lost your bearings utterly and wouldn't be in the least surprised to pass a troop of blackened miners coming off shift, there's always the rumble and tremble of a train passing somewhere on an unknown line even farther below. And it all happens in such orderly quiet: all these thousands of people passing on stairs and escalators, stepping on and off crowded trains, sliding off into the darkness with wobbling heads, and never speaking, like characters from *Night of the Living Dead*.

As I stood on the platform beneath another, fairly recent London civility—namely an electronic board announcing that the next train to Hainault would be arriving in four minutes—I turned my atten-

tion to the greatest of all civilities: the London Underground Map.
What a piece of perfection it is, created in 1931 by a forgotten hero
named Harry Beck, an out-of-work draftsman who realized that
when you are underground it doesn't actually matter where you are.
Beck saw—and what an intuitive stroke this was—that as long as
the stations were presented in their right sequence with their inter-
changes clearly delineated, he could freely distort scale, indeed
abandon it altogether. He gave his map the orderly precision of an
electrical wiring system, and in so doing created an entirely new,
imaginary London that has very little to do with the disorderly geography of the city above.

Here's an amusing trick you can play on people from Newfoundland or Lincolnshire. Take them to Bank Station and tell
them to make their way to Mansion House. Using Beck's map—
which even people from Newfoundland can understand in a moment—they will gamely take a Central Line train to Liverpool
Street, change to a Circle Line train heading east, and travel five
more stops. When eventually they get to Mansion House, they will
emerge to find they have arrived at a point two hundred feet farther down the same street, and that you have had a nice breakfast
and done a little shopping since you last saw them. Now take them
to Great Portland Street and tell them to meet you at Regent's
Park (that's right, same thing again!), and then to Temple Station
with instructions to rendezvous at Aldwych. What fun you can
have! And when you get tired of them, tell them to meet you at
Brompton Road Station. It closed in 1947, so you'll never have
to see them again.

The best part of Underground travel is that you never actually
see the places above you. You have to imagine them. In other cities, station names are drearily mundane: Lexington Avenue, Pots-
damer Platz, Third Street South. In London, by contrast, the
names nearly always sound sylvan and beckoning: Stamford Brook,
Turnham Green, Bromley-by-Bow, Maida Vale, Drayton Park.

That isn't a city up there, it's a Jane Austen novel. It's easy to imagine that you are shuttling about under a semimythic city from some golden pre-industrial age. Swiss Cottage ceases to be a busy road junction and becomes instead a gingerbread dwelling in the midst of the great oak forest known as St. John's Wood. Chalk Farm is an open space of fields where cheerful peasants in brown smocks cut and gather crops of chalk. Blackfriars is full of cowled and chanting monks, Oxford Circus has its bigtop, Barking is a dangerous place overrun with packs of wild dogs, Theydon Bois is a community of industrious Huguenot weavers, White City is a walled and turreted elysium built of the most dazzling ivory, and Holland Park is full of windmills.

The problem with losing yourself in these little reveries is that when you surface things are apt to be disappointing. I came up now at Tower Hill, and there wasn't a tower and there wasn't a hill. There isn't even any longer a Royal Mint (which I always preferred to imagine as a very large chocolate wrapped in green foil) on nearby Royal Mint Street, as it has been moved somewhere else and replaced with a building with lots of smoked glass. Much of what once stood in this noisy corner of London has been swept away and replaced with big buildings with lots of smoked glass. It was only eight years since I had last been here, but were it not for the fixed reference points of London Bridge and the Tower, I'd scarcely have recognized the neighborhood.

I walked along the painfully noisy street called the Highway, quietly agog at all the new development. It was like being in the midst of an ugly-building competition. For the better part of a decade architects had been arriving in the area and saying, "You think *that's* bad? Wait'll you see what *I* can do!" And there, towering proudly above all the clunky new offices, was the ugliest piece of bulk in London, the News International complex, looking like the central air-conditioning unit for the planet.

When I last saw it, in 1986, it stood forlornly amid acres of empty warehouses and puddly wasteground. The Highway, as I recalled it, was a comparatively sedate throughway. Now heavy lorries pounded along it, making the pavement shake and giving the air an unhealthy bluish tinge. The News International compound, housing the *Times*, *Sunday Times*, *Sun*, *News of the World*, and *Today* newspapers, was still surrounded with sinister fencing and electronic gates, but there was a new maximum-security reception center that looked like something you'd expect to find at a plutonium depot. Goodness knows what terrorist contingency they have allowed for, but it must be something ambitious. I'd never seen a more unbreachable-looking complex.

I presented myself at the security window and waited outside while my colleague was summoned. The most eerie thing about the scene now was how serene it was. The memory engraved in my skull was of throngs of demonstrators, police on horses, and angry pickets, for this was, during the long winter of 1986, the site of the biggest and most violent industrial dispute ever seen in London. On some nights crowds of several thousand would battle with police for hours.

It occurred to me that though I had worked at this vast and unsightly compound for seven months, I had never explored Wapping itself and was, of a sudden, keen to have a look at it. As it happened, my former colleague was not in, so I set off instead to investigate the neighborhood.

During the dispute it was not just inadvisable for a Murdoch employee to stroll through Wapping, it was positively dangerous. The pubs and cafés of the district teemed with disgruntled printers and visiting delegations of sympathizers—Scottish miners were particularly feared for some reason—who would happily have torn a wimpy journalist's limbs from his sockets to use as torches for that night's procession. One journalist who encountered some former printers in a pub some way from Wapping had a glass smashed in his face and, as I recall, nearly died, or at the very least failed to enjoy the rest of his evening.

So unsafe was it, particularly on nights of big demonstrations, that the police often wouldn't let anyone out of the compound until the small hours. Because we never knew when we would be set free, we had to form our cars into a line and then sit for hour upon hour in the freezing cold. Generally sometime after 1 A.M., when a significant portion of the braying throngs had been beaten back or dragged off to jail or had just gotten cold and hungry and gone home, the gates would be thrown open and a great fleet of News International trucks would roar down a ramp and out onto the Highway, where they would be met by a barrage of bricks and crush barriers from whatever was left of the mob. The rest of us, meanwhile, were instructed to make haste in convoy through the back lanes of Wapping and to disperse when we were a safe distance from the plant.

This worked well enough for several nights, but one evening we were sent on our way just as the pubs were shutting. As we were proceeding down some darkened, narrow street, suddenly people were stepping out of the shadows and into the road, kicking doors and heaving whatever came to hand. Ahead of me there were startling explosions of glass and intemperate shouting. To my deep and lasting astonishment someone about six cars ahead of me—a fussy little man from the foreign desk, whom even now I would happily drag over rough ground behind a Land Rover—got out to look at the damage to his car, as if he thought he might have run over a nail, bringing those of us behind to a halt. I remember watching in sputtering dismay as he tried to press back into position a flapping piece of trim, then turning my head to find at my window an enraged face—a white guy with dancing dreadlocks and an army surplus jacket—and everything took on a strange dreamlike quality. How odd, I thought, that a total stranger was

about to pull me from my car and beat me mushy for the benefit
of printworkers whom he had never met, who would mostly de-
spise him as an unkempt hippie, and who would certainly never
let him into their own union.

And all the while this was going on, some halfwit from the foreign
desk fifty yards ahead was walking slowly around his Peugeot, as-
sessing it deliberatively like someone about to buy a secondhand car,
and occasionally pausing to look with puzzlement at the bricks and
blows raining down on the cars behind him, as if it were some kind
of freak weather occurrence. Eventually, he got back in his car,
checked the rearview mirror, made sure his newspaper was still on
the seat beside him, put on his turn signal, checked the mirror again,
and pulled off—and my life was saved.

Six days later I took a job with *The Independent*.

It was thus very refreshing to walk without fear for my life through
the dozing streets of Wapping. I have never bought into that quaint
conceit about London's being essentially a collection of villages, but
to my delight and surprise Wapping did in fact rather feel like one.
Its shops were small and varied and the streets had cozy names:
Cinnamon Street, Waterman Way, Vinegar Street, Milk Yard. The
council estates were snug and cheery looking, and the looming warehouses had almost all been smartly renovated as flats. I instinctively
quivered at the sight of yet more glossy red trim and the thought of
these once-proud workplaces filled with braying twits named Selena
and Jasper, but it must be said that they have clearly brought some
prosperity to the neighborhood and doubtless saved the old warehouses from far sadder fates.

Near Wapping Old Stairs, I had a look at the river and tried to
imagine, without the tiniest measure of success, what these old
neighborhoods must have looked like in the eighteenth and nineteenth centuries when they teemed with workers and the wharves
were piled high with barrels of the spices and condiments that gave
the surrounding streets their names. As recently as 1960, over a

hundred thousand people worked on the docks or drew their livings
from it, and Docklands was still one of the busiest ports in the world.
By 1981, every London dock was closed. The view of the river from
Wapping now was as tranquil and undisturbed as a Constable landscape. I watched the river for perhaps thirty minutes and saw just
one boat go by. Then I turned and began the long trek back to
Hazlitt's.

chapter
5

I spent a couple of more days in London doing nothing much. I did a little research in a newspaper library, spent most of one afternoon trying to find my way through the complex network of pedestrian underpasses at Marble Arch, did a little shopping, saw some friends.

Everyone I saw said, "Gosh, you're brave!" when I revealed that I was planning to travel around Britain by public transport, but it never occurred to me to go any other way. The British are so lucky to have a relatively good public transport system (relative, that is, to what it will be when the Tories finish with it) and I think we should all try harder to enjoy it while it's still there. Besides, driving in Britain is such a dreary experience. There are far too many cars on the road, nearly double what there were when I first came to the country, and in those days people didn't actually drive their cars. They just parked them in the driveway and buffed them up once every week or so. About twice a year they would "get the car out"— those were the words they used, like that in itself was a big operation—and pootle off to visit relatives in East Grinstead or have a trip to someplace like Brighton or Eastbourne, and that was about it, apart from the buffing.

Now everyone drives everywhere for everything, which I don't understand because there isn't a single feature of driving in Britain that has even the tiniest measure of enjoyment in it. Just consider the average multistory car park, as they are known. You drive around for ages, and then spend a small eternity shunting into a space that is exactly two inches wider than the average car. Then, because you are parked next to a pillar, you have to climb over the seats and squeeze butt first out the passenger door, in the process transferring all the dirt from the side of your car to the back of your smart new jacket from Marks & Spencer. Then you go hunting for some distant pay-and-display machine, which doesn't make change or accept any coin introduced since 1976, and wait for an old guy who likes to read all the instructions on the machine before committing himself and then tries to insert his money through the ticket slot and maintenance keyhole.

Eventually you acquire a ticket to stick on the inside of your windshield and trek back to your car, where your wife greets you with a "Where have you *been*?" Ignoring her, you squeeze past the pillar, collecting a matching set of dust for the front of your jacket, discover that you can't reach the windshield as the door opens only three inches, so you just sort of throw the ticket at the dashboard (it flutters to the floor, but your wife doesn't notice so you say "Fuck it" and lock the door), and squeeze back out where your wife sees what a scruff you've turned into after she spent all that time dressing you, and beats the dust from you with paddled hands while saying, "Honestly, I can't take you *anywhere*."

And that's just the beginning. Arguing quietly, you have to find your way out of this dank hellhole via an unmarked door leading to a curious chamber that seems to be a composite of dungeon and urinal, or else wait two hours for the world's most abused and unreliable-looking elevator, which will take only two people and already has two people in it—an expressionless man whose wife is beating dust from his new Marks & Spencer jacket and berating him in clucking tones.

The remarkable thing is that everything about this process is intentionally—mark this, *intentionally*—designed to flood your life with unhappiness. From the tiny parking bays that can be got into only by maneuvering your car through a forty-six-point turn (why can't the spaces be angled, for crying out loud?), to the careful placing of pillars where they will cause maximum obstruction, to the ramps that are so dark and narrow and badly angled that you always bump the curb, to the remote, willfully unhelpful ticket machines (you can't tell me that a machine that can recognize and reject any foreign coin ever produced couldn't make change if it wanted to)—*all* of this is designed to make this the most dispiriting experience of your adult life. Did you know—this is a little-known fact but absolute truth—that when they dedicate a new multistory car park, the Lord Mayor and his wife have a ceremonial pee in the stairwell? It's true.

And that's just one tiny part of the driving experience. There are all the other manifold annoyances of motoring, like National Express bus drivers who swerve in front of you on motorways; eight-mile-long rows of traffic cones set out so that some guys on a crane can change a lightbulb; traffic lights on busy roundabouts that never let you advance more than twenty feet at a time; motorway service areas where you have to pay £4.20 for a minipot of coffee and a baked potato with a sneeze of cheddar in it, and there's no point in going to the shop because the men's magazines are all sealed in plastic and you don't need any *Waylon Jennings Highway Hits* tapes; morons with trailers who pull out of side roads just as you approach; some guy in a Morris Minor going eleven miles per hour through the Lake District and collecting a three-mile following because, apparently, he's always wanted to lead a parade; and other challenges to your patience and sanity nearly beyond endurance. Motor vehicles are ugly and dirty and they bring out the worst in people. They clutter every curbside; turn ancient market squares into disorderly jumbles of metal; spawn petrol stations, secondhand car lots, Kwik-Fit exhaust and muffler centers, and other dispiriting blights. They are horrible and awful and I wanted nothing to do with them on this trip. And besides, my wife wouldn't let me have the car.

Thus it was that I found myself late on a gray Saturday afternoon, on an exceptionally long and empty train bound for Windsor. I sat high on the seat in an empty carriage, and in fading daylight watched as the train slid past office blocks and out into the forests of council flats and snaking terraced houses of Vauxhall and Clapham. At Twickenham, I discovered why the train was so long and so empty. The platform was jammed solid with men and boys in warm clothes and scarves carrying glossy programs and little bags with tea flasks peeping out: obviously a rugby crowd from the Twickenham grounds. They boarded with patience and without pushing, and said "Sorry" when they bumped or inadvertently impinged on someone else's space. I admired this instinctive consideration for others, and was struck by what a regular thing that is in Britain and how little it is noticed. Nearly everyone rode all the way to Windsor—I presume there must be some sort of parking arrangement there; Windsor can't provide that many rugby fans—and formed a patient crush at the ticket barrier. An Asian man collected tickets in fast motion and said "Thank you" to every person who passed. He didn't have time to examine the tickets—you could have handed him a corn-flakes boxtop—but he did manage to find a vigorous salute for all, and they in turn thanked *him* for relieving them of their tickets and letting them pass. It was a little miracle of orderliness and goodwill. Anywhere else there'd have been someone on a box barking at people to form a line and not push.

The streets of Windsor were shiny with rain and unseasonally dark and wintry, but they were still filled with throngs of tourists. I got a room in the Castle Hotel on the High Street, one of those peculiarly higgledy-piggledy hotels in which you have to embark on an epic trek through a succession of wandering corridors and fire doors to reach your room. I had to go up one flight of stairs and, some distance farther on, down another in order to reach the distant wing in which my room was the very last. But it was a nice room and, I presumed, handy for Reading if I decided to exit through the window.

I dumped my pack and hastened back the way I'd come, keen to see a little of Windsor before the shops shut. I knew Windsor well because we used to shop there when we lived down the road in Virginia Water, and I strode with a proprietorial air, noting which shops had altered or changed hands over the years, which is to say most of them. Beside the handsome town hall stood Market Cross House, a building so perilously leaning that you can't help wonder if it was built that way intentionally with a distant view to pleasing Japanese visitors with cameras. It was now a sandwich bar, but, like most of the other shops on the pretty jumble of cobbled streets around it, it has been about a million things, usually tourist connected. The last time I was here, most of them were selling egg cups with legs; now they seemed to specialize in twee little pottery cottages and castles. Only Woods of Windsor, a company that manages to get more commercial mileage out of lavender than I would ever have thought possible, is still there selling soaps and toilet water. On Peascod Street, Marks & Spencer had expanded, Hammick's bookshop and Laura Ashley had changed locations, and the Golden Egg and Wimpy's restaurants were, not surprisingly, long gone (though I confess a certain fondness for the old-style Wimpy's with their odd sense of what constituted American food, as if they had compiled their recipes from a garbled telex). But I was pleased to note that Daniel's, the most interesting department store in Britain, was still there.

Daniel's is the most extraordinary place. It has all the features you expect of a provincial English department store—low ceilings, tiny obscure departments, frayed carpets held down with strips of electrician's tape, a sense that this space was once occupied by about eleven different shops and dwellings all with slightly different elevations—but it has the oddest assortment of things on sale: knicker elastic and collar snaps, buttons and pinking shears, six pieces of Portmeirion china, racks of clothing for very old people, a modest few rolls of carpet with the sorts of patterns you get when you rub your eyes too hard, chests of drawers with a handle missing, wardrobes on which one of the doors quietly swings open fifteen seconds after you experimentally shut it. Daniel's always puts me in mind of what Britain might have been like under communism.

It has long seemed to me unfortunate—and I'm taking the global view here—that such an important experiment in social organization was left to the Russians when the British clearly would have managed it so much better. All those things that are necessary to the successful implementation of a rigorous socialist system are, after all, second nature to the British. For a start, they like going without. They are great at pulling together, particularly in the face of adversity, for a perceived common good. They will queue patiently for indefinite periods and accept with rare fortitude the imposition of rationing, bland diets, and sudden inconvenient shortages of staple goods, as anyone who has ever looked for bread at a supermarket on a Saturday afternoon will know. They are comfortable with faceless bureaucracies and, as Mrs. Thatcher proved, tolerant of dictatorships. They will wait uncomplainingly for years for an operation or the delivery of a household appliance. They have a natural gift for making excellent, muttered jokes about authority without ever actually challenging it, and they derive universal satisfaction from the sight of the rich and powerful brought low. Most of those above the age of twenty-five already dress like East Germans. The conditions, in a word, are right.

Please understand I'm not saying that Britain would have been a happier, better place under communism, merely that the British would have done it properly. They would have taken it in stride, with good heart, and without excessive cheating. In point of fact, until about 1970 it wouldn't have made the slightest discernible difference to most people's lives, and might at least have spared us Robert Maxwell.

I rose early the next day and attended to my morning hygiene in a state of small excitation because I had a big day ahead of me. I was going to walk across Windsor Great Park. It is the most splendid park, stretching over forty square miles and incorporating into its ancient fabric every manner of sylvan charm: deep primeval woodlands, bosky dells, wandering footpaths and bridleways, formal and informal gardens, and a long, deeply fetching lake. Scattered picturesquely about are farms, woodland cottages, forgotten statues, a whole village occupied by estate workers and things that the Queen has brought back from trips abroad and couldn't think of anywhere else to put—obelisks and totem poles and other curious expressions of gratitude from distant outposts of the Commonwealth.

The news had not yet come out that there was oil under the park, so I didn't realize that I ought to drink things in carefully in case the next time I came this way it looked like an Oklahoma oil field. At this time, Windsor Great Park continued to enjoy a merciful obscurity, which I find mystifying in an open space so glorious on the very edge of London. Only once could I remember any reference to the park in the newspapers, a couple of years before when Prince Philip had taken a curious dislike to an avenue of ancient oaks and had instructed Her Majesty's Tree Choppers to remove them from the landscape.

I expect their branches had imperiled the progress through the park of his horses and plus-four, or whatever it is you call those bouncy, archaic contraptions he so likes to roam around in. You often see him and other members of the royal family in the park, speeding past in assorted vehicles on their way to polo matches or church services in the Queen Mother's private compound, the Royal Lodge. Indeed, because the public isn't allowed to drive on the park roads, a significant portion of the little traffic that passes is generated by royals. Once, on Boxing Day, when I was ambling along in a paternal fashion beside an offspring on a shiny new tricycle, I became aware with a kind of sixth sense that we were holding up the progress of a car, and turned to find that it was being driven by Princess Diana. As I hastened myself and my child out of the way, she gave me a smile that melted my heart, and since that time I have never said a word against the dear sweet girl, however pressed by those who think that she is a bit off her head because she spends £28,000 a year on leotards and makes occasional crank phone calls to hunky military men. (And who among us hasn't? is my unanswerable reply.)

I strode along the aptly named Long Walk from the base of Windsor Castle to the equestrian statue of King George III, known to locals as the copper horse, at the summit of Snow Hill, where I rested at the base and soaked up one of the most comely views in England: the majestic sprawl of Windsor Castle three miles away at the end of the Long Walk, with the town at its feet and, beyond, Eton, the misty Thames Valley, and the low Chiltern Hills. Deer grazed in picturesque herds in a clearing below and early morning strollers began to dot the long avenue framed by my splayed feet. I watched planes taking off from Heathrow and found on the horizon the faint but recognizable shapes of Battersea Power Station and the Post Office Tower. I can remember being very excited to discover that I could see London from way out here. It is, I believe, the only spot this far out where you can see central London. Henry VIII rode to this summit to hear the cannons from the Tower announce the execution of Anne Boleyn, though now all I could hear was the drone of airliners banking to land, and the startling yap of a large shaggy dog that appeared suddenly at my elbow—its owners following up a side hill—and offered me a large saliva specimen, which I declined.

I struck off through the park, past the grounds of the Royal Lodge, the pink Georgian house where the Queen and Princess Margaret spent their girlhoods, and through the surrounding woods and fields to my favorite corner of the park, Smith's Lawn. It must be the finest lawn in Britain, flat and flawlessly green and built on a heroic scale. There's almost never a soul up there, except when there's a polo match on. It took me the better part of an hour to cross it, though I went some distance out of my way to investigate a forlorn statue on the periphery, which turned out to be of Prince Albert, and another hour to find my way through the Valley Gardens and on to Virginia Water Lake, steaming softly in the autumnal morning air. It's a lovely piece of work, the lake, created by the Duke of Cumberland as a somewhat odd way of celebrating all those Scots he'd left inert or twitching on the battlefield of Culloden, and it is intensely picturesque and romantic in that way that only created landscapes can be, with sudden vistas perfectly framed by trees and a long decorative stone bridge. At the far end there is even a cluster of fake Roman ruins, opposite Fort Belvedere, the country home where Edward VIII made his famous abdication broadcast so that he could be free to go fishing with Goebbels and marry that sour-faced Simpson woman.

I mention this only because the nation seemed to be embarking on a similar monarchical crisis at this time. I must say, I can't begin to understand the attitudes of the British nation toward the royal family. For years—shall I be candid here for a moment?—I thought they were insupportably boring and only marginally more attractive than Mrs. Simpson, but everybody in England adored them. Then when, by a small miracle, they finally started doing arresting and erratic things and started making the *News of the World* on merit— when, in a word, they finally became *interesting*—the whole nation was suddenly saying, "Shocking. Let's get rid of them." Only that week, I had watched with open mouth a television program in which four pillars of British intellectual life sat around discussing whether the nation should dispense with Prince Charles and leapfrog to little Prince William. Now, putting aside for the moment the question of the wisdom of investing a lot of faith in the unmatured genetic output of Charles and Diana, which I would charitably describe as touching, it seemed to me to miss the whole point. If you are going to have a system of hereditary privilege, then surely you have to take what comes your way no matter how ponderous the poor fellow may be or how curious his taste in mistresses.

My own views on the matter are neatly encapsulated in a song of my own composition called "I'm the Eldest Son of the Eldest Son of the Eldest Son of the Eldest Son of the Guy Who Fucked Nell Gwyn," which I should be happy to send under separate cover upon receipt of £3.50 + 50p post and packaging.

In the meantime, you will have to imagine me humming this cheery ditty as I stepped smartly through the roar of traffic along the A30 and made my way down Christchurch Road to the sedate and leafy village of Virginia Water.

chapter
6

 y first sight of Virginia Water was on an unusually sultry
afternoon at the very end of August 1973, some five months after my
arrival in Dover. I had spent the summer traveling around in the
company of one Stephen Katz, who had joined me in Paris in April
and whom I had gratefully seen off from Istanbul some ten days
before. I was tired and road-weary, but very glad to be back in England. I stepped from a London train and was captivated instantly.
The village of Virginia Water looked tidy and beckoning. It was full
of lazy late-afternoon shadows and an impossible green lushness
such as could be appreciated only by someone freshly arrived from
an arid clime. Beyond the station rose the Gothic tower of Holloway
Sanitorium, a monumental heap of bricks and gables in parklike
grounds just beyond the station.

Two girls I knew from my hometown worked as student nurses at
the sanitorium and had offered me sleeping space on their floor and
the opportunity to ring their bath with five months of accumulated
muck. My intention was to catch a flight home from Heathrow the
next day; I was due to resume my listless university studies in two
weeks. But over many beers in a cheery pub called the Rose and

Crown, it was intimated to me that the hospital was always looking for menial staff and that I, as a native speaker of English, was a shoo-in. The next day, with a muzzy head and without benefit of reflection, I found myself filling in forms and being told to present myself to the charge nurse on Tuke Ward at 7 A.M. the following morning. A kindly little man with the intelligence of a child was summoned to take me to stores to collect a weighty set of keys and a teetering mountain of neatly folded hospital clothing—two gray suits, shirts, a tie, several white lab coats (what did they have in mind for me?)—and to deliver me to the male staff quarters across the road, where a crone with white hair showed me to a spartan room and, in a manner reminiscent of my old friend Mrs. Gubbins, issued a volley of instructions concerning the weekly exchange of soiled sheets for clean, the hours of hot water, the operation of the radiator, and other matters much too numerous and swiftly presented to take in, though I was rather proud to catch a passing reference to counterpanes. Been there, I thought.

I composed a letter to my parents telling them not to wait supper; passed a happy few hours trying on my new clothes and posing Betty Grable–style before the mirror; arranged my modest selection of paperback books on the windowsill; popped out to the post office and had a look around the village; dined at a little place called the Tudor Rose; and called in at a pub called the Trottesworth, where I found the ambience so agreeable and the alternative forms of amusement so nonexistent that I drank, I confess, an intemperate amount of beer, and returned to my new quarters by way of several shrubs and one memorably unyielding lamppost.

In the morning I awoke fifteen minutes late and found my way blearily to the hospital. Amid the melee of a shift change, I asked the way to Tuke Ward and arrived, hair askew and weaving slightly, ten minutes late. The charge nurse, a friendly fellow of early middle years, welcomed me warmly, told me where I'd find tea and biscuits and cleared off. I scarcely ever saw him after that. Tuke Ward was inhabited by long-stay male patients in a state of arrested insanity who, mercifully, seemed to look entirely after themselves. They fetched their own breakfasts from a wheeled cart, shaved themselves, made their own beds after a fashion, and, while I was momentarily engaged in a futile search for antacids in the staff loo, quietly departed. I emerged to find, to my confusion and alarm, that I was the only person left on the ward. I wandered puzzled through the day room, kitchen, and dormitories, and opened the ward door to find an empty corridor with a door to the world standing open at its far end. At that moment the phone in the ward office rang.

"Who's that?" barked a voice.

I summoned enough power of speech to identify myself and peered out the office window, expecting to see the thirty-three patients of Tuke Ward dashing from tree to tree in a desperate bid for freedom.

"Smithson here," said the voice. Smithson was the head nursing officer, an intimidating figure with muttonchops and a barrel chest. He'd been pointed out to me the day before. "You're the new boy, are you?"

"Yes, sir."

"Jolly there?"

I blinked, confused, and thought what odd turns of phrase the English had. "Well, actually it's very quiet."

"No, John Jolly, the charge nurse—is he there?"

"Oh. He's gone."

"Did he say when he'd be back?"

"No, sir."

"Everything under control?"

"Well, actually"—I cleared my throat—"it appears that the patients have escaped, sir."

"They've what?"

"Escaped, sir. I just went to the bathroom and when I came out—"

"They're supposed to be off the ward, son. They'll be on gardening detail or at occupational therapy. They leave every morning."

"Oh, thank Christ for that."

"I beg your pardon?"

"Thank goodness for that, sir."

"Yes, quite." He rang off.

I spent the rest of the morning wandering alone around the ward, looking in drawers and wardrobes and under beds, exploring store cupboards, trying to figure out how to make tea from loose leaves and a sieve, and, when my constitution proved up to it, having a private world skidding championship along the well-polished corridor that ran between the patients' rooms, complete with whispered and respectful commentary. When it got to be 1:30 and no one had told me to go to lunch, I dismissed myself and went to the staff dining hall, where I sat alone with a plate of beans, chips, and a mysterious item later identified to me as a Spam fritter, and noticed that Mr. Smithson and some of his colleagues, at a table across the room, were having a discussion of considerable mirth and, for some reason, casting merry looks in my direction.

When I returned to the ward, I discovered that several of the patients had returned in my absence. Most of them were slumped in chairs in the dayroom, sleeping off the exertions of a morning spent leaning on a rake or counting Rawl plugs into boxes, except for one dapper and well-spoken fellow in tweeds who was watching a cricket match on the television. He invited me to join him and, upon discovering that I was an American, enthusiastically explained to me this most bewildering of sports. I took him to be a member of staff, possibly the mysterious Mr. Jolly's afternoon replacement, possibly a visiting psychiatrist, until he turned to me, in the midst of a detailed explication of the intricacies of spin bowling, and said suddenly and conversationally, "I have atomic balls, you know."

"Excuse me?" I replied, my mind still on the other type of balls.

"Porton Down, 1947. Government experiments. All very hush-hush. You mustn't tell a soul."

"Ah . . . no, of course."

"I'm wanted by the Russians."

"Oh . . . ah?"

"That's why I'm here. Incognito." He tapped his nose significantly and cast an appraising glance at the dozing figures around us. "Not a bad place really. Full of madmen, of course. Positively teeming with lunatics, poor souls. But they do a lovely jam roly-poly on Wednesdays. Now this is Geoff Boycott coming up. Lovely touch. He'll have no trouble with Benson's delivery, just you see."

Most of the patients on Tuke Ward were like that when you got to know them—superficially lucid but, underneath, crazy as an overheated dog. It is an interesting experience to become acquainted with a country through the eyes of the insane, and, if I may say so, a particularly useful grounding for life in Britain.

And so my first permanent days in Britain passed. At night I went to the pub and by day I presided over a mostly empty ward. Each afternoon about four o'clock a Spanish lady in a pink coverall would appear with a clattering tea cart and the patients would stir to life to get a cup of tea and a slice of yellow cake, and from time to time the elusive Mr. Jolly dropped by to dispense medicines or reorder biscuits, but otherwise things were very quiet. I developed a passable understanding of cricket and my skidding became uncommonly accomplished.

The hospital, I came to discover, was its own little universe, virtually complete unto itself. It had its own carpentry shop and electricians, plumbers, and painters, its own bus and bus driver. It had a snooker room, a badminton court and swimming pool, a little shop selling toiletries and sweets, a chapel, a cricket pitch and social club, a podiatrist and hairdresser, kitchens, a sewing room, and a laundry. Once a week it showed movies in a kind of ballroom. It even had its own mortuary. The patients did all the gardening that didn't involve sharp tools and kept the grounds immaculate. It was a bit like a country club for crazy people. I liked it very much.

One day, during one of Mr. Jolly's periodic visits—I never did discover what he did during his absences—I was dispatched to a neighboring ward called Florence Nightingale to borrow a bottle of Thorazine to keep the patients docile. Flo, as it was known to the staff, was a strange and gloomy place, full of much more seriously demented people who wandered about or rocked ceaselessly in high-backed chairs. While the nurse in charge went off with jangling keys to sort out the Thorazine, I stared at the jabbering masses and gave thanks that I had given up hard drugs. At the far end of the room, there moved a pretty young nurse of clear and radiant goodness, caring for these helpless wrecks with boundless reserves of energy and compassion—guiding them to a chair, brightening their day with chatter, wiping dribble from their chins—and I thought, *This is just the sort of person I need*.

We were married sixteen months later in the local church, which I passed now as I made my way down Christchurch Road, shuffling along through papery leaves, under a tunnel of lofty boughs, humming the last eight bars of "Nell Gwyn." The big houses along Christchurch Road were unchanged, except for the addition on each of a security box and floodlights of the sort that come on for no reason late at night.

Virginia Water is an interesting place. It was built mostly in the 1920s and 1930s, with two small parades of shops and, surrounding them, a dense network of private roads winding through and around the famous Wentworth Golf Course. Scattered among the trees are rambling houses, often occupied by celebrities and built in a style that might be called Ostentatious English Vernacular, with busy roof-lines crowded with gables and fussy chimney pots, spacious and multiple verandas, odd-sized windows, at least one emphatic chimney breast, and acres of trailing roses over a trim little porch. It felt, when I first saw it, rather like walking into the pages of a 1937 *House & Garden*.

But what lent Virginia Water a particular charm back then, and I mean this quite seriously, was that it was full of wandering lunatics. Because most of the patients had been resident at the sanitorium for years and often decades, no matter how addled their thoughts or hesitant their gait, no matter how much they mumbled and muttered, adopted sudden postures of submission, or demonstrated any of a hundred other indications of someone comfortably out to lunch, most of them could be trusted to wander down to the village and find their way back again. Each day you could count on finding a refreshing sprinkling of lunatics buying fags or sweets, having a cup of tea, or just quietly remonstrating with thin air. The result was one of the most extraordinary communities in England, one in which wealthy people and lunatics mingled on equal terms. The shopkeepers and locals were quite wonderful about it, and didn't act as if anything was odd because a man with wild hair wearing a pajama jacket was standing in a corner of the baker's declaiming to a spot on the wall, or sitting at a corner table of the Tudor Rose with swiveling eyes and the makings of a smile, dropping sugar cubes into his minestrone soup. It was, and I'm still serious, a thoroughly heartwarming sight.

Among the five hundred or so patients at the sanitorium was a remarkable idiot savant named Harry. Harry had the mind of a small, preoccupied child, but you could name any date, past, present, or future, and he would instantly tell you what day of the week it was. We used to test him with a perpetual calendar and he was never wrong. You could ask him the date of the third Saturday of December 1935 or the second Wednesday of July 2017 and he would tell you faster than any computer could. Even more extraordinary, though it seemed merely tiresome at the time, was that several times a day he would approach members of the staff and ask them in a strange, bleating voice if the hospital was going to close in 1980. According to his copious medical notes, he had been obsessed with this question since his arrival as a young man in about 1950. The thing is, Holloway was a big, important institution, and there were never any plans to close it. Indeed, there were none right up until the stormy night in early 1980 when Harry was put to bed in a state of uncharacteristic agitation—he had been asking his question with increasing persistence for several weeks—and a bolt of lightning struck a back gable, causing a devastating fire that swept through the attics and several of the wards, rendering the entire structure suddenly uninhabitable.

It would make an even better story if poor Harry had been held to his bed by leather straps and perished in the blaze. Unfortunately for purposes of exciting narrative, all the patients were safely evacuated into the stormy night, though I like to imagine Harry with his lips contorted in a strange rapturous smile as he stood on the lawn, a blanket around his shoulders, his face lit by dancing flames, and watched the conflagration that he had so patiently awaited for thirty years.

The inmates were transferred to a special wing of a general hospital down the road at Chertsey, where they were soon deprived of their liberty on account of their unfortunate inclination to cause havoc in the wards and alarm the sane. In the meantime, the sanitorium quietly moldered away, its windows boarded or broken, its grand entrance from the road blocked by a heavy-duty metal gate topped with razor wire. I lived in Virginia Water for five years in the early 1980s when I was working in London and occasionally stopped to peer over the wall at the neglected grounds and general desolation. A series of developers had taken it over with ambitious plans to turn the site into an office park or conference center or compound of executive homes. They had set up some Portakabins and stern signs warning that the site was patroled by guard dogs, which, if the illustrations were to be believed, were barely under control, but nothing more positive than this was ever done. For well over a decade this wonderful old hospital, probably one of the dozen finest Victorian structures still standing, had just sat, crumbling and forlorn, and I had expected it to be much the same—indeed, was rehearsing an obsequious request to the watchman to be allowed to go up the drive for a quick peek since the building itself couldn't much be seen from the road.

So imagine my surprise when I crested a gentle slope and found a spanking new entrance knocked into the perimeter wall, a big sign welcoming me to Virginia Park, and, flanking a previously unknown vista of the sanitorium building, a generous clutch of smart new executive homes behind. With mouth agape, I stumbled up a freshly asphalted road lined with houses so new that there were still stickers on the windows and the yards were seas of mud. One of the houses had been done up as a show home and, as it was a Sunday, it was busy with people having a look. Inside, I found a glossy brochure full of architects' drawings of happy, slender people strolling around among handsome houses, listening to a chamber orchestra in the room where I had formerly watched movies in the company of twitching lunatics, or swimming in an indoor pool sunk into the floor of the great Gothic hall where I had once played badminton and falteringly asked the young nurse from Florence Nightingale for a date, with a distant view, if she could possibly spare the time, of marrying me. According to the rather sumptuous accompanying prose, residents of Virginia Park could choose among several dozen detached executive homes, a scattering of town houses and flats, and twenty-three grand apartments carved out of the restored sanitorium building, now mysteriously renamed Crosland House. The map of the site was dotted with strange names—Connolly Mews, Chapel Square, The Piazza—that owed little to its previous existence. How much more appropriate, I thought, if they had given them names like Lobotomy Square and Electroconvulsive Court. Prices started at £350,000.

I went back outside to see what I could get for my £350,000. The answer was a smallish but ornate home on a modest plot with an interesting view of a nineteenth-century mental hospital. I can't say that it was what I had always dreamed of. All the houses were built of red brick, with old-fashioned chimney pots, gingerbread trim, and other small nods to the Victorian age. One model, rather mundanely known as House Type D, even had a decorative tower. The result was that they looked as if they had somehow been pupped by the sanitorium. You could almost imagine them, given sufficient time, growing into sanitoriums themselves. Insofar as such a thing can work at all, it worked surprisingly well. The new houses didn't jar against the backdrop of the old sanitorium, and at least—something that surely wouldn't have happened a dozen years ago—that great old heap of a building, with all its happy memories for me and generations of the interestingly insane, had been saved. I doffed my hat to the developers and took my leave.

I had intended to stroll up to my old house, but it was a mile off and my feet were sore. Instead, I headed down Stroude Road, past the site of the old hospital social club, now replaced by a dwelling of considerable ugliness, and the scattered buildings that had once been quarters for nursing and domestic staff, and bet myself £100 that the next time I passed this way they would be gone and replaced by big houses with double garages.

I walked the two miles to Egham, and called at the house of a delightful lady named Mrs. Billen who is, among her many other selfless kindnesses, my mother-in-law. While she bustled off to the kitchen in that charming flutter with which all English ladies of a certain age receive sudden guests, I warmed my toes by the fire and reflected (for such was my state of mind these days) that this was the first English house I had ever been in, other than as a paying guest. My wife had brought me here as her young swain one Sunday afternoon many years before and we had sat, she and I and her family, tightly squeezed into this snug and well-heated lounge watching *Bullseye* and *The Generation Game* and other televisual offerings that seemed to me interestingly lacking in advanced entertainment value. This was a new experience for me. I hadn't seen my own family in what might be called a social setting since about 1958, apart from a few awkward hours at Christmases, so there was a certain cozy novelty in finding myself in the midst of so much familial warmth. It is something that I still very much admire in the British, though I confess a certain passing exultation when I learned that they were taking *Bullseye* off the air.

My mother-in-law—Mum—appeared with a tray of food such as made me wonder for a moment if she had mistaken me for a party of lumberjacks. As I greedily tucked into a delicious, steaming heap that brought to mind the Cairngorm Mountains re-created in comestible form, and afterward sat slumped with coffee and a happily distended stomach, we chattered away about this and that—the children, our impending move to the States, my work, her recent widowhood. Late in the evening—late, that is, for a couple of old-timers like us—she went into bustling mode again and, after making a great deal of industrious-sounding noise from every quarter of the house, announced that the guest room was ready. I found a neatly turned-down bed complete with hot-water bottle and, after the most cursory of ablutions, crawled gratefully into it, wondering why it is that the beds in the houses of grandparents and in-laws are always so deliciously comfortable. I was asleep in moments.

chapter
7

and so to Bournemouth, grandest of the south coast resorts. I
arrived at 5:30 in the evening in a driving rain. Night had fallen
heavily and the streets were full of swishing cars, their headlights
sweeping through bullets of shiny rain. I'd lived in Bournemouth
for two years in the 1970s and thought I knew it reasonably well,
but the area around the station had been extensively rebuilt, with
new roads and office blocks and one of those befuddling networks
of pedestrian subways that compel you to surface every few minutes
like a gopher to see where you are.

By the time I reached the East Cliff, a neighborhood of medium-
sized hotels perched high above a black sea, I was soaked through
and muttering. The one thing to be said for Bournemouth is that
you are certainly spoiled for choice with hotels. Among the many
gleaming palaces of comfort that lined every street for blocks around,
I selected an establishment on a side street for no reason other than
that I rather liked its sign: neat capitals in pink neon glowing beckoningly through the slicing rain. I stepped inside, shedding water,
and could see at a glance it was a good choice—clean, nicely old-
fashioned, attractively priced at £26 B&B according to a notice on

the wall, and with the kind of smothering warmth that makes your glasses steam and brings on sneezing fits. I decanted several ounces of water from my sleeve and asked for a single room for two nights.

"Is it raining out?" the reception girl asked brightly as I filled in the registration card between sneezes and pauses to wipe water from my face with the back of my arm.

"No, my ship sank and I had to swim the last seven miles."

"Oh, yes?" she went on in a manner that made me suspect she was not attending my words closely. "And will you be dining with us tonight, Mr."—she glanced at my water-smeared card—"Mr. Brylcreem?" I considered the alternative—a long slog through stair rods of rain—and felt inclined to stay in. Besides, between her cheerily bean-sized brain and my smeared scrawl, there was every chance they would charge the meal to another room. I said I'd eat in, accepted a key, and drippingly found my way to my room.

Among the many hundreds of things that have come a long way in Britain since 1973, few have come further than the average English hostelry. Nowadays you get a color TV, a coffee-making tray with a little packet of modestly tasty biscuits, a private bath with fluffy towels, a little basket of cotton wool balls in rainbow colors, and an array of sachets or little plastic bottles of shampoo, bath gel, and moisturizing lotion. My room even had an adequate bedside light and two soft pillows. I was very happy. I ran a deep bath, emptied into it all the gels and moisturizing creams (don't be alarmed; I've studied this closely and can assure you that they are all the same substance), and, as a fiesta of airy bubbles began their slow ascent toward a position some three feet above the top of the bath, returned to the room and slipped easily into the self-absorbed habits of the lone traveler, unpacking my knapsack with deliberative care, draping wet clothes over the radiator, laying out clean ones on the bed with as much fastidiousness as if I were about to go to my first high-school prom, arranging a travel clock and reading material with exacting precision on the bedside table, adjusting the lighting to a level of considered coziness, and finally retiring, in perky spirits and with a good book, for a long wallow in the sort of luxuriant foam seldom seen outside Jayne Mansfield movies.

Afterward, freshly attired and smelling bewitchingly of attar of roses, I presented myself in the spacious and empty dining salon and was shown to a table where the array of accoutrements—a wineglass containing a red paper napkin shaped into a floret, stainlesssteel salt and pepper shakers resting in a little stainless-steel boat, a dish containing wheels of butter carefully shaped like cogs, a smallnecked vase bearing a sprig of artificial lilies—instantly informed me that the food would be mediocre but presented with a certain wellpracticed flourish. I covered my eyes, counted to four, and extended my right hand knowing it would alight on a basket of bread rolls proffered by a hovering waiter—a mastery of timing that impressed him considerably, if I may say so, and left him in no doubt that he was dealing with a traveler who knew his way around creamy green soups, vegetables served with nested spoons, and circlets of toughened rawhide parading under the name *medallions of pork*.

Three other diners arrived—a rotund mother and father and an even larger teenaged son—whom the waiter thoughtfully seated in a place where I could watch them without having to crane my neck or reposition my chair. It is always interesting to watch people eat, but nothing provides more interest than the sight of a tableful of fat people tucking into their chow. It is a curious thing, but even the greediest and most rapacious fat people—and the trio before me could clearly have won championships for rapacity—never look as if they are enjoying themselves when they are dining. It is as if they are merely fulfilling some kind of long-standing obligation to maintain their bulk. When there is food before them, they lower their heads and Hoover it up, and in between times they sit with crossed arms staring uneasily at the room and acting as if they have never been introduced to the people sitting with them. But roll up a sweet trolley and everything changes. They begin to make rapturous cooing noises and suddenly their little corner of the room is full of happy conversation. Thus it was tonight. Such was the speed with which my dining partners consumed the provends set before them that they beat me by half a course and, to my frank horror, between them consumed the last of the profiteroles and Black Forest gateau from the sweet trolley. The boy, I noticed, had a double heap of both, the greedy fat pig.

I was left to choose between a watery dribble of trifle, a meringue confection that I knew would explode like a party popper as soon as I touched a spoon to it, or any of about a dozen modest cuplets of butterscotch pudding, each with a desultory nubbin of crusty yellow cream on top. Unhappily, I chose a butterscotch pudding, and as the tubby trio waddled past my table, their chins glistening with chocolate, I answered their polite, well-fed smiles with a flinty-hard look that told them not to try anything like that with me ever again. I think they got the message. The next morning at breakfast they took a table well out of my line of vision and gave me a wide berth at the juice trolley.

Bournemouth is a very fine place. For one thing it has the sea, which will be handy if global warming ever reaches its full potential, though I can't see much use for it at present, and there are the sinuous parks, collectively known as the Pleasure Gardens, that neatly divide the two halves of the town center and provide shoppers with a tranquil green place to rest on their long slog from one side of the town center to the other—though, of course, if it weren't for the parks there wouldn't be the long slog. Such is life.

The parks used to be described on maps as the Upper Pleasure Gardens and Lower Pleasure Gardens, but some councillor or other force for good realized the profound and unhealthy implications of placing *Lower* and *Pleasure* in such immediate proximity and successfully lobbied to have *Lower* removed from the title, so now you have the Upper Pleasure Gardens and the mere Pleasure Gardens, and lexical perverts have been banished to the beaches where they must find such gratification as they can by rubbing themselves on the groynes. Anyway, that's the kind of place Bournemouth is—genteel to a fault and proud of it.

Knowing already of the town's carefully nurtured reputation for gentility, I moved there in 1977 with the idea that this was going to be a kind of English answer to Bad Ems or Baden-Baden—manicured parks, palm courts with orchestras, swank hotels where men in white gloves kept the brass gleaming, bosomy elderly ladies in mink coats walking those little dogs you ache to kick (not out of cruelty, you understand, but from a simple, honest desire to see how far you can make them fly). Sadly, I have to report that almost none of this awaited me. The parks were very fetching, but instead of opulent casinos and handsome kursaals, they offered a small bandstand occupied on occasional Sundays by brass bands of mixed talent dressed like bus conductors, and small wooden erections—if you will excuse the term in the context of the Lower Pleasure Gardens—bedecked with colored glass pots with a candle inside, which I was assured were sometimes lit on calm summer evenings and thus were transformed into glowing depictions of butterflies, fairies, and other magical visions guaranteed to provide hours of healthy nocturnal enjoyment. I couldn't say because I never saw them lit, and in any case, a shortage of funds and the unconscionable tendency of youths to yank the pots from their frames and smash them at each other's feet for purposes of amusement meant that the structures were soon dismantled and taken away.

At first glance, the town looked largely unchanged, but in fact progress and the borough council had been at work everywhere. Christchurch Road, the main thoroughfare through the center, had been extensively pedestrianized and decorated with a curious glass-and-tubular-steel edifice that looked like a bus shelter for giants. Two of the shopping arcades had been nicely tarted up and there was now a McDonald's, Waterstones and Dillons bookshops, as well as one or two other establishments less directly connected to my personal requirements. Mostly, however, things had been subtracted. Beale's department store had closed its excellent book department, Dingle's had intemperately gotten rid of its food hall, and Beale-son's, yet another department store, had gone altogether. The International Store, a small supermarket, had likewise vanished, as had, more distressingly, an elegant little bakery, taking the world's best sugar doughnuts with it, alas, alas. On the plus side, there wasn't a scrap of litter to be found, whereas in my day Christchurch Road was an open-air litter bin.

Around the corner from the old vanished bakery on Richmond Hill were the splendid, vaguely art deco offices of the *Bournemouth Evening Echo,* where I worked for two years as a subeditor in a room borrowed from a Dickens novel: papers heaped in untidy stacks, gloomy lighting, two rows of hunched figures sitting at desks, and all of it bathed in a portentous, exhausting silence, the only noises the fretful scratchings of pencils and a soft but echoing *tunk* sound each time the minute hand on the wall clock clicked forward a notch. From across the road, I peered up at my old office windows now and shivered slightly.

After our marriage, my wife and I had gone back to the States for two years while I finished college, so my job at the *Echo* was not only my first real job in Britain, but my first real grown-up job, and throughout the two years I worked there I never ceased to feel like a fourteen-year-old masquerading as an adult, doubtless because nearly all my fellow subeditors were old enough to be my father, except for a couple of cadaverous figures at the far end who were old enough to be their fathers.

I sat next to a pair of kindly and learned men named Jack Straight and Austin Brooks, who spent two years patiently explaining to me the meaning of *sub judice,* the important distinction in English law between taking a car and stealing a car, and why, for reasons of potential libel, a suspect is never questioned or interrogated but "helping police with their inquiries." For my own safety, I was mostly entrusted with the job of editing reports from the two main women's clubs, the Townswomen's Guild and the Women's Institute. We received stacks and stacks of these daily, all seemingly written in the same florid hand and all saying the same numbing things: "A most fascinating demonstration was given by Mr Arthur Smoat of Pokesdown on the art of making animal shadows," "Mrs Evelyn Stubbs honoured the assembled guests with a most fascinating and amusing talk on her recent hysterectomy," "Mrs Throop was unable to give her planned talk on dog management because of her recent tragic mauling by her mastiff, Prince, but Mrs Smethwick gamely stepped into the breach with an hilarious account of her experiences as a free-lance funeral organist." Every one of them went on and on with page after page of votes of thanks, appeals for funds, long-winded accounts of successful jumble sales and coffee mornings, and detailed lists of who had supplied which refreshments and how delightful they all were. I have never experienced longer days.

The windows, I recall, could be opened only by means of a long pole. About ten minutes after we arrived each morning, one subeditor so old he could barely hold a pencil would begin scraping his chair about in an effort to get some clearance from his desk. It would take him about an hour to get out of his chair, and another hour to shuffle the few feet to the window and finagle it open with the pole, and another hour to lean the pole against the wall and shuffle back to his desk. The *instant* he was reseated, the man who sat opposite him would bob up, stride over, bang the window shut with the pole, and return to his seat with a challenging look on his face, at which point the old boy would silently and stoically begin the chair-scraping process all over again. This went on every day for two years through all seasons.

I never saw either one of them do a lick of work. The older fellow couldn't, of course, because he spent all but a few moments each day traveling to or from the window. The other guy mostly sat sucking on an unlit pipe and staring at me with a kind of smirk. Every time our gazes met, he would ask me some mystifying question to do with America. "Tell me," he would say, "is it true that Mickey Rooney never consummated his marriage with Ava Gardner, as I've read?" or "I've often wondered, and perhaps you can tell me, why is it that the nua-nua bird of Hawaii subsists only on pink-shelled mollusks when white-shelled mollusks are more numerous and of equal nutritive value, or so I've read?"

I would look at him, my mind fogged with Townswomen's Guild and Women's Institute reports, and say, "What?"

"You *have* heard of the nua-nua bird, I take it?"

"Er, no."

He would cock an eyebrow. "Really? How extraordinary." And then he'd suck his pipe.

It was altogether a strange place. The editor was a recluse who had his meals brought to his chamber by his secretary and seldom ventured out. I saw him only twice in all the time I was there, once when he interviewed me, a meeting that lasted three minutes and seemed to cause him considerable discomfort, and once when he opened the door that connected his room to ours, an event so unusual that we all looked up. Even the old boy paused in his endless shuffle to the window. The editor stared at us in a kind of frozen astonishment, clearly dumbfounded to find a roomful of subeditors on the other side of one of his office doors; he looked for a moment as if he might speak, then wordlessly retreated, shutting the door behind him. It was the last I ever saw of him. Six weeks later, I took a job in London.

Something else that had changed in Bournemouth was that all the little coffee bars had gone. There used to be one every three or four doors, with their gasping espresso machines and sticky tables. I don't know where holidaymakers go for coffee nowadays—yes, I do: the

Costa del Sol—but I had to walk nearly all the way to the Triangle, a distant point where local buses go to rest between engagements, before I was able to have a modest and refreshing cup.

Afterward, fancying a bit of an outing, I caught a bus to the neighboring town of Christchurch with a view to walking back. I got a seat at the top front of a yellow double-decker. There is something awfully exhilarating about riding on the top of a double-decker. You can see into upstairs windows and peer down on the tops of people's heads at bus stops (and when they come up the stairs a moment later, you can look at them with a knowing look that says, "I've just seen the top of your head") and there's the frisson of excitement that comes with careering round a corner or roundabout on the brink of catastrophe. You get an entirely fresh perspective on the world. Towns generally look more handsome from the top deck of a bus, but nowhere more so than Bournemouth. At street level, it's essentially like any other big English town—lots of building society offices and chain stores, all with big plate-glass windows—but upstairs you suddenly realize that you are in one of Britain's great Victorian communities. Bournemouth didn't even exist before about 1850—it was just a couple of farms between Christchurch and Poole—and then it positively boomed, throwing up piers and promenades, miles of ornate brick offices and plump, stately homes, most of them with elaborate corner towers and other busy embellishments that are generally now evident only to bus riders and window cleaners.

What a shame it is that so little of this Victorian glory actually reaches the ground. But then, of course, if you took out all that plate glass and made the ground floors of the buildings look as if they belonged to the floors above, we might not be able to see right into every Sketchley's dry cleaner and Leeds Permanent Building Society and Boots the Chemist, and what a sad loss that would be. Imagine passing a Sketchley's and not being able to see racks of garments in plastic bags and an assortment of battered carpet shampooers and a lady at the counter idly cleaning her teeth with a paper clip, and think how dreary life would be. Why, it's unthinkable.

I rode the bus to the end of the line, the parking lot of a big new Sainsbury's supermarket in Christchurch, and found my way through a network of pedestrian flyovers to the Highcliffe Road. About a half mile farther on, down a little side road, stood Highcliffe Castle, formerly the home of Gordon Selfridge, the department store magnate, and now a ruin.

Selfridge was an interesting fellow who provides a salutary moral lesson for us all. An American who spent his early career at Marshall Field in Chicago, he moved to England in 1906 with the intention of building in London the greatest shopping emporium in Europe. The British thought he was mad, particularly when they learned he was to build his store on Oxford Street, far away from the main shopping areas of Knightsbridge and Kensington, but by dint of hard work and total dedication he succeeded. For years, Selfridge was a model of decorum. He led a life of stern rectitude, early bedtimes, and tireless endeavor. He drank lots of milk and never fooled around. But in 1918 his wife died and the sudden release from marital bonds rather went to his head. He took up with a pair of Hungarian-American cuties known in music hall circles as the Dolly Sisters, and fell into rakish ways. With a Dolly on each arm, he took to roaming the casinos of Europe, gambling and losing lavishly. He dined out every night, invested foolish sums in racehorses and motorcars, bought Highcliffe Castle, and laid plans to build a 250-room estate at Hengistbury Head nearby. In ten swift years he raced through $8 million; lost control of Selfridge's; lost his castle and London home, his racehorses, and his Rolls-Royces; and eventually ended up living alone in a small flat in Putney and traveling by bus. He died penniless and virtually forgotten on May 8, 1947. But of course he had had the inestimable pleasure of bonking twin sisters, which is the main thing.

Today Highcliffe's stately Gothic shell stands amid a crowd of bungalows, an incongruous sight, except at the back where the grounds run down to the sea through a public parking lot. I'd have liked to know how the house had come to be in such a parlous and neglected state, but there was no one around its brooding eminence and there were no cars in the parking lot. I followed some rickety wooden steps down to the beach. The rain had stopped in the night, but the sky was threatening and there was a stiff breeze that made my hair and clothes boogie and had the sea in a frenzy of froth. I couldn't hear anything but the pounding of waves. Leaning steeply into the wind, I trudged along the beach in the posture of someone shouldering a car up a hill, passing in front of a long crescent of beach huts, all of identical design but painted in varying bright hues. Most were shut up for the winter, but about three quarters of the way along one stood open, rather in the manner of a magician's box, with a little porch on which sat a man and a woman in garden chairs, huddled in arctic clothing with lap blankets, buffeted by wind that seemed constantly to threaten to tip them over backward. The man was trying to read a newspaper, but the wind kept wrapping it around his face.

They both looked very happy—or if not happy exactly, at least highly contented, as if this were the Seychelles and they were drinking gin fizzes under nodding palms, rather than sitting half-perished in a stiff English gale. They were contented because they owned a little piece of prized beachfront property for which there was no doubt a long waiting list and—here was the true secret of their happiness—any time they wanted, they could retire to the hut and be fractionally less cold. They could make a cup of tea and, if they were feeling particularly rakish, have a chocolate digestive biscuit. Afterward, they could spend a happy half hour packing their things away and closing up hatches. And this was all they required in the world to bring themselves to a state of near rapture.

One of the charms of the British is that they have so little idea of their own virtues, and nowhere is this more true than with their happiness. You will laugh to hear me say it, but they are the happiest people on earth. Honestly. Watch any two Britons in conversation and see how long it is before they smile or laugh over some joke or pleasantry. It won't be more than a few seconds. I once shared a railway compartment between Dunkirk and Brussels with two French-speaking businessmen who were obviously old friends or colleagues. They talked genially the whole journey, but not once in two hours did I see either of them raise a flicker of a smile. You could imagine the same thing with Germans or Swiss or Spaniards or even Italians, but with Britons—never.

And the British are so easy to please. It is the most extraordinary thing. They actually like their pleasures small. That is why so many of their treats—tea cakes, scones, crumpets, rock cakes, rich tea biscuits, fruit Shrewsburys—are so cautiously flavorful. They are the only people in the world who think of jam and currants as thrilling constituents of a pudding or cake. Offer them something genuinely tempting—a slice of gateau or a choice of chocolates from a box—and they will nearly always hesitate and begin to worry that it's unwarranted and excessive, as if any pleasure beyond a very modest threshold is vaguely unseemly.

"Oh, I shouldn't really," they say.

"Oh, go on," you prod encouragingly.

"Well, just a small one then," they say and dartingly take a small one, and then get a look as if they have just done something terribly devilish. All this is completely alien to the American mind. To an American the whole purpose of living, the one constant confirmation of continued existence, is to cram as much sensual pleasure as possible into one's mouth more or less continuously. Gratification, instant and lavish, is a birthright. You might as well say "Oh, I shouldn't really" if someone tells you to take a deep breath.

I used to be puzzled by the curious attitude of the British to pleasure, and that tireless, dogged optimism of theirs that allowed them
to attach an upbeat turn of phrase to the direst inadequacies—
"Mustn't grumble," "It makes a change," "You could do worse,"
"It's not much, but it's cheap and cheerful," "Well, it was *quite*
nice"—but gradually I came around to their way of thinking and
my life has never been happier. I remember finding myself sitting in
damp clothes in a cold café on a dreary seaside promenade and
being presented with a cup of tea and a tea cake and going, "Ooh,
lovely!" and I knew then that the process had started. Before long
I came to regard all kinds of activities—asking for more toast in a
hotel, buying wool-rich socks at Marks & Spencer, getting two pairs
of pants when I really needed only one—as something daring, very
nearly illicit. My life became immensely richer.

I exchanged smiles now with the happy couple at their hut, and
trudged on along the beach to Mudeford, a hamlet standing on a
spit of sandy land between the sea and the reedy sprawl of Christchurch Harbour, with a handsome view across to Christchurch's ancient and majestic priory. Mudeford was once a refuge of smugglers,
but today it is little more than a small, rather tatty parade of shops
and a Volvo dealership surrounded by houses, all with jaunty nautical names: Saltings, Hove To, Sick over the Side.

I walked through it and on into Christchurch by way of a long,
messy street lined with garages, dusty-looking shops, and half-dead
pubs, thence on to Bournemouth through Tuckton, Southbourne,
and Boscombe. Time had not done many favors to most of these
places. Christchurch's and Southbourne's shopping precincts both
appeared to be locked in a slow, untidy spiral of decline, and at
Tuckton Bridge a once-lovely pub on the banks of the River Stour
had had its lawns sacrificed to make room for a large parking lot.
Now it was something called a Brewers Fayre, an offshoot of the
Whitbread organization. It was awful but clearly and depressingly
popular. Only Boscombe seemed to have picked itself up a little.

Once the main road through it had been ugly enough to make you gasp, full of blown litter, tacky shops, and cruelly unsympathetic supermarkets and department stores crammed into Victorian frontages. Now the street had been smartly pedestrianized along part of its length; the Royal Arcade, a nineteenth-century shopping center, was being done up with style and care, and the whole district was generously scattered with antique shops, which were considerably more interesting to look at than the previous range of tanning salons and bedding centers.

It was a long haul from Highcliffe to Bournemouth, ten miles or so altogether, and well into my daily happy hour by the time I reached East Overcliff Drive and the last leg to town. I paused to lean on a white fence rail and take in the view. The wind had died and in the pale evening light Poole Bay, as the sea at Bournemouth is called, was entrancing: a long, majestic curve of crumbly cliffs and wide golden beaches stretching from below the Isle of Wight to the purply Purbeck hills. Before me the lights of Bournemouth and Poole twinkled invitingly in the gathering dusk. Far below, Bournemouth's two piers looked cheerful and dashing, and far out at sea the lights of passing ships bobbed and blinked in the dusky light. The world, or at least this little corner of it, seemed a good and peaceful place, and I was immensely glad to be there.

Throughout this trip, I would have moments of quiet panic at the thought of ever leaving this snug and homey little isle. It was a melancholy business really, this little trip of mine, a bit like wandering through a much-loved home for the last time. The fact is, I liked it here. I liked it very much. It took only a friendly gesture from a shopkeeper, or a seat by the fire in a country pub, or a view like this to set me thinking that I was making a serious, deeply misguided mistake.

Which is why, if you were one of those cliff-top strollers in Bournemouth that mild evening, you may have seen a middle-aged American wandering past in a self-absorbed manner and muttering,

"Think of endless winter months of rain. Think of VAT at 17.5 percent. Think of loading your car to overflowing with rubbish on a Saturday and driving to the dump only to find that it is shut. Think of the strange, unshakable fondness of BBC1 for *Cagney and Lacey* repeats. Think of . . ."

chapter
8

I went to Salisbury on a big red double-decker bus that swayed down winding country roads and clattered through overhanging branches in a most exciting way. I like Salisbury very much. It's just the right size for a town—big enough for cinemas and bookshops, small enough to feel friendly and livable.

I picked my way through a busy market in the square and tried to imagine what the British see in these things. They always look so depressingly tawdry, with their upended crates and trodden lettuce leaves and grubby plastic awnings held together with clips. In French markets you pick among wicker baskets of glossy olives and cherries and little wheels of goat cheese, all neatly arrayed. In Britain you buy tea towels and ironing board covers from plastic beer crates. British markets never fail to put me in a gloomy and critical frame of mind.

Walking through the busy shopping streets now, I found it was the unattractive things that jumped out at me—Burger Kings and Prontaprints and Super Drugs and all the other manifold Enemies of the High Street, all of them with windows cluttered with an- nouncements of special offers and all of them shoehorned into buildings without even the most fleeting nod to their character or age. In the center of town, on a corner that ought to have been a visual delight, there stood a small building occupied by a Lunn Poly travel agency. Upstairs the structure was half-timbered and quietly glorious; downstairs, between outsized sheets of plate glass covered with handwritten notices of cheap flights to Tenerife and Málaga, the facade had been tiled—*tiled*—with a mosaic of little multitoned squares that looked as if they had been salvaged from a British Rail toilet. It was just awful. I stood before it and tried to imagine what combination of architects, corporate designers, and town planners could have allowed this to be done to a fine timber-framed seventeenth-century building, and could not. And the thing was that it was really not a great deal worse than many other frontages along the street.

It sometimes occurs to me that the British have more heritage than is good for them. In a country where there is so astonishingly much of everything, it is easy to look on it as a kind of inexhaustible resource. Consider the numbers: 445,000 ancient or historic buildings, 12,000 medieval churches, 1.5 million acres of common land, 120,000 miles of footpaths and public rights of way, 600,000 known sites of archaeological interest. In my Yorkshire village alone there are almost certainly more genuine seventeenth-century buildings than in the whole of North America, and that's just one obscure hamlet with a population comfortably under 100. Multiply that by all the other villages and hamlets in Britain and you see that the stockpile of ancient dwellings, barns, churches, pinfolds, walls, bridges, and other structures is immense almost beyond counting. There is so much of it everywhere that it's easy to believe that you can take away chunks of it—a half-timbered frontage here, some Georgian windows there, a few hundred yards of ancient hedge or drystone wall—and that there will still be plenty left. In fact, the country is being nibbled to death.

It astounds me how casual are the planning regulations in such a sensitive environment. Even in conservation areas a houseowner may remove all the original doors and windows, cover the roof with hacienda-style tiles and the facade with artificial stone cladding, take down the garden wall, crazy-pave the lawn, and add a plywood porch, and still be deemed, in the eyes of the law, to be maintaining the carefully preserved tone of the neighborhood. Just about the only thing he can't do, in fact, is tear the house down—but even that is a largely hypothetical legal nicety. In 1992, a development company in Reading that tore down five listed buildings in a conservation area was taken to court and fined all of £675.

Despite a certain stirring of consciousness in recent years, householders throughout the country can still do pretty much anything they want with their homes, farmers can still throw up mammoth tin sheds and grub up hedges, British Telecom can whip away red phone boxes and replace them with stainless-steel shower stalls, gasoline companies can erect huge flat canopies on every forecourt, and retailers can impose their plasticky corporate styles on the most architecturally sensitive of structures, and there's nothing you can do about it. Actually, there is one little thing you can do: withhold your custom. I am proud to tell you that I haven't gone into a Boots in years and won't until the company restores the frontages of its principal outlets in Cambridge, Cheltenham, York, and such others as I might care to add to the list from time to time, and I would willingly get drenched to the bone if I could find a single gas station within twenty miles of my home that didn't have a flying canopy.

Salisbury, I must point out in fairness, is actually much better at looking after itself than most other towns. Indeed, it is the very handsomeness of the place generally that makes the odd desecrations so difficult to bear. Moreover, it appears, little by little, to be getting better. The local authorities had recently insisted that a cinema owner preserve the half-timbered facade on a sixteenth-century building in the town center, and I noticed two places where developers appeared to be actually taking apart buildings that had been despoiled during the dark ages of the 1960s and 1970s and restoring them with diligence and care. One developer's board boasted that it did this sort of thing more or less always. May it prosper forever.

I would probably forgive Salisbury anything as long as it never messes with the Cathedral Close. There is no doubt in my mind that Salisbury Cathedral is the single most beautiful structure in England and the close around it the most beautiful space. Every stone, every wall, every shrub, is just right. It is as if every person who has touched it for seven hundred years has only improved it. I could live on a bench in the grounds. I sat on one now and gazed happily for a half hour at this exquisite composition of cathedral, lawns, and solemn houses. I'd have stayed longer except that it began to drizzle, so I got up to have a look around. I went first to the Salisbury Museum in the hope that there would be a kindly person behind the counter who would let me leave my knapsack while I looked at the museum and cathedral. (There was, bless him.) The Salisbury Museum is outstanding. I hadn't intended to linger, but it was packed with diverting Roman oddments and old pictures and little scale models of Old Sarum and the like, for which I am always a sucker.

I was particularly interested in the Stonehenge Gallery because I was going there on the morrow, so I read all the instructive labels attentively. I know this goes without saying, but Stonehenge really was the most incredible accomplishment. It took five hundred men just to pull each sarsen, plus a hundred more to dash around positioning the rollers. Just think about it for a minute. Can you imagine trying to talk six hundred people into helping you drag a fifty-ton stone eighteen miles across the countryside and muscle it into an upright position, and then saying, "Right, lads! Another twenty like that, plus some lintels and maybe a couple of dozen nice bluestones from Wales, and we can *party*!" Whoever was the person behind

Stonehenge was one dickens of a motivator, I'll tell you that.

From the museum, I wandered across the broad lawn to the cathedral. In the tragic event that you have never been there, I warn you now that Salisbury has long been the most money-keen of English cathedrals. I used to be pretty generally unsympathetic about ecclesiastical structures hectoring visitors for funds, but then I met the vicar of the University Church of St. Mary the Virgin in Oxford—the most-visited parish church in England—and learned that its three hundred thousand annual visitors between them deposit a miserly £8,000 in the collection boxes, since which time I have mellowed considerably. I mean to say, these are glorious structures and deserve our grateful support. But Salisbury, I must say, takes things a good step beyond what I would call discreet solicitation.

First, you have to pass a cinema-style ticket booth where you are encouraged to pay a "voluntary" admission charge of £2.50, then once inside you are repeatedly assaulted with further calls on your pocket. You are asked to pay to hear a recorded message or make a brass rubbing, to show your support for the Salisbury Cathedral Girl Choristers and the Friends of Salisbury Cathedral, and to help restore something called the Eisenhower flag, a seriously faded and tattered Stars and Stripes that once hung in Eisenhower's command post at nearby Wilton House. (I left 10p and a note saying, "But why did you let it get in such a state in the first place?") Altogether, I counted nine separate types of contributions boxes between the admission booth and the gift shop—ten if you include the one for votive candles. On top of that, you could hardly move through the nave without bumping into an upright display introducing the cathedral staff (there were smiling photographs of all of them, as if this were a Burger King) or discussing the Church's voluntary work overseas or glass cases with cutaway models showing how the cathedral had been constructed—diverting, I grant you, but surely more appropriate to the museum across the close. It was a mess. How long, I wonder, till you climb into an electric cart and are whirred through the "Salisbury Cathedral Experience" complete with animatronic stonemasons and monks like Friar Tuck? I give it five years.

Afterward, I collected my knapsack from the kindly man at the Salisbury Museum and trudged off to the central tourist office, where I presented the young man behind the counter with a complicated prospective itinerary through Wiltshire and Dorset, from Stonehenge to Avebury and on to Lacock, Stourhead Gardens, and possibly Sherborne, and asked him if he could tell me which buses I needed to catch that would let me see them all in three days. He looked at me as if I were dangerously eccentric and said, "Have you by any chance traveled by bus in Britain before?"

I assured him that I had, in 1973.

"Well, I think you'll find that things have changed a bit since then," he said.

He handed me a slender leaflet giving the bus times between Salisbury and points west and helped me locate the modest section dealing with journeys to Stonehenge. I had hoped to catch an early morning bus to Stonehenge with a view to proceeding on to Avebury for the afternoon, but this, I instantly apprehended, was an impossibility. The first bus to Stonehenge didn't leave until almost eleven in the morning. I gave a snort of disbelief.

"I believe you'll find the local taxi services will take you to Stonehenge, wait for you there, and bring you back for about twenty pounds," he suggested. "A lot of our American visitors find this very satisfactory."

I explained to him that though I was technically an American, I had lived in Britain long enough to be careful with my money, and, though I had not yet reached the point where I extracted coins one at a time from a little plastic squeeze pouch, I would not willingly part with £20 for any good or service that I couldn't take home with me and get years of faithful use out of afterward. I retired to a nearby coffee shop with a sheaf of bus timetables and, extracting from my knapsack a weighty *Great Britain Railway Passenger Timetable* purchased specially for this trip, began a lengthy cross-study of the various modes of public travel available through the ancient region of Wessex.

I was mildly astounded to discover that many substantial communities had no rail services at all—Marlborough, Devizes, and Amesbury, to name but three. None of the bus timetables appeared to interconnect in any meaningful way. Buses to places like Lacock were woefully infrequent and generally made the return journey more or less immediately, leaving you the choice of staying for fourteen minutes or seven hours. It was all most discouraging.

Frowning darkly, I went off to the offices of the local newspaper to find the desk of one Peter Blacklock, an old friend from *The Times* now working in Salisbury, who had once carelessly mentioned that he and his wife, Joan, would be delighted to put me up if I was ever passing through Salisbury. I had dropped him a line a few days before, telling him that I would call at his office at 4:30 on whatever day it was, but the note must never have reached him because when I arrived at 4:29 he was just easing himself out a back window. I'm joking, of course! He was waiting for me with twinkling eyes and gave every impression that he and the saintly Joan couldn't wait for me to eat their food, drink their liquor, muss the guest bed, and help them pass the night with a robust seven-hour version of my famous Nasal Symphony. They were kindness itself.

In the morning, I walked with Peter into town while he pointed out local landmarks—the spot where *As You Like It* was first performed, a bridge used by Trollope in the Barsetshire chronicles—and parted outside the newspaper offices. With two hours to kill, I pootled about aimlessly, peering into shops and drinking cups of coffee, before finally calling at the bus station, where a crowd of people was already waiting for the 10:55 to Stonehenge. The bus didn't arrive until after 11 and then it took nearly twenty minutes for the driver to dispense tickets since there were many tourists from foreign lands and few of them seemed able, poor souls, to grasp the idea that they needed to hand over money and acquire a little slip of paper before they could take a seat. I paid £3.95 for a return ticket on the bus, then a further £2.80 for admission at Stonehenge itself. "Can I interest you in a guidebook at two pounds sixty-five?" the ticket lady asked me and received in reply a hollow laugh.

Things had changed at Stonehenge since I was last there in the early 1970s. They've built a smart new gift shop and coffee bar, though there is still no interpretation center, which is entirely understandable. This is, after all, merely the most important prehistoric monument in Europe and one of the dozen most-visited tourist attractions in England, so clearly there is no point in spending foolish sums making it interesting and instructive. The big change is that you can no longer go right up to the stones and scratch I LOVE DENISE or whatever on them, as you formerly were able. Now you are held back by a discreet rope a considerable distance from the mighty henge. This has actually effected a considerable improvement. It means that the brooding stones aren't lost among crowds of daytrippers, but left in an undisturbed and singular glory.

Impressive as Stonehenge is, there comes a moment somewhere about eleven minutes after your arrival when you realize your fascination has peaked, and you spend another forty minutes walking around the perimeter rope looking at it only out of a combination of politeness, reluctance at being the first from your bus to leave, and a desire to get £2.80 worth of exposure from the experience. Eventually I wandered back to the gift shop and looked at the books and souvenirs, had a coffee in a plastic cup, then wandered back to the bus stop to wait for the 13:10 to Salisbury, and divided my time between wondering why they couldn't provide benches and where on earth I might go next.

chapter
9

among the many thousands of things that I have never been able to understand, one in particular stands out. That is the question of who was the first person who stood by a pile of sand and said, "You know, I bet if we took some of this and mixed it with a little potash and heated it, we could make a material that would be solid and yet transparent. We could call it glass." Call me obtuse, but you could stand me on a beach till the end of time and never would it occur to me to try to make it into windows.

Much as I admire sand's miraculous ability to be transformed into useful objects like glass and concrete, I am not a great fan of it in its natural state. To me, it is primarily a hostile barrier that stands between a parking lot and water. It blows in your face, gets in your sandwiches, swallows vital objects like car keys and coins. In hot countries, it burns your feet and makes you go "Ooh! Ah!" and hop to the water in a fashion that people with better bodies find amusing. When you are wet, it adheres to you like stucco, and cannot be shifted with a fireman's hose. But—and here's the strange thing— the moment you step on a beach towel, climb into a car, or walk across a recently vacuumed carpet, it all falls off.

For days afterward, you tip astounding, mysteriously undiminishing piles of it onto the floor every time you take off your shoes, and spray the vicinity with quantities more when you peel off your socks. Sand stays with you longer than many contagious diseases. And dogs use it as a lavatory. No, you may keep sand as far as I am concerned.

But I am prepared to make an exception for Studland Beach, where I found myself now, having had a nifty brainstorm the previous day on the Salisbury bus. I had dredged my memory banks and remembered a small promise I'd made to myself many years before: that one day I would walk the Dorset coast path, which runs for about a hundred miles through some of the most sumptuous scenery on England's southern coast, and now here I was on this sunny September morn, fresh off the Sandbanks ferry, clutching a knobby walking stick that I had treated myself to in a moment of impetuosity in Poole, and making my way around the regal sweep of this most fetching of beaches.

It was a glorious day to be abroad. The sea was blue and covered with dancing spangles, the sky was full of drifting clouds white as bedsheets, and the houses and hotels of Sandbanks behind me looked radiant, almost Mediterranean, in the clear air. I turned with a light heart and made my way along the moist, packed sand at the water's edge toward the village of Studland and beckoning green hills beyond. For much of its length, the beach is reserved for nudists, which always adds a measure of interest to any walk along it, though today in fact there wasn't a soul to be seen along its three fetching miles, nothing before me but virgin sand and behind only my own footprints.

Studland village is a pretty little place scattered among trees, with a Norman church and some fine views over the bay. I followed the path around the edge of the village and up the hill toward Handfast Point. Halfway along, I met a couple out walking two large black dogs of uncertain genetic background. The dogs were romping playfully in the tall grass, but, as always happens, at the first sight of me their muscles tautened, their eyes turned a glowing red, their incisors grew a sudden inch, and they were transformed into beasts of prey. In a trice they were at me, barking savagely, squabbling over sinew, and nipping at my dancing ankles with horrible yellowy teeth.

"Would you please get your animals off me!" I cried in a voice that sounded uncannily like that of Minnie Mouse.

The owner loped up and began attaching leashes. He had on some stupidly jaunty flat cap like Abbott and Costello would wear in a golfing short. "It's your stick," he said accusingly. "They don't like sticks."

"What, they only attack cripples?"

"They just don't like sticks."

"Well, then maybe your stupid wife should walk ahead with a sign saying, 'Look Out! Stick-Crazy Dogs Coming.'" I was, you may gather, a trifle upset.

"Look here, sunshine, there's no need to get personal."

"Your dogs attacked me for no reason. You shouldn't have dogs if you can't control them. And don't you call me sunshine, *bub*."

We stood glowering at each other. For one moment, it looked as if we might actually grapple and end up rolling around in the mud in an unseemly fashion. I restrained a wild impulse to reach out and flip his preposterous cap from his head. But then one of the dogs went for my ankles again and I retreated a few steps up the hill. I stood on the hillside, shaking my stick at them like some wild-haired lunatic. "And your hat's stupid, too!" I shouted as they huffed off down the hill. That done, I smoothed down my jacket, composed my features, and proceeded on my way. Well, honestly.

Handfast Point is a grassy cliff that ends in a sudden drop of perhaps two hundred feet to seriously frothy seas. It takes a special blend of nerve and foolishness to creep up to the edge and have a look. Just beyond it stand two stranded pinnacles of limestone known as Old Harry and Old Harry's Wife, all that remains of a land bridge that once connected Dorset to the Isle of Wight, eighteen miles away across the bay and just visible through a cloak of salty mists. Beyond the headland, the path climbed steeply to Ballard Down, a taxing slog for an old puffed-out flubba-wubba like me, but worth it for the view, which was sensational—like being on top of the world. For miles around, the Dorset hills rolled and billowed, like a shaken-out quilt settling onto a bed. Country lanes wandered among plump hedgerows and the hillsides were prettily dotted with woodlands, farms, and the creamy flecks of sheep. In the distance the sea, bright and vast and silvery blue, stretched away to a mountain of tumbling cumulus. Far below, the little resort community of Swanage huddled against a rocky headland on the edge of a horseshoe bay, and behind me lay Studland, the marshy flats of Poole Harbour and Brownsea Island, and beyond that a hazy infinity of meticulously worked farmland. It was beautiful beyond words.

I went over to a stone bench that had been thoughtfully conveyed to this lofty summit for the benefit of weary hikers like me— it really is extraordinary how often you encounter some little kindly gesture like this in Britain—and took out my Ordnance Survey 1:25,000 map for this corner of Dorset. As a rule, I am not terribly comfortable with any map that doesn't have a You Are Here arrow on it somewhere, but the Ordnance Survey maps are in a league of their own. Coming from a country where mapmakers tend to exclude any landscape feature smaller than, say, Pikes Peak, I am constantly impressed by the richness of detail on the OS 1:25,000 series maps. They include every wrinkle and divot on the landscape, every barn, milestone, wind pump, and tumulus. They distinguish between sand pits and gravel pits and between power lines strung from pylons and power lines strung from poles. This one even included the stone seat on which I sat now. It astounds me to be able to look at a map and know to the square meter where my buttocks are deployed.

In my idle perusal, I noticed that a mile or so to the west there stood a historic obelisk. Wondering why anyone would erect a monument in such a remote and challenging spot, I struck off along the crest of the hill to have a look. Well, it was the longest mile I can remember. I passed through grassy fields, through flocks of skittish sheep, over stiles and through gates. Eventually, I arrived at a modest, wholly unremarkable granite obelisk. The weathered inscription revealed that in 1887 the Dorset Water Board had run a pipe past this point. *Well, yippee,* I thought. Pursing my lips and referring once more to my map, I noticed that just a little farther on was something called the Giant's Grave, and I thought, *Now, that sounds interesting.*

So I plodded off to see it. And that's the trouble, you see. There is always some intriguing landmark just over the next contour line. You could spend your life moving from stone circle to Roman settlement (remains of) to ruined abbey, and never see but a fraction of them even in a small area, particularly if, like me, you seldom actually find them. I never found the Giant's Grave. I think I was close, but I can't be sure. The one drawback of these OS maps is that sometimes perhaps they give you too much detail. With so many possible landscape features to choose among, it's easy to convince yourself that you are pretty much wherever you want to be. You see a grove of trees and you stroke your chin and think, *Well, now, let's see, that must be Hanging Snot Wood, which means that that odd-looking hillock is almost certainly Jumping Dwarf Long Barrow, in which case that place·on the far hill must be Desperation Farm.* And so you strike off confidently until you come up against some obviously unexpected landscape feature like Portsmouth and realize that you have gone somewhat astray.

Thus it was that I spent a quiet, sweatily perplexed afternoon tramping through a large, forgotten, but very green and pretty corner of Dorset, looking for an inland route to Swanage. The more I plunged on, the less defined did the footpaths become. By mid-afternoon, I found myself increasingly crawling under barbed wire, fording streams with my pack on my head, wrenching my leg from bear traps, falling down, and longing to be elsewhere. Occasionally, I would pause to rest and try to identify some small point of congruence between my map and the surrounding landscape. Eventually I would rise, peel a cow pat from my seat, purse my lips, and strike off in an entirely new direction. By such means did I find myself, late in the afternoon and somewhat to my surprise, arriving footsore, travel soiled, and decorated about the extremities with interesting rivulets of dried blood, in Corfe Castle.

To celebrate my good fortune at finding myself anywhere at all, I went to the best hotel in town, an Elizabethan manor on the main street called Mortons House. It looked a thoroughly agreeable place and my spirits swelled. Moreover, it could accommodate me.

"Come far?" asked the girl at the desk as I filled in the registration card. The first rule of walking is, of course, to lie through your teeth.

"Brockenhurst," I said, impulsively naming a town thirty miles to the east.

"Goodness, that's a long way!"

I sniffed in a frankly manful way. "Yeah, well, I've got a good map."

"And where are you off to tomorrow?"

"Cardiff."

"Gosh! On foot?"

"Never go any other way." I hoisted my pack, picked up my room key, and gave her a man-of-the-world wink that would, I fancy, have made her swoon had I been but twenty years younger and considerably better looking, and not had a large dab of cowshit on the end of my nose.

I spent a few minutes turning a large white towel black, then hurried out to see the village before everything shut. Corfe is a popular and pretty place, a cluster of stone cottages dominated by the lofty, jagged walls of its picturesque and much-visited castle—everyone's favorite ruin after Princess Margaret. I treated myself to a pot of tea and a cake at the busy and cheerful little National Trust Tea Room, then hastened next door to the castle entrance. Admission was £2.90, which I thought a bit steep for a heap of rubble, and the place was closing in ten minutes, but I bought a ticket anyway because I didn't know when I might pass this way again. The castle, once one of the grandest in southern England, was pretty thoroughly dismantled by antiroyalists during the English Civil War, and then the townspeople helped themselves to most of what was left—much of the surrounding village is built of old castle stone—so there isn't a great deal to look at other than some ragged fragments of wall, but the views across the surrounding valley were exceedingly becoming, with the fading sunlight draping the hillsides in long shadows and a hint of evening mist creeping in among the hollows.

I had a long, hot bath at the hotel and then, feeling happily worn out, decided to content myself with such pleasures as Mortons House could provide. I had a couple of drinks in the bar, then was summoned to the dining room. There were eight other diners, all white-haired, well dressed, and nearly silent. Why are the English so quiet in hotel dining rooms? There wasn't a sound in the room but for the quiet scrapings of cutlery and murmured two-second conversations like:

"Supposed to be fine again tomorrow."

"Oh? That's good."

"Mmm."

And then silence.

Or:

"Soup's nice."

"Yes."

And then silence.

Given the nature of the hotel, I'd expected the menu to feature items like brown Windsor soup and roast beef and Yorkshire pudding, but of course things have moved on in the hotel trade. The menu now was richly endowed with ten-guinea words that you wouldn't have seen on an English menu ten years ago—"noisettes," "tartare," "duxelle," "coulis," "timbale"—and written in a curious inflated language with eccentric capitalizations. I had, and I quote, "Fanned Galia Melon and Cumbrian Air Dried Ham served with a Mixed leaf Salad," followed by "Fillet Steak served with a crushed Black Peppercorn Sauce flamed in Brandy and finished with Cream," which together were nearly as pleasurable to read as to eat.

I was greatly taken with this new way of talking and derived considerable pleasure from speaking it to the waiter. I asked him for a luster of water freshly drawn from the house tap and presented *au nature* in a cylinder of glass, and when he came around with the bread rolls I entreated him to present me a tonged rondelle of blanched wheat, oven baked and masked in a poppy-seed coating. I was just getting warmed up to this and about to ask for a fanned lap coverlet, freshly laundered and scented with a delicate hint of Lemon Daz, to replace the one that had slipped from my lap and now lay recumbent on the horizontal walking surface subjacent to my feet, when he handed me a card that said "Sweets Menu" and I realized that we were back in the no-nonsense world of English.

It's a funny thing about English diners. They'll let you dazzle them with piddly duxelles of this and fussy little noisettes of that, but don't mess with their puddings, which is my thinking exactly. All the dessert entries were for gooey dishes with good English names. I had sticky toffee pudding and it was splendid. As I finished, the waiter invited me to withdraw to the lounge where a caisson of fresh-roasted coffee, complemented by the chef's own selection of mint wafers, awaited. I dressed the tabletop with a small circlet of copper specie crafted at the Royal Mint and, suppressing a small eruction of gastrointestinal air, effected my egress.

Because I had strayed from the coast path, my first order of business the next morning was to find my way back to it. I left Corfe and lumbered heavily up a ferociously steep hill to the nearby village of Kingston. It was another glorious day and the views from Kingston over Corfe and its castle—suddenly distant and miniature—were memorable.

I picked up a mercifully level footpath and followed it for two miles through woods and fields along the crest of a secluded hanging valley to rejoin the coast path at a lonely and dramatic eminence called Houns-tout Cliff. The view once again was stunning: whale-back hills and radiant white cliffs, dotted with small coves and hidden beaches washed by a blue and infinite sea. I could see all the way to Lulworth, my destination for the day, some ten miles and many daunting whalebacks to the west.

I followed the path up steep hills and down. It was only ten in the morning, but already it was unseasonably warm. Most of the Dorset coast hills are no more than a few hundred feet high, but they are steep and numerous and I was soon sweaty, puffed out, and thirsty. I took off my pack and discovered with a groan that I had left my fancy new water bottle, bought in Poole and diligently filled that morning, back at the hotel. There's nothing like having nothing to drink to bring on a towering thirst. I plodded on, hoping against hope that there would be a pub or café in Kimmeridge, but as I approached from a high path above its lovely bay I could see that it was too small to be likely to offer anything.

Taking out my binoculars I surveyed the village from afar and discovered that there was a Portakabin of some type by the beachside parking lot. A little tearoom on wheels, perhaps. I hastened along the path, past a sadly neglected stone tower—one of many lookout follies built along the south coast in a more enterprising age—and down a steep path to the beach. Such was the distance involved that it took the better part of an hour. Crossing my fingers, I picked my way over the beach and went up to the Portakabin. It was a National Trust information center and it was closed.

I made an anguished face. I had a throat like sandpaper. I was many long miles from anywhere and there was no one around. At that moment, by a kind of miracle, an ice cream van came trundling over the hill playing a twinkly tune such as English ice cream vans always play (to attract the notice of children) and set up at the edge of the parking lot. I waited an impatient ten minutes while the young man in sole charge unhurriedly opened up various hatches and set out things. The instant the window slid open I asked him what he had to drink. He rooted around and announced that he had six small plastic bottles of Panda Cola. I bought them all and retired to the shady side of the van, where I feverishly removed the plastic lid from one and poured its life-saving contents down my gullet.

Now I don't want you to think for a moment that Panda Cola is in any way inferior to Coke, Pepsi, Dr Pepper, 7UP, Sprite, or any of the many other flavored drinks that unaccountably enjoy a larger patronage, or that serving a soft drink warm strikes me as remotely eccentric, but there was something curiously unsatisfying about the drinks I had just acquired. I drank one after another until my stomach was taut and sloshing, but I couldn't say that I actually felt refreshed. Sighing, I put the two remaining bottles in my knapsack, in case I had a syrup crisis later on, and continued on my way.

A couple of miles beyond Kimmeridge, at the far side of a monumentally steep hill, stands the little village of Tyneham, or what's left of it. In 1943, the British Army ordered Tyneham's inhabitants to evacuate the community as it wanted to practice lobbing shells into the surrounding hillsides. The villagers were solemnly assured that once Hitler was licked they could all come back. Fifty-one years later they were still waiting. Forgive my disrespectful tone, but this seems to me disgraceful, not simply because it's a terrible inconvenience to the inhabitants (especially those who might have forgotten to cancel their milk), but also for poor sods like me who have to hope that the footpath through the firing range is open, which it is but occasionally. In fact, on this day it was open—I had prudently checked before setting off—so I was able to wander up and over the steep hill out of Kimmeridge and have a look around the two grassy streets of roofless houses that are about all that remains of Tyneham. When I was last there in the late 1970s, Tyneham was forlorn, overgrown, and practically unknown—a proper little ghost town. Now the Dorset County Council has made it into something of a tourist attraction. It put up a big parking lot and restored the school and church as small museums, which rather suggests that Tyneham's abandonment is considered permanent.

I know the army needs some place for gunnery practice, but surely it could find some new and less visually sensitive location to blow up—Leeds, say. The odd thing was that I couldn't see any sign of devastation on the hillsides. Big red numbered targets were scattered strategically about, but they were uniformly unblemished, as was the landscape around them. Perhaps the army shoots Nerf balls or something. Who can say? Certainly not I, because my diminishing physical resources were entirely consumed by the challenge of hauling myself up a killer slope that led to the summit of Rings Hill, high above Worbarrow Bay. The view was sensational—I could see all the way back to Poole Harbour many miles to the east—but what commanded my attention was the cruel discovery that the path immediately plunged back down to sea level before starting back up an even more formidable flanking hill. I fortified myself with a Panda Cola and plunged on.

The neighboring eminence, called Bindon Hill, was a whopper.
It not only rose straight up to the lower reaches of the troposphere,
but then presented a lofty up-and-down ridge that ran on more or
less forever. By the time the straggly village of West Lulworth hove
into view and I began a long, stumbling descent, my legs seemed
able to bend in several new directions and I could feel blisters bubbling up between my toes. I arrived in Lulworth in the delirious
stagger of someone wandering in off the desert in an adventure
movie, sweat streaked, mumbling, and frothing little nose rings of
Panda Cola.

But at least I had surmounted the most challenging part of the
walk and now I was back in civilization, in one of the most delightful
small seaside resorts in England. Things could only get better.

chapter
10

Once many years ago, in anticipation of the offspring we would one day have, a relative of my wife's gave us a box of Ladybird children's books from the 1950s and 1960s. They all had titles like *Out in the Sun* and *Sunny Days at the Seaside,* and contained meticulously drafted, richly colored illustrations of a prosperous, contented, litter-free Britain in which the sun always shone, shopkeepers smiled, and children in freshly pressed clothes derived happiness and pleasure from innocent pastimes—riding a bus to the shops, floating a model boat on a park pond, chatting to a kindly policeman.

My favorite was a book called *Adventure on the Island.* There was in fact precious little adventure in the book—the high point, I recall, was finding a starfish suckered to a rock—but I loved it because of the illustrations (by the gifted and much-missed J. H. Wingfield), which portrayed an island of rocky coves and long views that was recognizably British, but with a Mediterranean climate and a tidy absence of pay-and-display car parks, bingo parlors, and the tackier sort of amusement arcades. Here commercial activity was limited to the odd cake shop and tearoom.

I was strangely influenced by this book, and for some years agreed to take our family vacations at the British seaside on the assumption that one day we would find this magic place where summer days were forever sunny, the water as warm as a sitz bath, and commercial blight unknown.

When at last we began to accumulate children, it turned out that they didn't like these books at all because the characters in them never did anything more lively than visit a pet shop or watch a fisherman paint his boat. I tried to explain that this was sound preparation for life in Britain, but they wouldn't have it and instead, to my dismay, attached their affections to a pair of irksome little clots called Topsy and Tim.

I mention this here because of all the little seaside places we went to over the years, Lulworth seemed the closest to this idealized image I had in my head. It was small and cheerful and had an engaging old-fashioned feel. Its little shops sold seaside-type things that harked back to a more innocent age—wooden sailboats, toy nets on poles, colorful beach balls held in long string bags—and its few restaurants were always full of happy trippers enjoying a cream tea. The intensely pretty, almost circular cove at the village's foot was strewn with rocks and boulders for children to clamber over and dotted with shallow pools in which to search for miniature crabs. It was altogether a delightful spot.

So imagine my surprise, when I emerged fresh-scrubbed from my hotel in search of drink and a hearty, well-earned dinner, to discover that Lulworth wasn't anything like I remembered. Its central feature was a vast and unsightly parking lot, which I had quite forgotten, and the shops, pubs, and guesthouses along the street to the cove looked dowdy and hard up. I went into a large pub and almost immediately regretted it. It had that sickly, stale smell of slopped beer and was full of flashing fruit machines. I was almost the only customer in the place, but nearly every table was covered with empty pint glasses and ashtrays overflowing with cigarette butts, crisp packets, and other disorderly detritus. My glass was sticky and the lager was warm. I drank up and tried another pub nearby, which was marginally less grubby but scarcely more congenial, with battered decor, loud music, and a more or less total lack of delight at the bestowal of my custom. It's small wonder (and I speak as an enthusiast) that so many pubs are losing their trade.

Discouraged, I repaired to a nearby restaurant, a place where my wife and I used to have crab salads and fancy ourselves genteel. Things had changed here, too. The menu had plunged downmarket to the scampi, chips, and peas level, and the food was heartily mediocre. But the truly memorable thing was the service. I have never seen such resplendent ineptitude in a restaurant. The place was packed, and it soon became evident that not one party was happy. Almost every dish that appeared from the kitchen had something on it that hadn't been ordered or lacked something that had. Some people sat foodless for ages while others at their table were presented all their courses more or less at once. (Naturally, no one complained.) I ordered a prawn cocktail, waited thirty minutes for it, and then discovered that several of the prawns were still frozen. I sent it back and never saw it again. Forty minutes later a waitress appeared with a plate of plaice, chips, and peas and couldn't find a taker so I had it, although I'd ordered haddock. When I finished, I calculated my bill from the menu, left the right money, minus a small reckoning for the frozen prawns, and departed.

Then I went back to my hotel, a place of deep and depressing cheerlessness, with nylon sheets and cold radiators, went to bed and read by the light of a seven-watt bulb, and made a small, heartfelt vow never to return to Lulworth so long as I might live.

In the morning I awoke to find rain falling over the hills in great blown sheets. I breakfasted, settled the bill, and spent a protracted period struggling into waterproof outerwear in the front hallway. It's a funny thing: I dress myself most days without incident, but give me a pair of waterproof pants to put on and it's as if I've never stood unaided. I spent twenty minutes crashing into walls and furniture, falling into potted plants, and, in one particularly notable outburst, hopping on one leg for some fifteen feet before wrapping my neck around a newel-post.

When at last I was fully kitted out, I caught a glimpse of myself in a full-length wall mirror and realized I looked like nothing so much as a large blue condom. Thus attired and accompanied on each step by an irritating rustle of nylon, I picked up my pack and walking stick and took to the hills. I proceeded up Hambury Tout, past Durdle Door and the steep-sided valley engagingly called Scratchy Bottom, and on up a steep, muddy, zigzagging path to a lonely, fog-shrouded eminence called Swyre Head. The weather was appalling and the rain maddening.

Indulge me for a moment, if you will. Drum on the top of your head with the fingers of both hands and see how long it takes before either it gets seriously on your nerves or everyone in the vicinity is staring at you. In either case, you will find that you are happy to stop it. Now imagine those drumming fingers are raindrops endlessly beating on your hood and that there's nothing you can do about it, and moreover that your glasses are two circles of steamy uselessness, that you are slipping around on a rain-slickened path a single misstep from a long fall to a rocky beach—a fall that would reduce you to little more than a smear on a piece of rock, like jam on bread. I imagined the headline—AMERICAN WRITER DIES IN FALL; WAS LEAVING COUNTRY ANYWAY—and plodded on, squinting Magoo-like, with feelings of foreboding.

It is twelve miles from Lulworth to Weymouth. In *The Kingdom by the Sea*, Paul Theroux gives the impression that you can walk it in an easy lope and still have time for a cream tea and to mock the locals, but I trust he had better weather than I. It took me most of the day. The walking beyond Swyre Head was mostly along mercifully flat, if lofty, cliffs high above a cadaverous gray sea, but the footing was treacherous and the going slow. At Ringstead Bay the hills abruptly ended in a final steep descent to the beach. I rode an ooze of flowing mud down the hill to the bay, pausing only long enough to belly into boulders and carry out a few tree-resiliency tests. At the bottom I pulled out my map and, making calipers of my fingers, worked out that I had covered only about five miles. It had taken most of the morning. Frowning at my lack of progress, I shoved the map into a pocket and moodily trudged on.

The rest of the day was a dreary, wet tramp along low hills above a pounding surf. The rain eased off and turned into an insidious drizzle—that special English kind of drizzle that hangs in the air and saps the spirit. About one o'clock Weymouth materialized from the mists across a long curve of bay, and I gave a small cry of joy. But its seeming nearness was a cruel deception. It took me nearly two hours to reach the town's outskirts, and another hour to walk along the endless front to the center, by which time I was tired and limping. I got a room in a small hotel on the front and spent a long time lying on the bed, booted and still condomed, before I could summon the strength to change into something less obviously mirth making, have a light wash, and hit the town.

I liked Weymouth a good deal more than I'd expected to. It has two claims to fame. In 1348 it was the place where the Black Death was introduced into England, and in 1789 it became the world's first seaside resort when that tedious lunatic George III started a fashion for sea bathing there. Today the town tries to maintain an air of Georgian elegance and generally nearly succeeds, though like most seaside resorts it has about it a whiff of terminal decline at least as far as tourism goes. The Gloucester Hotel, where George and his retinue stayed (it was a private house then), had recently closed and now Weymouth didn't have a single decent large hotel, a sad omission in an old seaside town. But I'm happy to report that it did have many good pubs and one outstanding restaurant, Perry's, all of them in the harborfront district, a renovated area with fishing smacks bobbing on the water and a jaunty nautical air that makes you half expect to see Popeye and Bluto come loping round the corner. Perry's was crowded and cheerful and a joy to the spirits after Lulworth. I had local mussels from Poole—after three days of hard walking it came as a shock to realize that Poole was still local—and a highly creditable sea bass, and afterward retired to the kind of dark and low-ceilinged pub where you feel as if you ought to be wearing a bulky Arran sweater and a captain's cap. I enjoyed myself very much and drank so much my feet stopped aching.

To the west of Weymouth stands the fifty-mile-long arc of Lyme Bay. Since the landscape just west of Weymouth is not particularly, or even fractionally, memorable, I took a taxi to Abbotsbury, and began my walk midway along Chesil Beach. I don't know what Chesil Beach is like toward the Weymouth end, but along this stretch it consisted of great drifts of small, kidney-shaped pebbles worn to a uniform smoothness by aeons of wave action. They are nearly impossible to walk on, since you sink to your ankle tops with every step. The coast path is on firmer ground immediately behind the beach, but leaves you unable to see over the stony dunes. Instead, you just hear the sea, crashing into the shore and the other side and sending endless successions of pebbles clattering along the water's edge. It was a walk of consummate tedium and my blisters soon began to throb. By the time I reached West Bay, early in the afternoon, I was ready for a good sit-down and something to eat.

West Bay is an odd little place, spread out in a higgledy-piggledy fashion across a duny landscape. It had something of the air of a gold-rush town, as if it had sprung up hurriedly, and it looked poor and gray and spray battered. I hunted around for someplace to eat and happened on a nondescript-looking establishment called the Riverside Café. I opened the door and found myself in the most extraordinary setting. The place was heaving. The air was thick with shrill London-style chatter and all the customers looked as if they had just stepped out of a Ralph Lauren advertisement. They all had sweaters slung casually around their shoulders and sunglasses perched on their heads. It was as if a little piece of Fulham or Chelsea had been magically wafted to this godforsaken corner of the Dorset coast.

Certainly I had never seen this kind of tempo outside a restaurant in London. Waiters and waitresses dashed everywhere trying to fulfill what appeared to be an inexhaustible demand to keep the customers fed and, above all, supplied with wine. It was quite extraordinary and it all rather went to my head. I'm not usually much of one for lunch, but the food smelled so wonderful and the ambience was so extraordinary that I found myself ordering like a trencherman. I had a starter of scallop and lobster terrine, an exquisite fillet of sea bass with green beans and a mountain of chips, and two glasses of wine, rounding it off with coffee and a generous slab of cheesecake. The proprietor, a jolly nice man named Arthur Watson, wandered among the tables and even called on me. He told me that until ten years before the place had been just a traditional seaside café doing roast lunches and burger and chips, and little by little it had begun introducing fresh fish and fancier foods and found there was a clamor for it. Now it was packed out every mealtime and had just been named the *Good Food Guide*'s restaurant of the year for Dorset, but it still did burgers and it still did chips with everything, and I thought that was just wonderful.

It was after three when I emerged from the Riverside with a light head and heavy everything else. Taking a seat on a bench, I pulled out my map and realized with a snort of dismay that I was still ten miles from Lyme Regis, with the 626 feet of Golden Cap, the highest hill on the south coast, standing between me and it. My blisters throbbed, my legs ached, my stomach was grotesquely gorged, and a light rain was beginning to fall.

As I sat there, a bus pulled up. I got up and put my head in the open door. "Going west?" I said to the driver. He nodded. Impulsively, I lumbered aboard, bought a ticket, and took a seat toward the back. The trick of successful walking, I always say, is knowing when to stop.

chapter
II

I spent the night in Lyme Regis and passed the following morning poking about in the town before catching a bus to Axminster and a train on to Exeter, a process that consumed considerably more time than I had expected. Daylight was fading by the time I stepped from Exeter Central Station into a light but annoying rain.

I wandered through the city examining hotels from the street, but they all seemed a bit grand for me, and eventually ended up at the central tourist office, feeling mildly lost and far from home. I wasn't quite sure what I was doing here. I looked through racks of leaflets for shire horse centers, petting zoos, falconry centers, miniature pony centers, model railways, butterfly farms, and something called—I jest not, I regret to say—Twiggy Winkie's Farm and Hedgehog Hospital, none of which seemed to address my leisure requirements. Nearly all the leaflets were depressingly illiterate, particularly with regard to punctuation—I sometimes think that if I see one more tourist leaflet that says "Englands Best" or "Britains Largest," I will go and torch the place—and they all seemed so pathetically modest in what they had to offer. Nearly all of them padded out their lists of featured attractions with things like "Free Car Park," "Gift Shop and Tearoom," and the inevitable "Adventure Playground" (and then were witless enough to show you in the photograph that it was just a climbing frame and a couple of plastic animals on springs). Who goes to these places? I couldn't say, I'm sure.

There was a notice on the counter saying that the office booked rooms, so I asked the helpful lady if she would secure me lodgings. She interviewed me candidly with regard to how much I was prepared to pay, which I always find embarrassing and frankly un-English, and by a process of attrition we established that I fell into a category that could be called cheap but demanding. It happened that the Royal Clarence Hotel was doing a special deal with rooms at £25 a night if you promised not to steal the towels, and I leaped at that because I'd passed it on the way in and it looked awfully nice, a big white Georgian place on the cathedral square. And so it proved to be. The room was newly decorated and big enough for hotel room Olympics—wastebin basketball, furniture steeplechase, jumping onto the bed by means of a swing on the bathroom door and a well-timed leap, and other perennial favorites of the lone traveler. I had a short but vigorous workout, showered, changed, and hit the streets famished.

Exeter is not an easy place to love. It was extensively bombed during the war, which gave the city fathers a wonderful opportunity, enthusiastically seized, to rebuild most of it in concrete. It was only a little after six in the evening, but the city center was practically dead. I wandered around beneath gloomy street lights, looking in shop windows and reading those strange posters—bills, as they are known in the trade—for provincial newspapers that you always find in Britain. I have an odd fascination with these because they are always either wholly unfathomable to nonlocals (LETTER BOX RAPIST STRIKES AGAIN, BEULAH FLIES HOME) or so boring that you can't imagine how anyone could possibly have thought they would boost sales (COUNCIL STORM OVER DUSTBINS CONTRACT, PHONE

NOTES FROM A SMALL ISLAND

BOX VANDALS STRIKE AGAIN). My favorite—this is a real one, which I saw many years ago in Hemel Hempstead—was WOMAN, 81, DIES.

Perhaps I took all the wrong streets, but there seemed to be no restaurants anywhere in central Exeter. I was only looking for something modest that didn't have "Fayre," "Vegan," or "Copper Kettle" in the title, but all that happened was I kept wandering down restaurantless streets and coming up against monstrous relief roads with massive roundabouts and complicated pedestrian crossings that clearly weren't designed to be negotiated on foot by anyone with less than six hours to spare. Finally, I happened on a hilly street with a few modest eateries and plunged randomly into a Chinese restaurant full of foreboding at the prospect of trying to feed myself with chopsticks. Am I alone in thinking it odd that a people ingenious enough to invent paper, gunpowder, kites, and any number of other useful objects, and who have a noble history extending back three thousand years, haven't yet worked out that a pair of knitting needles is no way to capture food? I spent a perplexed hour stabbing at rice, dribbling sauce across the tablecloth, and lifting finely poised pieces of meat to my mouth only to discover that they had mysteriously vanished and weren't to be found anywhere. By the time I finished, the table looked as if it had been at the center of a violent argument. I paid my bill and slunk out the door and back to the hotel, where I watched a little TV and snacked on the copious leftovers that I found in sweater folds and trouser cuffs.

In the morning, I rose early and went out for a look around the town. Exeter was locked in a foggy gloom, though the cathedral square was very handsome and the cathedral, I was impressed to find, was open even at eight in the morning. I sat for some time at the back and listened to the morning choir practice, which was quite wonderful. Then I wandered down to the old quay area to see what I might find there. It had been artily renovated with shops and museums, but all of them were closed at this time of day—or perhaps this time of year—and there wasn't a soul about.

By the time I returned to the High Street, the shops were opening. I hadn't had breakfast because it wasn't included in my special room rate, so I was feeling immoderately peckish and began a hunt for cafés, but again Exeter seemed strangely lacking. In the end, I went into Marks & Spencer to buy a sandwich.

Although the store had only just opened, the food hall was busy and there were long queues at the tills. I took a place in a line behind eight other shoppers. They were all women and they all did the same mystifying thing: They acted surprised when it came time to pay. This is something that has been puzzling me for years. Women will stand there watching their items being rung up, and then when the till lady says, "That's four pounds twenty, love" or whatever, they suddenly look as if they've never done this sort of thing before. They go "Oh!" and start rooting in a flustered fashion in their handbags for their purses or checkbooks, as if no one had told them that this might happen.

Men, for all their many shortcomings, like washing large pieces of oily machinery in the kitchen sink or forgetting that a painted door stays wet for more than thirty seconds, are generally pretty good when it comes to paying. They spend their time in line doing a wallet inventory and sorting through their coins. When the till person announces the bill, they *immediately* hand over an approximately correct amount of money, keep their hands extended for the change however long it takes or however foolish they may begin to look if there is, say, a problem with the till roll, and then—mark this—they pocket their change *as they walk away,* instead of deciding that now is the time to search for the car keys and reorganize six months' worth of receipts.

And while we're on this rather daring sexist interlude, why is it that women never push toothpaste tubes up from the bottom and always try to get somebody else to change a lightbulb? How are they able to smell and hear things that are so clearly beyond the range of human acuity, and how do they know from another room that you are about to dip a finger into the icing of a freshly made cake? Why, above all, do they find it so unsettling if you spend more than four minutes a day on the toilet? This last is another long-standing mystery to me. A woman of my close acquaintance and I regularly have surreal conversations that run something like this:

"What are you doing in there?" (This said in an edgy tone.)

"I'm descaling the kettle. What do you think I'm doing in here?"

"You've been in there half an hour. Are you reading?"

"No."

"You're reading, aren't you? I can hear the pages."

"Honestly, I'm not." That is to say, I *was* reading until a minute ago but now of course I'm talking to you, dear.

"Have you covered up the keyhole? I can't see anything."

"Please tell me that you're not down on your hands and knees trying to look through the keyhole at your husband having a bowel movement in his own bathroom. Please."

"You come out of there now. You've been in there for nearly three quarters of an hour just *reading*."

As she retreats, you sit there thinking, *Did all that really just happen or have I wandered into some kind of Dada exhibition?* And then, shaking your head, you return to your magazine.

Still, it must be said that women are great with children, vomit, and painted doors—three months after a painted door has dried they will still be touching it tentatively, as if suspecting it might turn on them—which makes up for a lot, so I smiled benignly at the parade of flustered ladies ahead of me until it was my turn to demonstrate to the ones following how to do this sort of thing properly, but frankly I don't think they took it in.

I ate my sandwich on the street, then returned to the hotel, gathered up my things, settled the bill, stepped back outdoors, and thought, *Now what?* I wandered back to the rail station and had a look at the flickering television screens announcing arrivals and departures. I thought about catching a train to Plymouth or Penzance but the next one wasn't for two hours. There was, however, a train to Barnstaple leaving shortly. It occurred to me that I could go there, then make my way by bus along the luscious north Devon coast to Taunton or Minehead. I could stop en route at Lynton and Lynmouth, and possibly Porlock and Dunster—all pretty and diverting little communities. It seemed a capital idea.

I asked the man in the ticket window for a one-way ticket to Barnstaple. He told me one way was £8.80, but he could do me a round trip for £4.40.

"You wouldn't care to explain the logic of that to me, would you?" I asked.

"I would if I could, sir," he responded with commendable frankness.

I took my pack and ticket to the requisite platform, where I sat on a bench and passed the time watching the station pigeons. They really are the most amazingly panicky and dopey creatures. I couldn't imagine an emptier, less satisfying life. Here are instructions for being a pigeon: (1) Walk around aimlessly for a while, pecking at cigarette butts and other inappropriate items. (2) Take fright at someone walking along the platform and fly off to a girder. (3) Have a shit. (4) Repeat.

The platform televisions weren't working and I couldn't understand the announcements—it took me ages to work out that "Eczema" was actually Exmouth—so every time a train came in, I had to get up and make inquiries. For reasons that elude rational explanation, British Rail always puts the destination on the front of the train, which would be awfully handy if passengers were waiting on the tracks, but not perhaps ideal for those boarding it from the side. Most of the other passengers evidently couldn't hear the announcements, because when the Barnstaple train eventually came in, half a dozen of us formed a patient queue beside a BR employee and asked him if this was the Barnstaple train.

For the benefit of those unfamiliar with British life, I should explain that there is a certain ritual involved in this. Even though you have heard the conductor tell the person ahead of you that this is the Barnstaple train, you still have to say, "Excuse me, is this the Barnstaple train?" When he acknowledges that the large linear object three feet to your right is indeed the Barnstaple train, you have to point to it and say, "*This* one?" Then when you board the train, you must additionally ask the carriage generally, "Excuse me, is this the Barnstaple train?" to which most people will say that they think it is, except for one man with a lot of parcels who will get a panicked look and hurriedly gather up his things and get off.

You should always take his seat since you will generally find that he has left behind a folded newspaper and an uneaten bar of chocolate, and possibly a nice pair of sheepskin gloves.

Thus it was that I found myself sliding out of Exeter Central Station while a man laden with parcels trotted along beside my window mouthing sentiments I couldn't decipher through the thick glass, and taking stock of my new possessions—a *Daily Mirror* and a Kit Kat, but unfortunately no gloves. We rattled out through the Exeter suburbs and into the lush Devon countryside. I was on what was called the Tarka Line—something to do with that story about Tarka the otter, which evidently was written somewhere in the vicinity. The hilly landscape was gorgeous and extravagantly green. You could be excused for thinking that the principal industry of Britain is the manufacture of chlorophyll. We chuntered along among wooded hills, scattered farms, churches with square towers that made them look like leftover pieces from a very large chess set. I soon settled into that happy delirium that the motion of a train always induces in me, and only half noted the names of the little villages we passed through—Pinhead, West Stuttering, Bakelite, Ham Hocks.

It took over an hour and a half to cover the thirty-eight miles to Barnstaple, where I alighted and headed into town over a long bridge over the swift-flowing River Taw. I wandered around for half an hour through narrow shopping streets and a large, drafty covered market thinly arrayed with people selling handicraft items, and felt content that there was no need to linger here. Barnstaple used to be a major rail interchange, with three stations, but now there is just the one with its infrequent pootling service to Exeter, and a bus station overlooking the river. I went into the bus station and found two women sitting in an office beyond an open door, talking together in that quaint "Oi be drinkin' zoider" accent of this part of the world.

I asked them about buses to Minehead, about thirty miles to the east along the coast. They looked at me as if I'd asked for connections to Tierra del Fuego.

"Oh, you won't be gittin to Moinhead this toim of year, you won't be," said one.

"No buses to Moinhead arter firrrrst of Octobaaarrrr," chimed in the second one.

"What about Lynton and Lynmouth?"

They snorted at my naïveté. This was England. This was 1994.

"Porlock?"

Snort.

"Dunster?"

Snort.

The best they could suggest was that I take a bus to Bideford and see if I could catch another bus on from there. "They may be runnin the Scarrrrrlet Loin out of Bideforrrrrd, they may be, oi they may, they may—but can't be sartin."

"Will there be more people like you there?" I wanted to say but didn't. The only other option they could suggest was a bus to Westward Ho!, but there didn't seem much point since I couldn't go anywhere else from there, and anyway I couldn't face spending the night in an ejaculation, as it were. I thanked them and departed.

I stood outside in a froth of uncertainty and tried to think what to do next. All my carefully laid plans were coming unraveled. I retired to the curiously named Royal and Fortescue Hotel, where I ordered a tuna sandwich and a cup of coffee from a mute and charmless waitress, and rooted in my pack for my timetable, where I discovered that I had twenty-three minutes to eat my sandwich, drink my coffee, and waddle the mile to the railway station to catch a train back to Exeter, where I could start again.

I swallowed my sandwich nearly whole when it came, gulped two sips of coffee, threw some money on the table, and fled for the station, terrified that I would miss the train and have to spend the night in Barnstaple. I just made it. When I got to Exeter, I marched straight up to the TV screens, determined to take the first train to anywhere.

Thus it was that I found myself in the hands of fate and bound for the little seaside resort of Weston-super-Mare.

chapter
12

the way I see it, there are three reasons never to be unhappy.

First, you were born. This in itself is a remarkable achievement. Did you know that each time your father ejaculated (and frankly he did it quite a lot) he produced roughly 25 million spermatozoa—enough to repopulate Britain every two days or so? For you to have been born, not only did you have to be among the few batches of sperm that had even a theoretical chance of prospering—in itself quite a long shot—but you then had to win a race against 24,999,999 or so other wriggling contenders, all rushing to swim the English Channel of your mother's vagina in order to be the first ashore at the fertile egg of Boulogne, as it were. Being born was easily the most remarkable achievement of your whole life. And think: You could just as easily have been a flatworm.

Second, you are alive. For the tiniest moment in the span of eternity you have the miraculous privilege to exist. For endless aeons you did not. Soon you will cease to be once more. That you are able to sit here right now in this one never-to-be-repeated moment, reading this book, eating bonbons, dreaming about hot sex with that scrumptious person from accounts, speculatively sniffing your armpits, doing whatever you are doing—just *existing*—is really wondrous beyond belief.

Third, you have plenty to eat, you live in a time of peace, and "Tie a Yellow Ribbon Round the Ole Oak Tree" will never be number one again.

If you bear these things in mind, you will never be truly unhappy—though in fairness I must point out that if you find yourself alone in Weston-super-Mare on a rainy Tuesday evening, you may come close.

It was only a little after six when I stepped from the Exeter train and ventured into the town, but already the whole of Weston appeared to be indoors beyond drawn curtains. The streets were empty, dark, and full of slanting rain. I walked from the station through a concrete shopping precinct and out onto the blustery seafront. Most of the hotels along the front were dark and evidently shut for the winter, and the few that were open didn't look particularly enticing. I walked a mile or so to a cluster of three brightly lit establishments at the far end of the promenade and randomly selected a place called the Birchfield. It was fairly basic, but clean and reasonably priced. You could do worse, and I have.

I gave myself a cursory grooming and wandered back into town in search of dinner and diversion. I had an odd sense that I had been here before, which patently I had not. My only acquaintance with Weston was that John Cleese had once told me (I'm not really dropping names—I was interviewing him for a newspaper article; he is a jolly nice fellow, by the way) that he and his parents had lived in a flat in Weston, and that when they moved out Jeffrey Archer and his parents moved in, which I thought was kind of remarkable—the idea of these two boys in short trousers saying hello and then one of them going on to greatness. What made Weston feel familiar was, of course, that it was just like everywhere else. It had Boots and Marks & Spencer and Dixons and W. H. Smith and all the rest of it. I realized with a kind of

dull ache that there wasn't a single thing here that I hadn't seen
a million times already.

I went into a pub called the Britannia Inn, which was un-
friendly without being actually hostile, and had a couple of lonely
pints, then ate at a Chinese restaurant, not because I craved Chinese but because it was the only place I could find open. I was
the only customer. As I quietly scattered rice and sweet-and-sour
sauce across the tablecloth, there were some rumbles of thunder
and, a moment later, the heavens opened—and I mean opened. I
have seldom seen it rain so hard in England. The rain clattered
onto the street like a shower of ball bearings and within minutes
the restaurant window was wholly obscured with water, as if
someone were running a hose over it. Because I was a long walk
from my hotel, I spun out the meal, hoping the weather would
ease off, but it didn't, and eventually I had no choice but to step
out into the rainy night.

I stood beneath a shop awning next door and wondered what
to do. Rain battered madly on the awning and rushed in torrents
through the gutters. All along the road, it poured over the sides
of overstretched gutters and fell to the pavement in an endless
staccato beat. With my eyes closed, it sounded like I was in the
midst of some vast, insane tap-dancing competition. Pulling my
jacket above my head, I waded out into the deluge, then sprinted
across the street and impulsively took refuge in the first bright
open thing I came to—an amusement arcade. Wiping my glasses
with a bandana, I took my bearings. The arcade was a large room
full of brightly pulsating machines, some of them playing electronic tunes or making unbidden *kerboom* noises, but apart from
an overseer sitting at a counter with a drooping cigarette and a
magazine, there was no one in the place, so it looked eerily as if
the machines were playing themselves.

With the exception of those crane things that give you three mi-
croseconds to try to snatch a stuffed animal with a grabber bucket

and in which the controls don't actually correspond to the movements of the crane, I don't understand arcade games at all. Generally I can't even figure out where to insert the money or, once it's inserted, how to make the game start. If by some miracle I manage to surmount these two obstacles, I invariably fail to recognize that the game has come to life and that I am wasting precious seconds feeling in remote coin-return slots and searching for a button that says START. Then I have thirty confused seconds of being immersed in some frantic mayhem without having the faintest idea what's going on, while my children shout, "You've just blown up Princess Leia, you stupid shit!" and then it says, "Game Over."

This is more or less what happened to me now. For no reason that I can possibly attach a rational explanation to, I put 50p into a game called *Killer Kickboxer* or *Kick Your Fucking Brains Out* or something like that, and spent about a minute punching a red button and waggling a joystick while my character, a muscular blond fellow, kicked uselessly at drapes and threw magic discs into thin air while a series of equally muscular but unscrupulous Orientals assaulted him with kidney chops and flung him repeatedly to the carpet.

I had a strange hour in which I wandered in a kind of trance, feeding money into machines and playing games I couldn't follow. I drove racing cars into bales of hay and obliterated friendly troops with lasers and unwittingly helped zombie mutants do unspeakable things to a child. Eventually I ran out of money and stepped out into the night. I had just a moment to note that the rain had eased a little and that the street was flooded, evidently from a clogged drain, when a red Ford Fiesta sped through the puddle at great speed and unusually close to the curb, transferring nearly all the water from the puddle and onto me.

As I stood there spluttering and gasping, the car slowed, three close-cropped heads popped out the windows and shouted some happy greeting along the lines of "Nyaa-nyaa, nyaa-nyaa!," and it sped off. Glumly, I trudged back along the prom, squelching with each step and shivering with cold. I don't wish to reduce this cheery chronicle to pathos, but I had only recently recovered from a fairly serious bout of pneumonia. I won't say that I nearly died, but I was ill enough to watch daytime television, and I certainly didn't want to be in that condition again. To add to my indignity, the Fiesta came past on a victory lap and its pleasure-starved occupants slowed to offer me another triumphal "Nyaa-nyaa" before speeding off into the night with a screech and brief, uncontrolled fishtail slide that unfortunately failed to bury them in a lamppost.

By the time I reached my distant hotel, I was feeling thoroughly chilled and wretched. So imagine my consternation, if you will, when I discovered that the reception area was in semidarkness and the door was locked. I looked at my watch. It was only nine o'clock, for God's sake. What kind of town was this? There were two door-bells, and I tried them both but without response. I tried my room key in the door and of course it didn't work. I tried the bells again, leaning on them both for many minutes and growing increasingly angry. When this elicited no satisfaction, I banged on the glass door with the flat of my hand, then with a fist, and finally with a stout boot and a touch of frenzy. I believe, on reflection, I may also have filled the quiet streets with shouting.

Eventually the proprietor appeared at the top of some basement stairs, looking surprised. "I'm so sorry, sir," he said mildly as he let me in. "Have you been out there long?"

Well, I blush to think at how I ranted at the poor man. I used immoderate language. I accused him and his fellow townspeople of appalling shortages of intelligence and charm. I told him that I had just passed the dreariest evening of my life in this god-forsaken hellhole of a resort, that I had been soaked to the skin by a carful of young men who between them were ten IQ points short of a moron, that I had walked a mile in wet clothes and had now spent nearly half an hour shivering in the cold because I had been locked out of my own hotel at nine o'clock in the bloody evening.

"May I remind you," I went on in a shrill voice, "that two hours ago you said good-bye to me, watched me go out the door and disappear down the street. Did you think I wasn't coming back? That I would sleep in a park and return for my things in the morning? Or is it merely that you are a total imbecile? Please tell me because I would very much like to know."

The proprietor flinchingly soaked up my abuse and responded with fluttering hands and a flood of apologies. He offered me a tray of tea and sandwiches, to dry and press my wet clothes, to escort me to my room and turn on my radiator personally. He did everything but fall to my feet and beg me to run him through with a saber. He positively *implored* me to let him bring me something warming on a tray.

"I don't want anything but to go to my room and count the minutes until I get out of this fucking dump!" I shouted, perhaps a trifle theatrically but to good effect, and stalked up the stairs to the second floor where I plodded about heatedly in the corridor for some minutes and realized that I didn't have the faintest idea which was my room. There was no number on the key.

I returned to the reception area, now once more in semidarkness, and put my head by the basement door. "Excuse me," I said in a small voice, "could you please tell me what room I'm in?"

"Number twenty-seven, sir," came a voice from the darkness.

I stood for some time without moving. "Thank you," I said.

"It's quite all right, sir," came the voice. "Have a good night."

I frowned and cleared my throat. "Thank you," I said again and retired to my room, where the night passed without further incident.

In the morning, I presented myself in the sunny dining room and, as I had feared, the proprietor was waiting to receive me. Now that

I was dry and warm and well rested, I felt terrible about my outburst of the night before.

"Good morning, sir!" he said brightly as if nothing had happened, and showed me to a window table with a nice view of the sea. "Sleep all right, did you?"

I was taken aback by his friendliness. "Uh, yes. Yes, I did as a matter of fact."

"Good! Splendid! Juice and cereal on the trolley. Please help yourself. Can I get you the full English breakfast, sir?"

I found this unmerited bonhomie unbearable. I tucked my chin into my chest and in a furtive grumble said, "Look, here, I'm very sorry for what I said last night. I was in a bit of a temper."

"It's quite all right, sir."

"No really, I'm, um, very sorry. Bit ashamed, in fact."

"Consider it forgotten, sir. So—full English breakfast, is it?"

"Yes, please."

"Very good, sir!"

I've never had such good or friendly service anywhere, or felt more like a worm. He brought my food promptly, chattering away about the weather and what a glorious day it promised to be. I couldn't understand why he was so forgiving. Only gradually did it occur to me what a strange sight I must have presented—a middle-aged man with a rucksack, visiting a place like Weston out of season for no evident reason, fetching up at his hotel and bellowing and stomping about over a trifling inconvenience. He must have thought I was mad, an escaped lunatic perhaps, and that this was the safest way to approach me. Either that, or he was just an extremely nice person. In either case, I salute him now.

Weston was surprisingly lovely in morning sunshine. Out in the bay, an island called Flat Holm basked in the clear, clean air and beyond it rose the green hills of Wales, twelve miles or so across the water. Even the hotels that I had disdained the night before didn't look half bad.

I walked to the station and took a train to Chepstow and a bus on to Monmouth through the famous Wye Valley. The valley was as beautiful as I remembered it from years before—dark woods, winding river, lonely white farmhouses high up on steep slopes—but the villages between were rather astonishingly charmless and seemed to consist mostly of gas stations, pubs with vast parking lots, and gift shops. I watched out for Tintern Abbey, made famous of course by the well-known Wordsworth poem "I Can Be Boring Outside the Lake District Too," and was disappointed to find that it didn't stand out in the country as I recalled but on the edge of an unmemorable village.

Monmouth, however, seemed to be a fine, handsome town with a sloping High Street and an imposing town hall. In front of it stood a statue of Charles Stewart Rolls, son of Lord and Lady Llangattock, "pioneer of ballooning, motoring and aviation, who died in a crash at Bournemouth in July 1910," according to the inscription. He was shown holding a model of an early biplane, which made him look rather like King Kong swatting away attacking craft. There was no indication of what his local connection might be. The Monmouth Bookshop on Church Street had a book of mine in the window, and so of course gets a mention here.

I had it in mind to do another little walk while the weather was fine, so I didn't linger. I bought a pasty in a baker's and ate it as I found my way to the Wye. I picked up a riverside path by the town's handsome stone bridge and followed it north along the Welsh bank. For the first forty minutes, I was accompanied by the ceaseless roar of traffic on the A40, but at a place called Goldsmith's Wood the river bent sharply away from the road and I was suddenly in another, infinitely more tranquil world. Birds fussed and twittered in the trees above and small, unseen creatures plinked into the water at my ap-

proach. The river, sparkling and languid and framed by hills of au-
tumn-colored trees, was very beautiful and I had it all to myself. A
mile or two farther on, I paused to study the map and noticed a spot
on a nearby hill called King Arthur's Cave. Well, I couldn't pass
that up, so I lumbered keenly up the hill and poked around among
likely spots, pausing from time to time to consult the map and
scratch my head. After about an hour of clambering over boulders
and fallen trees, and to my mild astonishment, I actually found the
cave. It wasn't much—just a shallow chamber hewn by nature from
a limestone cliff face—but I had a pleasing sense of being its first
visitor in years. At any rate, there were none of the usual signs of
recent visitation—graffiti and abandoned beer cans—which may
make it unique in Britain, if not the world.

Because time was getting on, I decided to take a shortcut through
the hilly woods, but I neglected to note that I was at the uppermost
of a very tight band of contour lines. In consequence, I found myself
a moment later descending a more or less perpendicular hill in an
entirely involuntary fashion, bounding through the woods with great
leaps and outflung arms in a manner oddly reminiscent of George
Chakiris in *West Side Story,* except of course that this was Wales and
George Chakiris didn't shit himself with terror, before eventually,
after several bouncing somersaults and an epochal eighty-yard slide
on the stomach, ending up on the very lip of a giddy precipice, with
a goggle-eyed view of the glittery Wye a hundred feet below. I cast
my gaze back along my suddenly motionless body to find that my
left foot had fortuitously snagged on a sapling. Had the sapling not
been there, I would not be here.

Muttering, "Thank you, Lord," I hauled myself to my feet, dusted
twigs and leaf mold from my front, and clambered laboriously back
up the hill to the path I had so intemperately forsaken. By the time
I reached the riverbank another hour had gone. It took another hour
or so to hike on to Symonds Yat, a spacious wooded bluff and well-
known beauty spot at the top of a formidable hill, with long views

in many directions. It was exceedingly fetching—a hang glider's vista over the meandering river and a flawless, arcadian landscape of undulant fields and clustered woodlands stretching off to the distant Black Mountains.

"Not bad," I said, "not bad at all," and wondered if there was anywhere nearby where I could get a cup of tea and possibly change my pants.

chapter
13

There are certain things that you have to be British, or at least older than me, or possibly both, to appreciate: skiffle music, saltcellars with a single hole, Marmite (an edible yeast extract with the visual properties of an industrial lubricant), Gracie Fields singing "Sally," George Formby doing anything, jumble sales, making sandwiches from bread you've sliced yourself, really milky tea, boiled cabbage, the belief that household wiring is an interesting topic for conversation, steam trains, toast made under a gas grill, thinking that going to choose wallpaper with your mate constitutes a reasonably fun day out, wine made out of something other than grapes, unheated bedrooms and bathrooms, erecting windbreaks on a beach (why, pray, are you *there* if you need a windbreak?), and cricket. There may be one or two others that don't occur to me at the moment.

I'm not saying that these things are bad or boring or misguided, merely that their full value and appeal yet elude me. Into this category I would also tentatively insert Oxford.

Now, I have the greatest respect for the university and its eight hundred years of tireless intellectual toil, but I must confess that I'm

not entirely clear what it's *for*, now that Britain no longer needs
colonial administrators who can quip in Latin. I mean to say, you
see all these dons and students striding past, absorbed in deep dis-
cussions about the Leibniz-Clarke controversy or post-Kantian aes-
thetics, and you think, *Most impressive, but perhaps a tad indulgent
in a country with three million unemployed and where the last great
invention was the jet engine?* Only the night before there had been
an item on *News at Ten* in which the anchorman had been radiant
with joy to announce that the Samsung Corporation was building a
new factory in Tyneside that would provide jobs for eight hundred
people willing to wear orange boiler suits and do t'ai chi for a half
hour every morning. Now call me an unreconstructed Philistine, but
it seems to me—and I offer this observation in a spirit of friendship—that when a nation's industrial prowess has plunged so low
that it is reliant on Korean firms for its future economic security,
then perhaps it is time to readdress one's educational priorities and
maybe give a little thought to what's going to put some food on the
table in about 2010.

I remember once years ago watching a special international edition of *University Challenge*—the program known in America as *College Bowl*—between a team of British students and a team of
American students. The British team won so handily that a kind of
embarrassed hush fell over the proceedings, as the Britons cranked
out one correct answer after another while the Americans just
frowned and fidgeted and thought (you could see it in their eyes),
What the hell's metempsychosis? The final score was something like
12,000 to 2, and it left the Britons wretched with embarrassment
since nothing causes the British deeper unease than to be seen to
do exceptionally well at something. But here's the thing. I am certain
beyond the tiniest measure of doubt that if you tracked down the
competitors to see what has become of them since, you would find
that every one of the Americans was pulling down $850,000 a year
trading bonds or running a corporation, while the British were study-

ing the tonal qualities of sixteenth-century choral music in Lower Silesia and wearing sweaters with holes in them.

But don't worry. Oxford has been preeminent since the Middle Ages, and I am sure that it will remain so long after it has become the University of Oxford (Sony UK), Ltd. The university, it must be said, has become infinitely more commercial-minded. At the time of my visit, it was just finishing a successful five-year £340 million fund-raising campaign, which was most impressive, and it had at last learned the value of corporate sponsorship. If you look through the university prospectus you'll find it littered with references to things like the All-New Shredded Wheat (No Added Sugar or Salt) Chair of Eastern Philosophy, and the Harris Carpets Why-Pay-More Thousands of Rolls in Stock at Everyday Low Prices School of Business Management.

This business of corporate sponsorship is something that seems to have crept into British life generally in recent years without being much remarked upon. Nowadays you have the Canon League, the Coca-Cola Cup, the Ever-Ready Derby, the Embassy World Snooker Championships. The day can't be far off when we get things like the Kellogg's Pop Tart Queen Mother, the Mitsubishi Corporation Proudly Presents Regent's Park, and Samsung City (formerly Newcastle).

But I digress. My gripe with Oxford has nothing to do with fund raising or how it educates its students. My gripe with Oxford is that so much of it is so ugly. Come with me down Merton Street and I will show you what I mean. Note, as we stroll past the back of Christ Church College, the studied calm of Corpus Christi, the honeyed glow of seven-hundred-year-old Merton, that we are immersed in an architectural treasure house, one of the densest assemblages of historic buildings in the world, and that Merton Street presents us with an unquestionably becoming prospect of gabled buildings, elaborate wrought iron gates, and fine seventeenth- and eighteenth-century town houses. Several of the houses have been mildly disfigured by the careless addition of electrical wires to their facades (something that other, less intellectually distracted nations would put inside), but never mind. They are easily overlooked. But what is this inescapable intrusion at the bottom? Is it an electrical substation? A halfway house designed by the inmates? No, it is the Merton College Wardens' Quarters, a little dash of mindless 1960s excrescence foisted on an otherwise largely flawless street.

Now come with me while we backtrack to Kybald Street, a forgotten lane lost amid a warren of picturesque little byways between Merton Street and the High. At its eastern extremity Kybald Street ends in a pocket-sized square that positively cries out for a small fountain, a shade tree, and maybe some benches. But what we find instead is a messy jumble of double- and triple-parked cars. Now on to Oriel Square: an even messier jumble of abandoned vehicles. Then on up the street called Cornmarket (avert your gaze; this is *truly* hideous), past Broad Street and St. Giles (still more automotive messiness), and finally let us stop, exhausted and dispirited, outside the unconscionable concrete eyesore that is the university's administrative offices on Wellington Square. No, let's not. Let's pass back down Cornmarket, through the horrible, low-ceilinged, ill-lit drabness of the Clarendon Shopping Centre, out onto Queen Street, past the equally unadorable Westgate Shopping Centre and central library with its heartless, staring windows, and come to rest at the outsized pustule that is the head office of Oxfordshire County Council. We could go on through the district of St. Ebbes, past the brutalist compound of the magistrates' courts, along the bleak sweep of Oxpens Road, with its tire and exhaust centers and pathetically underlandscaped ice rink and parking lots, and out onto the busy squalor of Park End Street, but I think we can safely stop here at the county council building and save our weary legs.

Now none of this would bother me a great deal except that everyone, but everyone, you talk to in Oxford thinks that it is one of the

most beautiful cities in the world, with all that that implies in terms
of careful preservation and general livability. Now I know that Oxford has moments of unutterable beauty. Christ Church Meadow,
Radcliffe Square, the college quads, Catte Street and Turl Street,
Queens Lane and much of the High Street, the botanic garden, Port
Meadow, University Parks, Clarendon House, the whole of north
Oxford—all very fine. It has the best collection of bookshops in the
world, some of the most splendid pubs, and the most wonderful
museums of any city of its size. It has a terrific indoor market. It has
the Sheldonian Theatre. It has the Bodleian Library. It has a scattering of prospects that melt the heart.

But there is also so much that is so wrong. How did it happen?
This is a serious question. What sort of mad seizure was it that
gripped the city's planners, architects, and college authorities in the
1960s and 1970s? Did you know that it was once seriously proposed
to tear down Jericho, a district of fine artisans' homes, and to run a
relief road right across Christ Church Meadow? These ideas weren't
just misguided, they were criminally insane. And yet on a lesser scale
they were repeated over and over throughout the city. Just look at
the Merton College Wardens' Quarters—which is not by any means
the worst building in the city. What a remarkable series of improb-
abilities were necessary to its construction. First, some architect had
to design it, had to wander through a city steeped in eight hundred
years of architectural tradition, and with great care conceive of a
structure that looked like a toaster with windows. Then a committee
of finely educated minds at Merton had to show the most extraordinary indifference to their responsibilities to posterity and say to
themselves, "You know, we've been putting up handsome buildings
since 1264; let's have an ugly one for a change." Then the planning
authorities had to say, "Well, why not? Plenty worse elsewhere."
Then the whole of the city—students, dons, shopkeepers, office
workers, members of the Oxford Preservation Trust—had to acqui-
esce and not kick up a fuss. Multiply this by, say, two hundred or

three hundred or four hundred and you have modern Oxford. And you tell me that it is one of the most beautiful, well-preserved cities in the world? I'm afraid not. It is a beautiful city that has been treated with gross indifference and lamentable incompetence for far too long, and every living person in Oxford should feel a little bit ashamed.

Goodness me! What an outburst! Let's lighten up and go look at some good things. The Ashmolean, for instance. What a wonderful institution, the oldest public museum on Planet Earth and certainly one of the finest. How is it that it is always so empty? I spent a long morning there politely examining the antiquities, and had the place all to myself but for a party of schoolchildren who could occasionally be sighted racing between rooms pursued some moments later by a harried-looking teacher, then strolled over to the Pitt-Rivers and University museums, which are also very agreeable in their quaint, welcome-to-the-1870s sort of way. I trawled through Blackwell's and Dillons bookshops, poked about at Balliol and Christ Church, ambled through University Parks and Christ Church Meadow, ranged out through Jericho and among the stolid, handsome mansions of north Oxford.

Perhaps I'm too hard on poor old Oxford. I mean it is basically a wonderful place, with its smoky pubs and bookshops and scholarly air, as long as you fix your gaze on the good things and never go anywhere near Cornmarket or George Street. I particularly like it at night when the traffic dies away enough that you don't need an oxygen mask and the High Street fills up with those mysteriously popular doner kebab vans, which tempt me not at all (how can anyone eat something that looks so uncannily as if it has been carved from a dead man's leg?) but do have a kind of Hopperish glow about them. I like the darkness of the back lanes that wander between high walls, where you half expect to be skewered and dismembered by Jack the Ripper or possibly a doner kebab wholesaler. I like wandering up St. Giles to immerse myself in the busy

conviviality of Brown's Restaurant—a wonderful, friendly place
where, perhaps uniquely in Britain, you can get an excellent Cae-
sar salad and a bacon cheeseburger without having to sit among
pounding music and a lot of ersatz Route 66 signs. Above all, I
like to drink in the pubs, where you can sit with a book and not
be looked on as a social miscreant; where you can be among
laughing, lively young people and lose yourself in reveries of what
it was like when you, too, had energy and a flat stomach and
thought of sex as something more than a welcome chance to lie
down for a while.

I'd impetuously said I would stay for three nights when I
booked into my hotel, and by midmorning of the third day I was
beginning to feel a little restless, so I decided to have a walk to
Sutton Courtenay for no reason other than that George Orwell is
buried there and it seemed about the right distance. I walked
out of the city by way of a water meadow to North Hinksey and
onward toward Boar's Hill through an area called, with curious
indecisiveness, Chilswell Valley or Happy Valley. It had rained in
the night and the heavy clay soil stuck to my boots and made the
going arduous. Soon I had an accumulation of mud that doubled
the size of my feet. A bit farther on, the path had been covered
with gravel, presumably to make the going easier, but in fact the
gravel stuck to my muddy boots so that it looked as if I were walking
around with two very large currant buns on my feet. At the top of
Boar's Hill I stopped to savor the view—it's the one that led
Matthew Arnold to pen the oft-quoted lines about "dreaming
spires," and it has been cruelly despoiled by those marching electricity pylons that Oxfordshire has in greater abundance than any
other county I know—and to scrape the mud from my boots with
a stick.

Boar's Hill has some lovely big houses but I don't think I could happily settle there. I noted three driveways with signs saying NO TURNING. Now tell me, just how petty do you have to be, how ludicrously possessive of your little piece of turf, to put up a sign like that? What harm can there possibly be in some lost or misdirected person's turning a car around in the edge of your driveway? I always make a point to turn around in such driveways, whether I need to or not, and I urge you to join me in this practice if the opportunity presents itself. It is always a good idea to toot your horn two or three times to make sure that the owner sees you.

I reached Abingdon by way of a back lane from Sunningwell. Abingdon has some of the nicest public housing I think I've ever seen—huge sweeps of lawn and neat houses—and a small, handsome, strikingly curious town hall raised off the ground on stone pillars as if somebody was expecting a forty-day flood, but that's as much as I'm prepared to say for Abingdon. It has the most appalling shopping precinct, which I later learned had been created by sweeping away a raft of medieval houses, and a kind of dogged commitment to ugliness around its fringes.

Sutton Courtenay seemed considerably farther on than I recalled it from the map, but it was a pleasant walk with frequent views of the Thames, and it was worth the effort of getting there because it is a charming place, with some fine homes, three agreeable-looking pubs, and a little green with a war memorial, beside which stands the churchyard where not only George Orwell lies, but also the Prime Minister H. H. Asquith. Call me a perennial Iowa farmboy, but I never fail to be impressed by how densely packed with achievement is this little island. How remarkable it is that in a single village churchyard you find the graves of two men of global stature. We in Iowa would be proud of either one of them—indeed we would be proud of Chester the Wonder Horse or the guy who invented traffic cones or pretty much anyone at all.

I walked into the graveyard and found Orwell's grave. It had three

straggly rosebushes growing out of it and some artificial flowers in a
glass jar, before a simple stone with a terse inscription:

> HERE LIES ERIC ARTHUR BLAIR
> BORN JUNE 25TH 1903
> DIED JANUARY 21ST 1950

Not much sentiment there, what? Nearby was the grave of Herbert
Henry Asquith. It was one of those tea caddy tombs, and it was
sinking into the ground in an alarming manner. His inscription, too,
was mysteriously to the point. It said simply:

> EARL OF OXFORD AND ASQUITH
> PRIME MINISTER OF ENGLAND
> APRIL 1908 TO DECEMBER 1916
> BORN 12 SEPTEMBER 1852
> DIED 15 FEBRUARY 1928

Notice anything odd there? I bet you did if you are Scottish or
Welsh. The whole place was a bit strange. I mean to say here was a
cemetery containing the grave of a famous author that was made as
anonymous as if he had been buried a pauper, and another of a man
whose descendants had apparently forgotten exactly what he was
prime minister of and that looked seriously in danger of being swallowed by the earth. Next to Asquith lay one Ruben Loveridge "who
fell asleep 29th April 1950" and nearby was a grave shared by two
men: "Samuel Lewis 1881–1930" and "Alan Slater 1924–1993."
What an intriguing little community this was—a place where men
are entombed together and they bury you if you fall asleep.

On second thought, I think we Iowans would be content to let
the British keep Orwell and Asquith as long as we could have the
guy who was buried alive.

chapter
14

i suspended my principles and rented a car for three days. Well,
I had to. I wanted to see the Cotswolds and it doesn't take long to
work out that you can't see the Cotswolds unless you have your own
motive power. As long ago as 1933, J. B. Priestley was noting in
English Journey that even then, in those golden days when Britain's
railway system reached into almost every corner of the country and
even stately homes sometimes had their own stations, there was just
one line through the Cotswolds. Now there isn't even that, except
for one that runs uselessly along the edges.

So I rented a car in Oxford and set off with that giddying sense
of unbounded possibility that comes when I find myself in charge
of two tons of unfamiliar metal. My experience with rental cars is
that generally they won't let you leave a city until they have had a
chance to say good-bye to most of it. Mine took me on a long tour
through Botley and Hinksey, on a nostalgic swing past the sprawling
Rover car factory at Cowley, and out through Blackbird Leys, before
taking me twice around a roundabout and flinging me, like a space-
craft in planetary orbit, back toward town. I was powerless to do
anything about this, largely because my attention was preoccupied

with trying to turn off the back windshield wiper, which seemed to
have a mind of its own, and figuring out how to remove an opaque
cloud of foamy washing fluid from the front windshield, which shot
out in great obscuring streams no matter which switch I pushed or
stalk I waggled.

At least it gave me a chance to see the little-known but intriguing
Potato Marketing Board building at Cowley, into whose parking lot
I pulled to turn the car around when I realized I was utterly lost.
The building was a substantial 1960s edifice, four stories high and
large enough, I would have guessed, to accommodate four hundred
or five hundred workers. I got out to wipe the window with some
pages torn from an owner's manual I found in the glove compartment, but found myself staring at the arresting grandeur of the Potato Marketing Board HQ. The scale of it was quite astounding.
How many people does it take to market potatoes, for goodness'
sake? There must be doors in there marked DEPARTMENT OF KING
EDWARDS and UNUSUAL TOPPINGS DIVISION, people in white shirts
sitting around long tables while some guy with a flip chart is earnestly outlining plans for the autumn campaign for Pentland
Squires. What a strange, circumscribed universe they must live in.
Imagine devoting the whole of your working life to edible tubers,
losing sleep because somebody else was made number two in Crisps
and Reconstituteds or because the Maris Piper graph is in a tailspin.
Imagine their cocktail parties. It doesn't bear thinking about.

I returned to the car and spent some time experimenting with the
controls and thinking how much I hated these things. Some people
are made for cars and some people aren't. It's as simple as that. I
hate driving cars and I hate thinking about cars and I hate talking
about cars. I especially hate it when you get a new car and go into
the pub, because somebody will always start quizzing you about it,
which I dread because I don't even understand the questions.

"See you've got a new car," they'll say. "How's it drive?"

I'm lost already. "Well, like a *car*. Why, have you never been in one?"

And then they start peppering you with questions. "What sort of mileage you get? How many liters is the engine? What's the torque? Got twin overhead cams or double-barreled alternator cum carburetor with a full pike and a double-twist dismount?" I can't for the life of me understand why anyone would want to know all this about a machine. You don't take that kind of interest in anything else. I've been waiting years for somebody in a pub to tell me he's got a new refrigerator so I can say, "Oh, really? How many gallons of freon does that baby hold? What's its BTU rating? How's it *cool*?"

This car had the usual array of switches and toggles, each illustrated with a symbol designed to confound. Really now, what is one to make of a switch labeled |Ø|? How can anyone be expected to work out that a rectangle that looks like a television set with poor reception indicates the rear-window heater? In the middle of this dashboard were two circular dials of equal size. One clearly indicated speed, but the other totally mystified me. It had two pointers on it, one of which advanced very slowly and the other of which didn't appear to move at all. I looked at it for ages before it finally dawned on me—this is true—that it was a clock.

By the time I found my way to Woodstock, ten miles north of Oxford, I was quite exhausted and very happy to bump to a halt against a curb and abandon the thing for a few hours. I must say I liked Woodstock very much. Its Georgian houses had a confident, almost regal air; its pubs were numerous and snug, its shops interesting and varied, and their frontages uniformly unspoiled. There wasn't a piece of brass in town that didn't gleam. The post office had an old-fashioned black-and-silver sign, far more elegant and classy than that red-and-yellow logo it uses now, and even Barclays Bank had somehow managed to resist the urge to cover the front of its building with lots of aqua-blue plastic.

The High Street was busy with shunting Volvos and tweedy shoppers with raffia baskets slung over their arms. I ambled along the
shops, pausing now and again to peer into windows, and past the
proud stone houses before coming abruptly to the entrance to Blenheim Palace and Park. Beneath an imposing ornamental arch there
was a ticket booth and a sign saying that admission for an adult was
£6.90, though closer inspection revealed that this included entrance
to the palace tour, butterfly house, miniature train, adventure playground, and whole cornucopia of other cultural diversions. Lower
down, the sign noted that admission to the grounds alone was 90p.
I may be easily fooled, but nobody takes 90p from me without good
reason. I had a trusty Ordnance Survey map and could see that this
was a public right-of-way, so I strode through the gate with a sneer
and my hand on my wallet, and the man in the ticket booth wisely
decided not to tamper with me.

The transformation when you pass through the gate is both immediate and stunning. On one side you are in a busy little town, on
the other in a rural arcadia of the sort that seems incomplete without a couple of Gainsborough figures ambling by. Before me spread
two thousand acres of meticulously composed landscape—stout
chestnuts and graceful sycamores, billiard table lawns, an ornamental lake bisected by an imposing bridge, and in the center of it
all the monumental baroque pile of Blenheim Palace. It was very
fine.

I followed the curving road through the grounds, past the palace
and busy visitors' parking lot, and on around the periphery of the
Pleasure Gardens. I would come back to check this out, but at the
moment I was headed across the park and to an exit on the other
side on the Bladon road. Bladon is a nondescript little place trem-
bling under the weight of passing trucks, but in its center is the
churchyard where Winston Churchill lies buried. It had begun to
rain and, as it was a long tramp up a busy road, I began to wonder
if this was worth the effort, but when I reached it I was glad

I had. The churchyard was lovely and secluded and Churchill's grave so modest that it took some finding among the tumbling gravestones. I was the only visitor. Churchill and Clemmie shared a simple and seemingly forgotten plot, which I found surprisingly touching and impressive. Coming as I do from a country where even the most obscure and worthless of presidents get huge memorial libraries when they pop their clogs—even Herbert Hoover, way out in the Iowa cornfields, has a place that looks like the headquarters of the World Trade Organization—it was remarkable to think that Britain's greatest twentieth-century statesman was commemorated with nothing more than a modest statue in Parliament Square and this simple grave. I was impressed by this commendable show of restraint.

I retraced my steps to Blenheim and had a nose around the Pleasure Gardens and other outdoor attractions. "Pleasure Gardens" apparently was short for "It's a Pleasure to Take Your Money," since it seemed largely dedicated to helping visitors to part with further sums in a gift shop and tearoom or by buying garden gates, benches, and other such items produced by the Blenheim Estate Sawmill. Dozens of people poked around happily, seemingly undisturbed by the thought that they had paid £6.90 for the privilege of looking at the sorts of items they could see for free at any garden center. As I left the gardens and walked back toward the palace, I took the opportunity to study the miniature steam train. It ran over a decidedly modest length of track across one corner of the grounds. The sight of fifty English people crouched on a little train in a cold gray drizzle waiting to be taken two hundred yards and thinking they were having fun is one that I shall not forget in a hurry.

I followed a paved path to the front of the palace and over Vanbrugh's sumptuous bridge to the mighty, absurdly egocentric column that the first Duke of Marlborough erected at the top of a hill overlooking the palace and lake. It really is the most extraordinary edifice, not only because it is lofty and impressive, but because it dominates the view from at least a hundred palace windows. What kind of person, I wondered, would erect a one-hundred-foot-high column to himself in his own grounds? How striking was the contrast with the simple grave of dear old Winnie.

Maybe I'm a bit simple, but it has always seemed to me that the scale of Blenheim Palace and the scale of Marlborough's achievement are curiously disproportionate. I can understand how in a moment of mad rejoicing a grateful nation might have awarded him, say, a two-week timeshare for life in the Canaries and maybe a set of cutlery or a coffee maker, but I can't for the life of me comprehend how a scattering of triumphs in obscure places like Oudenaarde and Malplaquet could be deemed to have entitled the conniving old fart to one of the great houses of Europe and a dukedom. More extraordinary still to my mind is the thought that nearly three hundred years later the Duke's heirs can litter the grounds with miniature trains and bouncing castles, charge admission, and enjoy unearned positions of rank and privilege simply because a distant grandsire happened to have a passing talent for winning battles. It seems a most eccentric arrangement to me.

I remember once reading that the tenth Duke of Marlborough, on a visit to one of his daughters' homes, announced in consternation from the top of the stairs that his toothbrush wasn't foaming properly. It turned out that his valet had always put toothpaste on his brush for him, and as a consequence the Duke was unaware that dental implements didn't foam up spontaneously. I rest my case.

As I was standing there taking in the view and reflecting on the curious practice of primogeniture, some well-groomed young woman on a bay horse bounded past very near to where I was standing. I've no idea who she was, but she looked rich and privileged. I gave her a little smile, such as one habitually gives strangers in an open place, and she stared flatly back at me as if I was not important enough to smile at. So I shot her. Then I returned to the car and drove on.

I spent two days driving through the Cotswolds and didn't like it
at all—not because the Cotswolds were unlovely but because the car
was. You are so sealed off from the world in a moving vehicle, and
the pace is all wrong. I had grown used to moving about at walking
speed or at least at British Rail speed, which is often of course much
the same thing. So it was with relief, after a day spent dashing about
through various Chippings and Slaughters and Tweeness-upon-the-
Waters that I abandoned the car in a parking lot in Broadway and
took to my feet.

The last time I had seen Broadway, on an August afternoon some
years before, it had been a nightmare of sclerotic traffic and flocks
of shuffling daytrippers, but now, out of season, it seemed quiet and
forgotten, its High Street nearly empty. It's an almost absurdly pretty
place with its steeply pitched roofs, mullioned windows, prolific gables, and trim little gardens. There is something about that golden
Cotswold stone—the way it absorbs sunlight and then feeds it back
so that even on the dullest days villages like Broadway seem to be
basking in a perennial soft glow. This day, in fact, was sunny and
gorgeous, with just a tang of autumn crispness in the air, which gave
the world a marvelous clean, fresh-laundered feel. Halfway along the
High Street I found a signpost for the Cotswold Way, a long-
distance footpath, and plunged off down a track between old buildings. I followed a narrow trail across a sunny meadow and up the
long slope toward Broadway Tower, an outsized folly high above the
village. The view from the top over the broad Vale of Evesham, was,
as always from such points, sensational—gently undulating trape-
zoids of farmland rolling off to a haze of distant wooded hills. Britain
still has more landscape that looks like an illustration from a children's storybook than any other country I know—a remarkable

achievement in such a densely crowded and industrially minded little island. And yet I couldn't help feel that the view may have been
more bucolic and rewarding ten or perhaps twenty years ago.

It is easy to forget, in a landscape so timeless and fetching, so
companionably rooted to an ancient past, how easily it is lost. The
panorama before me incorporated electricity pylons, scattered housing estates, and the distant sunny glints of cash-and-carry warehouses. Far worse, the dense, carefully knitted network of hedgerows
was showing distinct signs of becoming frayed and disjointed, like
the pattern on a candlewick bedspread that has been picked off by
idle fingers. Here and there fragments of overgrown hedge stood
stranded and forlorn in the midst of otherwise featureless fields.

Between 1945 and 1985 England lost ninety-six thousand miles
of hedgerows, enough to girdle the earth four times. So muddled
has been government policy toward the countryside that for a period
of twenty-four years farmers could actually get one grant to plant
hedgerows and another to grub them up. Between 1984 and 1990,
despite the withdrawal of government money to plow up hedgerows,
a further fifty-three thousand miles were lost. You often hear it said
(and I know because I once spent three days at a symposium on
hedgerows; the things I do to keep my children in Reeboks) that
hedgerows are in fact a transitory feature of the landscape, a relic of
the enclosure movements, and that trying to save them merely
thwarts the natural evolution of the countryside. Indeed, increasingly
in Britain you hear the view that conservation of all types is fussy,
retrograde, and an impediment to progress. I have before me as I
write a quote from Lord Palumbo, a leading developer, arguing that
the whole vague notion of heritage "carries the baggage of nostalgia
for a non-existent golden age which, had it existed, might well have
been the death of invention," which is so fatuous it breaks my heart.
Quite apart from the consideration that if you followed that argument to its logical conclusion you would tear down Stonehenge and
the Tower of London, in point of fact many hedgerows have been

there for a very, very long time. In Cambridgeshire, I know of a particularly lovely hedge, called Judith's Hedge, that is older than Salisbury Cathedral, older than York Minster, older indeed than all but a handful of buildings in Britain, and yet no statute stands between it and its destruction. If the road needed widening or the owners decided they preferred the property to be bounded by fenceposts and barbed wire, it would be the work of but a couple of hours to bulldoze away nine hundred years of living history. That's insane. At least half the hedgerows in Britain predate the enclosure movements and perhaps as many as a fifth date back to Anglo-Saxon times. Anyway, the reason for saving hedgerows isn't because they have been there forever and ever, but because they clearly and unequivocally enhance the landscape. They are a central part of what makes England England. Without them, it would just be Indiana with steeples.

It gets me a little wild sometimes. The British enjoy possibly the most comely, the most parklike, the most carefully composed countryside the world has ever known, a product of centuries of tireless, instinctive improvement, and sometimes they seem so exasperatingly *blind* to it. In half a generation much of it could be gone forever. We're not talking here about "nostalgia for a non-existent golden age." We're talking about something that is green and living and incomparably beautiful. So if one more person says to me, "Hedgerows aren't really an ancient feature of the landscape, you know," I shall very likely punch him in the hooter. I'm a great believer in Voltaire's famous maxim, "Sir, I may not agree with what you say, but I shall defend to the death your right to be a complete asshole," but there comes a time when a line must be drawn.

I struck off down a wooded back lane to Snowshill, three miles away. The leaves were golden and rustly and the sky vast and blue and empty but for an occasional slow-moving wedge of migrating birds. It was a wonderful day to be abroad—the kind of day that has you puffing your chest and singing "Zip-a-Dee-Doo-Dah" in the voice of Paul Robeson. Snowshill drowsed in the sunshine, a cluster of stone cottages gathered around a sloping green. I bought an entrance ticket to Snowshill Manor, now in the hands of the National Trust but from 1919 to 1956 the home of an eccentric character named Charles Wade, who devoted his life to accumulating a vast and unfocused assortment of stuff, some of it very good, some of it little more than junk—clavichords, microscopes, Flemish tapestries, snuff and tobacco boxes, maps and sextants, samurai armor, penny-farthing bicycles, you name it—until he had filled his house so full that there was no room left for him. He spent his last years living happily in an outbuilding, which, like the house, has been preserved as it was on the day he died. I enjoyed it very much, and afterward, as the sun sank in the west and the world filled with long shadows and a vague, entrancing, autumny smell of woodsmoke, I hiked back to my car a happy man.

I spent the night in Cirencester and the next day, after a pleasant look around the little Corinium Museum, with its outstanding but curiously little-known collection of Roman mosaics, coins, and other artifacts, drove on to Winchcombe to see the real thing *in situ*. On a hill above Winchcombe, you see, there is a little-visited site so singular and wonderful that I hesitate even to mention it. Most of the relatively few visitors who intrude upon this tranquil corner of the Cotswolds generally content themselves with a look around Sudeley Castle or a hike to the remote hump of the famous Belas Knap long barrow. But I headed straight for a grassy hillside path called the Salt Way, so named because in medieval times salt was conveyed along it. It was an enchanting walk through open countryside, with long views across sharply defined valleys that seemed never to have seen a car or heard the sound of a chainsaw.

At a place called Cole's Hill the path plunged abruptly into a seriously overgrown wood, dark and primeval in feel and all but impenetrable with brambles. Somewhere in here, I knew, was my goal—a site listed on the map as "Roman villa (remains of)." For perhaps half an hour, I hacked through the growth with my stick before I came upon the foundations of an old wall. It looked like nothing much—the remains of an old pigsty perhaps—but a few feet farther on, all but obscured by wild ivy, were more low walls, a whole series of them, on both sides of the path. The path itself was paved with flagstones underneath a carpet of wet leaves, and I knew that I was in the villa. In one of the relict chambers, the floor had been carefully covered with plastic fertilizer bags weighted with stones at each corner. This was what I had come to see. I had been told about this by a friend but had never really believed it. For underneath those bags was a virtually complete Roman mosaic, about five feet square, exquisitely patterned and flawlessly preserved but for a tiny bit of fracturing around the edges.

I cannot tell you how odd it felt to be standing in a forgotten wood in what had once been, in an inconceivably distant past, the home of a Roman family, looking at a mosaic laid at least sixteen hundred years ago when this was an open sunny space, long before this ancient wood grew up around it. It is one thing to see these things in museums, quite another to come upon one on the spot where it was laid. I have no idea why it hadn't been gathered up and taken away to someplace like the Corinium Museum. I presume it is a terrible oversight, but I am so grateful to have had the chance to see it. I sat for a long time on a stone, riveted with wonder and admiration. I don't know which seized me more, the thought that people in togas had once stood on this floor chatting in vernacular Latin or that it was still here, flawless and undisturbed, amid this tangle of growth.

This may sound awfully stupid, but for the first time it dawned on me in a kind of profound way that all those Roman antiquities I had gazed at all these years hadn't been created with a view to ending up one day in museums. Because the mosaic was still in its original setting, because it hadn't been roped off and placed inside a modern building, it was still clearly and radiantly a *floor* and not merely some diverting artifact. This was something meant to be walked on and used, something that had unquestionably felt the shuffle of Roman sandals. It had a strange kind of spell about it that left me quietly agog.

After a long time, I got up and carefully put back all the fertilizer bags and reweighted them with stones. I picked up my stick, surveyed my work to make sure all was in order, then turned and began the long process of hacking my way back to that strange and careless place that is the twentieth century.

Postscript: Months later, after the British publication of this book, someone with local knowledge wrote to tell me that the mosaic wasn't Roman at all, but a Victorian replica. Poop.

chapter
15

I returned my rental car to Oxford and decided to make for Milton Keynes. I selected it as my destination on the basis of a quick look at a road map, assuming that it would be easy enough to get there by train. In fact, such are the idiosyncrasies of the British Rail route system, I had to go all the way back to London and catch an Underground train to Euston Station and then finally a train to Milton Keynes—an overall journey of perhaps 120 miles in order to travel between two towns about 30 miles apart.

It was costly and time-consuming and left me feeling a tiny bit fractious, not least because the train from Euston was crowded and I sat facing a bleating woman and her ten-year-old son, who kept knocking my shins with his dangling legs and irritating me by staring at me with piggy eyes while picking his nose and eating the issue. It was strangely riveting. He appeared to regard his nose as a kind of midfaced snack dispenser. I tried to absorb myself in a book, but I found my gaze repeatedly rising against my wishes to find him staring at me with a smug look and a busy finger. It was quite repellent and I was very pleased, when the train finally pulled into Milton Keynes, to be able to get my rucksack down from the overhead rack and drag it across his head as I departed.

Milton Keynes—it rhymes with *jeans*—was one of thirty-two "new towns" that were built after the war during that brief but heady period when *social engineering* didn't seem an ominous term, at least to those doing the engineering. These model communities were to be at the forefront of a thrusting, prosperous, forward-looking, thoroughly revitalized Britain—in newsreel footage it looks as if they were trying to re-create the 1939 New York World's Fair on a national scale—and Milton Keynes was in many ways the quintessence of the movement.

I didn't hate Milton Keynes immediately, which I suppose is as much as you could hope for the place. You step out of the station and into a big open piazza lined on three sides with buildings of reflective glass, and have an instant sense of spaciousness such as you almost never get in English towns. The town itself stood on the slope of a small hill a good half mile away, beyond a network of pedestrian tunnels and over a large open space shared by parking lots and those strange new-town trees that never seem to grow.

In many respects, Milton Keynes was much superior to any new town I had seen before. The underpasses were faced with polished granite and were largely free of graffiti and the permanent murky puddles that seem to be a design feature of other planned communities. The town itself was a strange amalgam of styles. The grassless, shady strips along the centers of the main boulevards gave them a vaguely French air. The landscaped light-industrial parks around the fringes looked German. The grid plan and numbered street names recalled America. The buildings were of the featureless sort you find around any international airport. In short, it looked anything but English.

The oddest thing was that there were no shops and no one about. I walked for some distance through the central core of the town, up one avenue and down another and through the shadowy streets that connected them. Every parking space was full and there were signs of life behind the gaping office windows, but almost no passing traffic and never more than one or two other pedestrians along the endless vistas of road. I knew there was a vast shopping mall in the town somewhere because I had read about it, but I couldn't for the life of me find it, and I couldn't even find anyone to ask. The annoying thing was that nearly all the buildings looked like they might be shopping malls. I kept spotting likely-looking contenders and going up to investigate, only to find that they were the headquarters for an insurance company or something.

I ended up wandering some distance out into a residential area— a boundless expanse of neat, numbingly identical yellow-brick homes, winding streets, and pedestrian walkways lined with never-grow trees—but there was still no one around. From a hilltop I spied a sprawl of blue roofs about three quarters of a mile off and thought that might be the shopping mall and headed for it. The pedestrian walkways, which had seemed rather agreeable to me at first, began to become irritating. They wandered lazily through submerged cuttings, nicely landscaped but with a feeling of being in no hurry to get you anywhere. Clearly they had been laid out by people who had thought of it as a two-dimensional exercise. They followed circuitous, seemingly purposeless routes that must have looked pleasing on paper, but gave no consideration to the idea that people, faced with a long walk between houses and shops, would mostly like to get there in a reasonably direct way. Worse still was the sense of being lost in a semisubterranean world cut off from visible landmarks. I found myself frequently scrambling up banks just to see where I was, only to discover that it was nowhere near where I wanted to be.

Eventually, at the end of one of these muttered scrambles, I found that I was beside a busy dual carriageway exactly opposite the blue-roofed sprawl I had begun searching for an hour earlier. I could see signs for Texas Homecare and a McDonald's and other such places. But when I returned to the footway I couldn't begin to work out how to get over there. The paths forked off in a variety of directions, disappearing around landscaped bends, none of which proved remotely rewarding when looked into. In the end I followed one sloping path back up to street level, where at least I could see where I was, and walked along it all the way back to the train station, which now seemed so absurdly remote from the residential areas that clearly only a total idiot could possibly have thought that Milton Keynes would be a paradise for pedestrians. It was no wonder that I hadn't passed a single person on foot all morning.

I reached the station far more tired than the distance walked would warrant and gasping for a cup of coffee. Outside the station there was a map of the town, which I hadn't noticed on the way in, and I studied it, dying to know where the goddamn shopping mall was. It turned out that I had been about a hundred feet from it on my initial reconnoiter of the town center, but had failed to recognize it.

Sighing, and feeling an unaccountable determination to see this place, I headed back through the pedestrian subways, over the open ground, and back through the lifeless core of office buildings to see it, reflecting as I went what an extraordinary piece of work it was for a planner, confronted with a blank sheet of paper and a near infinity of possibilities for erecting a model community, to decide to put the shopping center a mile from the railway station.

It seems almost impossible to believe, but the shopping center was even worse designed than the town around it. Indeed, it must be a source of mirth wherever shopping mall designers forgather. It was absolutely enormous—more than a million square feet—and it contained every chain store that there has ever been or will ever be. But it was dark and determinedly unlovely and built along two straight, featureless parallel avenues that must run for half a mile. Unless in my delirium I overlooked them, and I think not, there was no food court, no central gathering place, nowhere much to sit, no design feature to encourage you to warm to this place to even the most fractional degree. It was like being in the world's largest bus station. The rest rooms were few and hard to find, and in consequence were as crowded with users as if it were half time at a football match.

I had a cup of coffee in the grubbiest McDonald's I ever hope to visit and, clearing a space among the accumulated litter left by earlier users of my table, sat with my railway timetable and accompanying route map and felt a stab of despair at the discovery that the options before me were to go back to London or onward to Rugby, Coventry, or Birmingham. I had no desire to do any of these. It seemed like days, rather than mere hours, since I had dropped off my rental car in Oxford and set off for the station with the simpleminded plan of traveling from Oxford to Cambridge by way of a lunchtime break at Milton Keynes.

Time was leaking away. I had, in some remote, half-forgotten life, sat at a kitchen table in a house in the Yorkshire Dales and worked out that I could comfortably cover the whole country in six or, at the outside, seven weeks. And that included airy plans to go practically everywhere—the Channel Islands, Lundy, Shetland, virtually all the cities. I had read John Hillaby's book *Journey Through Britain* and he *walked* from Land's End to John o'Groats in eight weeks. Surely, with the assistance of a fleet modern public-transport system, I could see most of Britain in six or seven weeks. But now here I was, having used up nearly half my allotted time, and I hadn't even penetrated as far as the Midlands.

So, in a dim frame of mind, I gathered up my things, trudged back to the station, and caught a train to London where, in effect, I would have to start all over again. I didn't know where to go, so I did what I often do. As the train marched through the rolling, autumn-bare farmlands of Buckinghamshire, I spread out a map and lost myself in the names. This is, to me, one of the deep and abiding pleasures of life in Britain.

There is almost no area of British life that isn't touched with a kind of genius for names. Select any area of nomenclature at all, from prisons (Wormwood Scrubs, Strangeways) to pubs (the Cat and Fiddle, the Lamb and Flag) to wild flowers (stitchwort, lady's bedstraw, blue fleabane, feverfew) to the names of soccer teams (Sheffield Wednesday, Aston Villa, Queen of the South) and you are in for a spell of enchantment. But nowhere, of course, are the British more gifted than with place names. Of the thirty thousand named places in Britain a good half, I would guess, are notable or arresting in some way. There are villages that seem to hide some ancient and possibly dark secret (Husbands Bosworth, Rime Intrinseca, White-ladies Aston) and villages that sound like characters from a bad nine-teenth-century novel (Bradford Peverell, Compton Valence, Langton Herring, Wootton Fitzpaine). There are villages that sound like fer-tilizers (Hastigrow), shoe deodorizers (Powfoot), breath fresheners (Minto), dog food (Whelpo), toilet cleansers (Potto, Sanahole, Durno), skin complaints (Whiterashes, Sockburn), and even a Scot-tish spot remover (Sootywells). There are villages that have an atti-tude problem (Seething, Mockbeggar, Wrangle) and villages of strange phenomena (Meathop, Wigtwizzle, Blubberhouses). There are villages without number whose very names summon forth an im-age of lazy summer afternoons and butterflies darting in meadows (Winterbourne Abbas, Weston Lullingfields, Theddlethorpe All Saints, Little Missenden). Above all, there are villages almost with-out number whose names are just endearingly inane—Prittlewell, Little Rollright, Chew Magna, Titsey, Woodstock Slop, Lickey End, Stragglethorpe, Yonder Bognie, Nether Wallop, and the practically unbeatable Thornton-le-Beans. (Bury me there!)

One small but seldom-noted feature is how often these engagingly named places cluster together. In just one compact area south of Cambridge, for instance, you can find Blo Norton, Rickinghall In-ferior, Hellions Bumpstead, Ugley, and the memorably inspired Shellow Bowells. I had an impulse to go there now—to sniff out

Shellow Bowells, as it were, and find what makes Norton Blo and Rickinghall Inferior—but as I glanced over the map my eye caught a line across the landscape called, with seductive resonance, the Devil's Dyke. I had never heard of it, but it sounded awfully promising. I felt better already.

And so it was I was to be found late the next morning tramping a back lane outside the Cambridgeshire hamlet of Reach looking for the dike's start. It was a grim and ghostly day. Fog filled the air and visibility was next to nothing. The dike rose up suddenly, almost alarmingly, out of the soupy grayness, and I clambered up to its top. It is a strange and brooding eminence, particularly in thick fog and out of season. Built during the darkest of the dark ages some thirteen hundred years ago, the Devil's Dyke is a long, straight earthen embankment that rises up to sixty feet above the surrounding landscape and runs for seven and a half miles between Reach and Ditton Green. Disappointingly, no one knows why it is called the Devil's Dyke. The name isn't recorded before the sixteenth century. Standing as it does in the midst of flat fenlands, it has a kind of menacing, palpably ancient air, but also a feeling of monumental folly. It required an obviously immense commitment of labor to construct, but it didn't take a whole lot of tactical genius to realize that all an invading army had to do was go around it, which is what all of them did, and within no time at all the Devil's Dyke had ceased to have any use at all except to show people in the fen country what it felt like to be sixty feet high.

Still, it offers an agreeable, easy stroll along its grassy summit, and on this bleak morning I had it all to myself. Not until I reached the approximate midway point did I begin to see other people, mostly exercising their dogs on the broad sward of Newmarket Heath and looking ghostly in the unearthly fog. The dike runs right through

the grounds of Newmarket Racecourse, which I thought rather jolly
though I couldn't see a damn thing, and thence on through pros-
perous-looking horse country. Gradually the fog began to thin and
between the skeletal trees I glimpsed a succession of large stud
farms, each with a white-fenced paddock, a big house, and a sprawl
of ornate stable blocks with cupolas and weather vanes that made
them look uncannily like a modern Tesco's supermarket. Pleasant
as it was to have an easy, flat ramble along such a well-defined route,
it was also a trifle dull. I walked for a couple of hours without passing
anyone and then abruptly the dike ended in a field outside Ditton
Green, and I was left standing there with an unsettling sense of
anticlimax. It was only a little after two in the afternoon and I was
nowhere near tired. I knew that Ditton had no railway station, but
I had presumed I could catch a bus to Cambridge, and indeed in
the local bus shelter I discovered that I could—if I waited two days.
So I trudged four miles to Newmarket down a busy road, had an
idle look around there, then caught a train to Cambridge.

One of the sustaining pleasures of a long tramp in the country,
particularly out of season, is the thought that eventually you will find
a room in a snug hostelry, have a series of drinks before a blazing
fire, and then dine on hearty viands to which the day's exercise and
fresh air have clearly entitled you. But I arrived in Cambridge feeling
fresh and untaxed and entitled to nothing. Worse still, presuming
that the walk would be more challenging than it was and that I might
arrive late, I had booked a room in the University Arms Hotel in the
expectation that it would have the requisite blazing fire, the hearty
viands, and something of the air of a senior common room. In fact,
as I discovered to my quiet dismay, it was an overpriced modern
block and my gloomy room was lamentably at odds with its description in my guidebook.

I had a listless look around the city. Now Cambridge, I know, is
a very fine city and a great place for names—Jesus Green and
Christ's Pieces alone take some beating—but I couldn't make myself

warm to it this day. The central market was a tatty mess, there seemed a discouraging surfeit of concrete structures scattered around the center, and everything was drenched in a cheerless drizzle. I ended up nosing around in secondhand bookshops. I was looking for nothing in particular, but in one I came across an illustrated history of Selfridge's department store and I took it eagerly from the shelf, hoping for an explanation of how Highcliffe Castle had fallen into dereliction and, better still, for prurient anecdotes involving Selfridge and the libidinous Dolly Sisters.

Alas, this appeared to be a sanitized version of the Selfridge story. I found only a single passing mention of the Dollys, suggesting that they were a couple of innocent waifs in whom Selfridge took a benign and avuncular interest. Of Selfridge's precipitate decline from rectitude there was scarcely a mention and of Highcliffe Castle nothing at all. So I put the book back and, realizing that somehow everything I did this day would be touched with disappointment, I went and had a pint of beer in an empty pub, a mediocre dinner in an Indian restaurant, a lonely walk in the rain; and finally I retired to my room, where I discovered that there was nothing at all of note on television, and realized that I had left my walking stick in Newmarket.

I retired with a book only to discover that the bedside lightbulb was gone—not burned out but gone—and passed the remaining hours of the evening lying inert on the bed and watching a *Cagney & Lacey* rerun on TV, partly out of a curious interest to detect what it is about this ancient program that so besots the controller of BBC1 (only possible answer: Sharon Gless's chest) and partly because of its guaranteed narcotic effect. I fell asleep with my glasses on and awoke at some indeterminate hour to find the TV screen a frantic, noisy blizzard. I got up to switch it off, tripped heavily over some unyielding object, and managed the interesting trick of turning off the TV with my head. Curious to know how I had managed this, in case I decided to make it a party piece, I discovered that the offending object was my stick, which was not in Newmarket after all but on the floor, lodged between a chair and a bed leg.

Well, that's one good thing, I thought and, gracing my nostrils with two walrus tusks of tissue to stanch a sudden flow of blood, climbed wearily back into bed.

chapter
16

Nothing gives the English more pleasure, in a quiet but determined sort of way, than to do things oddly. They put milk in their
tea, drive on the wrong side of the road, pronounce Cholmondeley
as "Chumley" and Belvoir as "Beaver," celebrate the Queen's birth-
day in June even though she was born in April, and dress their palace
guards in bearskin helmets that make them look as if, for some private and unfathomable reason, they are wearing fur-lined wastebas-
kets on their heads.

Almost every realm of British life you could care to name, from
the rules of cricket to the running of Parliament, is predicated on a
system guaranteed to confound foreigners (that is, of course, the
whole purpose of it), but in one area British practice rises to a zenith
so rarefied that most Britons themselves are left in a state of profound
confusion. I refer to that ancient and complex assemblage of privileged pointlessness known as the aristocracy.

If you have always been confused by why some people in Britain
are called Sir This while others are Lord That, and others are the
Earl of Such and Such or Viscount Something or Other, worry not.
I'm here to help you. But I must also warn you. Like most things

rooted in centuries of British tradition, it is an immensely complicated business.

So complicated, in fact, that the bible on the subject, *The Complete Peerage*, fills nine fat volumes. A companion work, *Debrett's
Correct Form*, which deals with how aristocrats should be addressed
and who sits where at dinner, runs to 422 densely printed pages. So
arcane are the workings of the system that only a handful of people
at the College of Arms in London—the HQ of the aristocracy—can
truly be said to understand it. There, officers with such splendidly
florid titles as First Rouge Dragon Pursuivant, Garter King of Arms,
and First Bluemantle Pursuivant rule on protocol, succession, and
titular deportment.

One complicating factor is that just because someone is called
Lord or Viscount or Marquess doesn't necessarily mean that he is
one. The relatives of some, but by no means all, aristocrats are allowed by custom to use what are called courtesy titles. The higher
you move up the noble scale, the more freely courtesy titles are employed. The eldest son of the Duke of Leinster, for instance, may
style himself the Marquess of Kildare. He isn't a marquess at all—
that is to say, he isn't allowed to sit in the House of Lords or to
enjoy any privileges of lordship—but nonetheless the title is his to
use. The son of this pretend-marquess may call himself the Earl of
Offaly, while his son is known as Viscount Leinster. If one person
in the chain dies, everybody moves up a position, rather like a game
of work-up in baseball.

To complicate matters, many aristocrats have over the centuries
accumulated a multiplicity of titles. The Duke of Beaufort, the Marquess of Worcester, Lord Botecourt, the Earl of Worcester, and Lord
Herbert de Herbert are all one person. Most aristocrats also have
what you might call a civilian name, and some of these are no less
impressive than their titles. Viscount Massereene and Ferrard, in
addition to his already ambitious title, also revels in the decidedly
chewy name John Clotworthy Talbot Foster White-Melville Skef-

fington. Altogether some forty thousand lordly titles are in use in Britain, but the actual number of nobles is only a tiny fraction of that—a little under twelve hundred, or barely 0.2 percent of the British population.

The primary perk of ennoblement is admission to what has been called the best club in London: the House of Lords. Only a small number of those entitled to attend ever actually do so, which is just as well since there are only 250 seats, and many of those who attend seldom speak. The champion nonspeaker appears to have been the twelfth Earl of Waldegrave, who took his seat in the Lords in 1936 but didn't feel sufficiently moved to speak until 1957. Members of the Lords are excused from jury service, forbidden to vote in national elections, and given the right to be hanged by a rope made of silk rather than hemp, though since capital punishment was outlawed in England forty years ago the privilege is somewhat academic.

True nobility begins with the Queen and the members of her immediate and extended families, including the three royal dukedoms of Kent, Gloucester, and Cornwall. Below them, in descending order of precedence, come two archbishops, 25 nonroyal dukes, 27 marquesses, 162 earls and countesses, 99 viscounts, 24 bishops, and 880 barons and baronesses. It is, to say the least, a tight-knit little circle, one in which intermarriage is not just common but, at the higher levels, practically de rigueur. All 25 of the nonroyal dukes are related by blood or marriage. Five are directly descended from that frolicsome and merry monarch Charles II and his various mistresses.

In terms of prestige and grandeur, the dukes are in a league of their own. A duke is always accorded his full title. Lesser nobles may be alternatively addressed as Lord. Thus the Marquess of Bath is sometimes referred to as Lord Bath. With a duke this would never happen.

A very few titles can be passed through the female line, but most cannot. If the Duke of Devonshire, say, fails to produce a son and heir, the title will die out. On average about four or five noble titles disappear each year. At this rate, it has been calculated, the hereditary nobility will vanish altogether by 2175. I certainly hope so.

I bring this up here because the next morning, after gently removing the tissues from my swollen nostrils and checking out of my Cambridge hotel, I set off for Worksop on a literally noble quest—to track down the ancestral home of one of Britain's most extraordinary and eccentric of nobles, the fifth Duke of Portland.

So I caught a train to Peterborough and then another on the main line north. I hadn't slept particularly well on account of an unsettling dream involving *Cagney & Lacey* and the discovery that I hadn't filed a U.S. tax return since 1975 (they threatened to turn me over to that guy who takes his shirt off in the opening credits, so you can imagine the state of my bedclothes when I awoke with a gasp about dawn), and I was looking forward to one of those quiet, soothing journeys that only trains can provide.

So it was with some dismay that I discovered that the seat behind me was occupied by Cellphone Man. These people are getting to be a real nuisance, aren't they? This one was particularly irritating because his voice was loud and self-satisfied and littered with moronspeak, and his calls were so clearly pointless:

"Hello, Clive here. I'm on the ten-oh-seven and should be at HQ by thirteen hundred hours as expected. I'm going to need a rush debrief on the Pentland Squire scenario. What say? No, I'm out of the loop on Maris Pipers. Listen, can you think of *any* reason why anyone would employ a total anus like me? What's that? Because I'm the sort of person who's happy as a pig in shit just because he's got a mobile phone? Hey, *interesting* concept." Then a few moments of silence and "Hello, love. I'm on the ten-oh-seven. Should be home by five. Yes, just like every other night. No reason to tell you at all except that I've got this phone and I'm a complete fuckwit. I'll call again from Doncaster for no reason." Then: "Clive here. Yeah, I'm still on the ten-oh-seven but we had a points failure at

Grantham, so I'm looking now at an ETA of thirteen-oh-two rather than the forecast thirteen hundred hours. If Phil calls, will you tell him that I'm still a complete fuckwit?" And so it went all morning.

I watched eagerly out the window for Retford, where I would have to alight to catch an onward bus to Worksop. Retford had long been something of a mystery to me on account of its near-total anonymity. For seven years, I had passed through it every time I traveled from my home in Yorkshire to London. It was one of the main stops on the east coast line, but I had never seen anyone get on or anyone get off there. On my British Rail route map, Retford was accorded capital letters, giving it equal typographical standing with Liverpool, Leicester, Nottingham, Glasgow, and all the other substantial communities of Britain, and yet I knew nothing about it. In fact, I don't believe I had even heard of it before I saw its lonely station for the first time from the train. More than that, I had never met anyone who had been there or knew anything about it. My *AA Book of British Towns* included lavish and kindly descriptions of every obscure community you could think to name—Kirriemuir, Knutsford, Prestonpans, Swadlincote, Bridge of Allan, Duns, Forfar, Wigtown—but on Retford it maintained a stern and mysterious silence. Clearly, it was time to check this place out.

So it was with some keenness that I found myself, some two hours after setting off and alone among the many passengers, alighting in Retford, and walking into town through a clinging mist of rain. Retford, I am pleased to report, is a delightful and charming place even under the sort of oppressive gray clouds that make far more celebrated towns seem dreary and tired. Its centerpiece is a large and handsome market square lined with a picturesque jumble of noble Georgian buildings. Beside the main church stood a weighty black cannon with a plaque saying CAPTURED AT SEVASTAPOL 1855, which I thought a remarkable piece of initiative on the part of the locals—it's not every day, after all, that you find a Nottinghamshire market town storming a Crimean redoubt and bringing home booty—and the shops seemed prosperous and well ordered. I can't say that I felt like spending my holidays here, but I was pleased to have seen it at last and to have found it trim and likable.

I had a cup of tea in a little shop, then caught a bus to Worksop, a place of similar size and tempo (and which, by the by, *does* get an entry in the *AA Book of British Towns*). Retford and Worksop apparently had had a contest to see which of them would house the headquarters of Bassetlaw District Council, and Worksop had evidently lost since the offices were there. They were predictably hideous and discordant, but the rest of the town seemed agreeable enough in a low-key sort of way.

Worksop is the unofficial capital of a compact region known as The Dukeries. The seats of five historic dukedoms—Newcastle, Portland, Kingston, Leeds, and Norfolk—are all within twenty miles of each other in this obscure corner of the North Midlands, though Leeds and Portland are now extinct and the others, I gather, have mostly gone away. (The Duke of Newcastle, according to Simon Winchester in *Their Noble Lordships*, lives in a modest house in Hampshire, which I trust has taught *him* the folly of not investing in bouncing castles and miniature steam trains.)

My target was Welbeck Abbey, former home of the Portlands and reputedly one of the finest stately homes in England. The Portlands haven't lived there since 1954 on account of a similar unfortunate lack of prescience with regard to adventure playgrounds and petting zoos. The fifth Duke of Portland, one W.J.C. Scott-Bentinck (1800–1879), has long been something of a hero of mine. Old W.J.C., as I like to think of him, was one of history's great recluses and went to the most extraordinary lengths to avoid all forms of human contact. He lived in just one small corner of his stately home and communicated with his servants through notes passed to him through a special message box cut into the door to his rooms. Food was conveyed to him in the dining room by means of a miniature railway running from the kitchen. In the event of chance encounters, he would stand stock still and servants were instructed to pass him as they would a piece of furniture. Those who transgressed this instruction were compelled to skate on the Duke's private skating rink until exhausted. Sightseers were allowed to tour the house and grounds—"so long," as the Duke put it, "as you would be good enough not to *see* me."

For reasons that can only be guessed at, the Duke used his considerable inheritance to build a second mansion underground. At its peak, he had fifteen thousand men employed on its construction, and when completed it included, among much else, a library nearly 250 feet long and the largest ballroom in England, with space for up to two thousand guests—rather an odd thing to build if you never have guests. A network of tunnels and secret passageways connected the various rooms and ran for considerable distances out into the surrounding countryside. It was as if, in the words of one biographer, "he anticipated nuclear warfare." When it was necessary for the Duke to travel to London, he would have himself sealed in his horse-drawn carriage, which would be driven through a tunnel one and a half miles long to a place near Worksop Station and loaded onto a special flatcar for the trip to the capital. There, still sealed, it would be driven to his London residence, Harcourt House.

When the Duke died, his heirs found all of the aboveground rooms devoid of furnishings except for one chamber in the middle of which sat the Duke's commode. The main hall was mysteriously floorless. Most of the rooms were painted pink. The one upstairs room in which the Duke had resided was packed to the ceiling with hundreds of green boxes, each of which contained a single dark brown wig. This was, in short, a man worth getting to know.

I strolled out of Worksop to the edge of Clumber Park, a neighboring National Trust holding, and found what I hoped was a path to Welbeck Abbey, some three or four miles away. It was a long walk along a muddy woodland track. According to the footpath signs, I was on something called the Robin Hood Way, but this didn't feel

much like Sherwood Forest. It was mostly a boundless conifer plan-
tation, a sort of farm for trees, and it seemed eerily, preternaturally
still and lifeless. It was the kind of setting where you half expect to
stumble on a body half covered with leaves, which is my great dread
because the police would interview me and I would immediately
become a suspect on account of an unfortunate inability to answer
questions like "Where were you on the afternoon of Wednesday, the
third of October, at four P.M.?" I could imagine myself sitting in a
windowless interview room, saying, "Let's see, I think I might have
been in Oxford, or maybe it was the Dorset coast path. Jeez, *I* don't
know." And the next thing you know I'd be sewing mailbags in
Wormwood Scrubs prison.

Things got stranger. An odd wind rose in the treetops, making
them bend and dance, but didn't descend to earth, so that at ground
level everything was calm, which was a little spooky; and then I
passed through a steep sandstone ravine with tree roots growing
weirdly like vines along its face. Between the roots, the surface was
covered with hundreds of carefully scratched inscriptions, with
names and dates and occasional twined hearts. The dates covered
an extraordinary span: 1861, 1947, 1962, 1990. This seemed a
strange place indeed. Either this was a popular spot for lovers or
some couple had been going steady for a very long time.

A little farther on I came to a lonely gatehouse with a machicolated
roofline. Beyond it stood a sweep of open field full of stubbly winter
wheat, and beyond that, just visible through a mantle of trees, was
a large and many-angled green copper roof—Welbeck Abbey, or so
at least I hoped. I followed the path around the periphery of the
field, which was immense and muddy. It took me nearly three quarters of an hour to make my way to a paved lane, but I was sure now
that I had found the right place. The lane passed alongside a narrow,
reedy lake, and this, according to my trusty OS map, was the only
body of water for miles. I followed the lane for perhaps a mile until
it ended at a rather grand entrance beside a sign saying PRIVATE—

NO ENTRY, but with no other indication of what lay beyond.

I stood for a moment in a lather of indecision (the name I would like, incidentally, if I am ever ennobled: Lord Lather of Indecision) and decided to venture up the drive just a little way—just enough to at least glimpse the house that I had come so far to see. So I walked on cautiously. The grounds were meticulously and expensively groomed, but well screened with trees, so I walked a little farther. After a few hundred yards the trees thinned and opened out into lawns. There was a kind of assault course, with climbing nets and logs on stilts. What *was* this place? A bit farther on, beside the lake, there was an odd paved area—like a parking lot in the middle of nowhere—which I realized, with a small cry of joy, must have been the Duke's famous skating rink. Now I was so far into the grounds that it hardly mattered. I strode on until I was square in front of the house. It was grand but curiously characterless and it had been clumsily modified with a number of new extensions. Beyond in the distance was a cricket pitch with an elaborate pavilion. There was no one around, but there was a parking lot with several cars. This was clearly some kind of institution—perhaps a training center for something like IBM. So why was it so anonymous? I was about to go up and have a look in the windows when a door opened and a man in a uniform emerged and strode toward me with a severe look on his face. As he neared me, I could see his jacket said MOD SECURITY. MOD is Ministry of Defence. Oh-oh.

"Hello," I said with a big foolish smile.

"Are you aware, sir, that you are trespassing on government property?"

I wavered for a moment, torn between giving him a tourist-from-Iowa act ("You mean this isn't Hampton Court Palace? Shit, I just gave a cab driver a hundred seventy-five pounds") and fessing up. I fessed. In a small, respectful voice, I told him about my long fascination with the fifth Duke of Portland and how I had ached to see this place for years and couldn't resist just having a peep at it after

coming all this way, which was exactly the right thing to do because
he evidently had an affection for old W.J.C. himself. He escorted
me smartishly to the edge of the property and kept up something of
a bluff manner, but he seemed quietly pleased to have someone who
shared his interests. He confirmed that the paved area was the skating rink and pointed out where the tunnels ran, which was pretty
much everywhere. They were still sound, he told me, though they
weren't used any longer except for storage. The ballroom and other
underground chambers, however, were still regularly employed for
functions and as a gymnasium. The MOD had just spent a million
pounds refurbishing the ballroom.

"What is this place anyway?" I asked.

"Training center, sir" was all he would say, and in any case we
had reached the end of the drive. He watched to make sure I went.
I walked back across the big field, then paused at the far end to look
at the Welbeck Abbey roof rising through the treetops. I was pleased
to know that the Ministry of Defence had maintained the tunnels
and underground rooms, but it seemed an awful shame that the
place was so formidably shut to the public. It isn't every day after
all that the British aristocracy produce someone of W.J.C. Scott-
Bentinck's rare and extraordinary mental loopiness, though in fairness it must be said they give it their best shot.

And with this thought to chew on, I turned and began the long
trudge back to Worksop.

chapter
17

I spent a pleasant night in Lincoln, wandering its steep and ancient streets before and after dinner, admiring the squat, dark immensity of the cathedral and its two Gothic towers, and looking
forward very much to seeing it in the morning. I like Lincoln, partly
because it is pretty and well preserved but mostly because it seems
so agreeably remote. H. V. Morton, in his book *In Search of England,* likened it to an inland St. Michael's Mount standing above
the great sea of the Lincolnshire plain, and that's exactly right. If
you look on a map, it's only just down the road a few miles from
Nottingham and Sheffield, but it feels far away and quite forgotten.
I like that very much.

Just about the time of my visit there was an interesting report in
The Independent about a long-running dispute between the dean of
Lincoln Cathedral and his treasurer. Six years earlier, it appears, the
treasurer, along with his wife, their daughter, and a family friend,
had taken the cathedral's treasured copy of the Magna Carta off to
Australia for a six-month fund-raising tour. The tour was a financial
disaster. It lost over £500,000—a pretty hefty bill, when you think
about it, for four people and a piece of parchment. Most of this the

Australian government had graciously covered, but the cathedral was still left nursing a £56,000 loss. The upshot is that the dean leaked the story to the press, causing outrage and consternation among the cathedral chapter; the Bishop of Lincoln held an inquiry at which he commanded the chapter to resign; the chapter refused to resign; and now everybody was mad at pretty much everybody else. This had been going on for six years.

So when I stepped into the lovely, echoing immensity of Lincoln Cathedral the following morning I was rather hoping that there would be hymnals flying about and the unseemly but exciting sight of clerics wrestling in the transept, but in fact all was disappointingly calm. On the other hand, it was wonderful to be in a great ecclesiastical structure so little disturbed by shuffling troops of tourists. When you consider the hordes that flock to Salisbury, York, Canterbury, Bath, and so many of the other great churches of England, Lincoln's relative obscurity is something of a small miracle. It would be hard to think of a place of equal architectural majesty less known to outsiders—Durham perhaps.

The whole of the nave was filled with ranks of padded metal chairs. I've never understood this. Why can't there be wooden pews in these cathedrals? Every English cathedral I've ever seen has been like this, with semistraggly rows of chairs that can be stacked or folded away. Why? Do they clear the chairs away for barn dancing or something? Whatever the reason, they always look cheap and out of keeping with the surrounding splendor of soaring vaults, stained glass, and Gothic tracery. What a heartbreak it is sometimes to live in an age of such consummate cost-consciousness. Still, it must be said that the modern intrusions do help to underline how extravagantly deployed were the skills of medieval stonemasons, glaziers, and wood-carvers, and how unstinting was the use of materials.

I would like to have lingered, but I had a vital date to keep. I needed to be in Bradford by midafternoon in order to see one of the most exciting visual offerings in the entire world. On the first

Saturday of every month, you see, Pictureville Cinema, part of the large and popular Museum of Photography, Film, and Something Else, shows an original, uncut version of *This Is Cinerama*. It is the only place in the world now where you can see this wonderful piece of cinematic history, and this was the first Saturday of the month.

I can't tell you how much I was looking forward to this. I fretted all the way that I would miss my rail connection at Doncaster and then I fretted again that I would miss the one at Leeds, but in fact I reached Bradford in plenty of time—nearly three hours early, in fact, which made me tremble slightly, for what is one to do in Bradford with three hours to kill?

Bradford's role in life is to make every place else in the world look better in comparison, and it does this very well. Nowhere on this trip would I see a city more palpably forlorn. Nowhere would I pass more vacant shops, their windows soaped or covered with tattered posters for pop concerts, in other, more vibrant communities like Huddersfield and Pudsey, or more office buildings festooned with TO LET signs. At least one shop in three in the town center was empty and most of the rest seemed to be barely hanging on. Soon after this visit, Rackham's, the main department store, would announce it was closing. Such life as there was had mostly moved indoors to a characterless compound called the Arndale Centre. (And why is it, by the way, that sixties shopping centers in Britain are always called the Arndale Centre? I have yet to find anyone who can supply an answer.) But mostly Bradford seemed steeped in a perilous and irreversible decline.

Once this was one of the greatest congregations of Victorian architecture anywhere, but you would scarcely guess it now. Scores of wonderful buildings were swept away in the 1950s, 1960s, and 1970s to make room for wide new roads and angular office buildings with painted plywood insets beneath each window. Nearly everything in the city suffers from well-intentioned but misguided meddling by planners. Many of the busier streets have the kind of pedestrian

crossing that you have to negotiate in stages—one stage to get to an
island in the middle, then another long wait with strangers before
you are given four seconds to sprint to the other side—which makes
even the simplest errands tiresome, particularly if you want to make
a catercorner crossing and have to wait at four sets of lights to travel
a net distance of perhaps thirty yards. Worse still, along many of the
main inner relief roads the hapless pedestrian is forced into a series
of bleak and menacing underpasses that meet in large circles, open
to the sky but always in shadow, and so badly drained, I'm told, that
someone once drowned in one during a flash downpour.

You won't be surprised to hear that I used to wonder about these
planning insanities a lot, and then one day I got a book from my
local library called *Bradford—Outline for Tomorrow* or something
like that. It was from the late fifties or early sixties and it was full of
black-and-white architects' drawings of gleaming pedestrian precincts peopled with prosperous, confidently striding, semi–stick figures, and office buildings of the type that loomed over me now, and
I suddenly saw, with a kind of astonishing clarity, what the planners
were trying to do. I mean to say, they genuinely thought they were
building a new world—a Britain in which the brooding, soot-
blackened buildings and narrow streets of the past would be swept
away and replaced with sunny plazas and shiny modern offices, libraries, schools, and hospitals, all linked with brightly tiled underground passageways where pedestrians would be safely segregated
from the passing traffic. Everything about it looked bright and clean
and fun. There were even pictures of women with strollers stopping
to chat in the sunken open-air circles. And what we got instead was
a city of empty, peeling office blocks, discouraging roads, pedestrian
drains, and economic desolation. Perhaps it would have happened
anyway, but at least we would have been left with a city of crumbling
old buildings instead of crumbling new ones.

Nowadays, in a gesture that is as ironic as it is pathetic, the local
authorities are desperately trying to promote their meager stock of

old buildings as tourist attractions. In a modest cluster of narrow streets on a slope just enough out of the city center to have escaped the bulldozer, there still stand some three dozen large and striking warehouses—though that word barely does them justice—mostly built between 1860 and 1874 in a confident neoclassical style that makes them look like merchant banks rather than woolsheds, which together make up the area known as Little Germany (so called because Germans for a time dominated the woolen trade). Once there were many other districts like this—indeed, the whole of central Bradford as late as the 1950s consisted almost wholly of warehouses, mills, banks, and offices singlemindedly dedicated to the business of accumulating, sorting, and trading wool. And then—goodness knows how—the wool business just leaked away. It was, I suppose, the usual story of overconfidence and lack of investment followed by panic and retreat. In any case, the mills went, the offices grew dark, the once-bustling Wool Exchange—the central market for wool traders—dwindled to a dusty nothingness, and now you would never guess that Bradford had ever known greatness.

Of all the once-thriving wool precincts in the city—Bermondsey, Cheapside, Manor Row, Sunbridge Road—only the few dark buildings of Little Germany survive in any number, and even this promising small neighborhood seems bleak and futureless. At the time of my visit two thirds of the buildings were covered in scaffolding, and the other third had TO LET signs on them. Those that had been renovated looked smart and well done, but they also looked permanently vacant, and they were about to be joined in their gleaming, well-preserved emptiness by the two dozen others now in the process of being renovated.

What a good idea it would be, I thought, if the government ordered the evacuation of Milton Keynes and made all the insurance companies and other firms decamp to places like Bradford in order to bring some life back to real cities. Then Milton Keynes could become as Little Germany is now, an empty place that people could

stroll through and wonder at. But it will never happen, of course.
Obviously, the government would never order such a thing, but it
won't even happen through market forces because companies want
big modern buildings with lots of parking, and nobody wants to live
in Bradford, and who can blame them? And anyway, even if by some
miracle they find tenants for all these wonderful old relics, Little
Germany will never be anything more than a small, well-preserved
enclave in the heart of a dying city.

Still, Bradford is not without its charms. The Alhambra Theatre,
built in 1914 in an excitingly effusive style with minarets and towers,
has been sumptuously and skillfully renovated and remains the most
wonderful place to see a pantomime. (One of the great British
Christmas traditions and something I positively adore, by the way.
Within weeks of this visit, I would be back to see Billy Pearce in
Aladdin. Laugh? I soaked the seat.) The Museum of Film, Photography, Imax Cinema, and Something Else (I can never remember
the exact name) has brought a welcome flicker of life to a corner of
the city that previously had to rely on a dowdy indoor ice rink for
its diversion value, and there are some good pubs. I went into one
now, the Mannville Arms, and had a pint of beer and a bowl of chili.
The Mannville is well known in Bradford as the place where the
Yorkshire Ripper, a notorious murderer of the 1970s, used to hang
out, though it ought to be famous for its chili, which is outstanding.

Afterward, with an hour still to kill, I walked over to the Museum
of Television, Photography, and Whatever, which I admire, partly
because it is free and partly because I think it is deeply commendable to put these institutions in the provinces. I had a look through
the various galleries, and watched in some wonder as throngs of
people parted with substantial sums of cash to see the two o'clock
Imax show. I've been to these Imax screenings before and frankly I
can't understand their appeal. I know the screen is massive and the
visual reproduction theoretically stunning, but the films are always
so incredibly *dull*, with their earnest, leaden commentaries about

Man's conquest of this and fulfilling his destiny to do that—this latest offering that had the crowds flocking in was actually called *Destiny in Space*—when any fool can see that what everybody really wants is to go on a roller-coaster ride and experience a little here-comes-my-lunch aerial dive bombing.

The people at Cinerama Corporation understood this well some forty years ago and made a death-defying roller-coaster ride the focus of their advertising campaign. The first and last time I saw *This Is Cinerama* was in 1956 on a family trip to Chicago. The movie had been on general release since 1952, but such was its popularity in the big cities, and its unavailability in places like Iowa, that it ran for years and years, though it must be said that by the time we saw it most of the audience consisted of people in bib overalls chewing on stalks of grass. My memories of it were vague—I was just four years old in the summer of 1956—but fond, and I couldn't wait to see it now.

Such was my eagerness that I hastened out of the Museum of Various Things Involving Celluloid and across to the nearby entrance of the Pictureville Cinema half an hour early and stood, alone in a freezing drizzle, for fifteen minutes before the doors were opened. I bought a ticket, stipulating a place in the center of the auditorium and with plenty of room for vomiting, and found my way to my seat. It was a splendid cinema, with plush seats and a big curving screen behind velvet curtains. For a few minutes it looked as if I was going to have the place to myself, but then others started coming in and by two minutes to showtime it was pretty well full.

At the stroke of two, the room darkened and the curtains opened perhaps fifteen feet—a fraction of their total sweep—and the modest portion of exposed screen filled with some introductory footage by Lowell Thomas sitting in an obviously fake study filled with globe-trotting objects, preparing us for the wonder we were about to behold. Now you must put this in its historical context. Cinerama was created in a desperate response to television, which in the early

1950s was threatening to put Hollywood clean out of business. So this prefatory footage, filmed in black and white and presented in a modest rectangle the shape of a television screen, was clearly intended to implant a subliminal reminder that this was the sort of dull, inadequate image audiences had lately grown accustomed to. After a brief but not uninteresting rundown on the history of the cinematic arts, Thomas told us to sit back and enjoy the greatest visual spectacle the world had ever seen. Then he disappeared, rich orchestral music rose from every quarter, the curtains drew back and back and back to reveal a majestic curved screen, and suddenly we were in a world drenched in color, on a roller coaster on Long Island, and gosh was it good.

I was in heaven. The 3-D effect was far better than you would expect with such a simple and ancient projection system. It really was like being on a roller coaster, but with one incomparable difference: This was a 1951 roller coaster, rising high above parking lots full of vintage Studebakers and DeSotos and thundering terrifyingly past crowds of people in capacious trousers and colorful baggy shirts. This wasn't a movie. It was time travel.

I really mean that. Between the 3-D wizardry, the stereophonic sound, and the sparkling sharpness of the images, it was like being thrust magically back forty years in time. This had a particular resonance for me because in the summer of 1951, when this footage was being shot, I was curled up in my mother's abdomen, increasing in body weight at a rate that I wouldn't match until I quit smoking thirty-five years later. This was the world I was about to be born into, and what a delightful, happy, promising place it seemed.

I don't think I have ever spent three such happy hours. We went all over the world, for *This Is Cinerama* wasn't a movie in a conventional sense but a travelogue designed to show this wonder of the age to best effect. We glided through Venice on gondolas, watched from the quaysides by people in capacious trousers and baggy colorful shirts; listened to the Vienna Choir Boys outside the Schönbrunn Palace; watched a regimental tattoo at Edinburgh Castle; saw a long segment of *Aida* at La Scala (bit boring, that); and concluded with an airplane flight over the whole of America. We soared above Niagara Falls—a place I had been to the summer before, but this was quite unlike the tourist-clogged nightmare I had visited, with its forests of viewing towers and international hotels. This Niagara Falls had a backdrop of trees and low buildings and thinly used parking lots. We visited Cypress Gardens in Florida, where young waterskiers with names like Chip and Betty put on a show just for us; flew low over the rippling farm fields of Middle America; and had an exciting landing at Kansas City Airport. We brushed over the Rockies, dropped into the staggering vastness of the Grand Canyon, and flew through the formidable, twisting gorges of Zion National Park while the plane banked sharply past alarming outcrops of rock and Lowell Thomas gravely but happily announced that such a cinematic feat had never before been attempted—and all of this to a swelling stereophonic rendition of "God Bless America" by the Mormon Tabernacle Choir, which began with a melodic hum and rose to a full-throated let's-give-those-Krauts-a-licking crescendo. Tears of joy and pride welled in my sockets and it was all I could do to keep from climbing onto my seat and crying, "Ladies and gentlemen, this is *my* country!"

And then it was over and we were shuffling out into the drizzly twilit bleakness of Bradford, which was something of a shock to the system, believe me. I stood by a bronze statue of J. B. Priestley, who was a Bradford lad, and stared at the bleak, hopeless city before me and thought, *Yes, I am ready to go home*.

But first, I additionally thought, *I'll just have a curry.*

chapter
18

i forgot to mention curry houses earlier in my brief list of Bradford's glories, which was a terrible oversight. Bradford may have lost a wool trade but it has gained a thousand excellent Indian restaurants, which I personally find a reasonable swap as I have a strictly limited need for bales of fiber but can take about as much Indian food as you care to shovel at me.

The oldest of the Bradford curry houses, I'm told, and certainly one of the best and cheapest, is the Kashmir, just up the road from the Alhambra. There is a proper restaurant upstairs, with white tablecloths, gleaming cutlery, and poised, helpful waiters, but aficionados descend to the basement where you sit with strangers at long Formica-topped tables. This place is so hard core that it doesn't bother with cutlery. You just scoop the food in with hunks of nan bread and messy fingers. For £3 I had a small feast that was rich, delicious, and so hot that it made my fillings sizzle.

Afterward, bloated and sated and with a stomach bubbling away like a heated beaker in a mad-scientist movie, I stepped out into the Bradford evening and wondered what to do with myself. It was just after six o'clock on a Saturday night, but already the place felt dead.

I was acutely and uncomfortably aware that my home and dear family were just over the next range of hills. For some reason I had it in my head that it would be cheating to go home now with the trip half finished, but then I thought, *Sod it. I'm cold and lonesome and I'm not about to spend a night in a hotel twenty miles from my own home.* So I walked to Forster Square station, took a rattling, empty train to Skipton and a cab to the little Dales village where I live, and had the driver drop me down the road so that I could approach the house on foot.

What a joy it is to arrive after dark at a snug-looking house, its windows filled with welcoming light, and know that it is yours and that inside is your family. I walked up the drive and looked through the kitchen window, and there they all were, gathered around the kitchen table playing Monopoly, bless their wholesome little hearts. I stared at them for ages, lost in a glow of affection and admiration and feeling like Jimmy Stewart in *It's a Wonderful Life* when he gets to spy on his own life. And then I went in.

Now I can't possibly write about this sort of thing without making it sound like an episode from *The Waltons,* so what I'm going to do is distract your attention for a moment from this animated and heartwarming reunion in a Yorkshire Dales kitchen and tell you a true but irrelevant story.

In the early 1980s, I was freelancing a lot in my spare time, principally for airline magazines. I got the idea to do an article on remarkable coincidences and sent off a query letter to one of these publications, which expressed serious interest and promised payment of $500 if published—a sum of money I could very handily have done with. But when I came to write the article, I realized that, although I had plenty of information about scientific studies into the probabilities of coincidence, I didn't have nearly enough examples of remarkable coincidences themselves to give the article sufficient zip or to fill fifteen hundred words of space. So I wrote a letter to the magazine saying I wouldn't be able to deliver and left it on the top of my typewriter to post the next day. Then I dressed myself in respectable clothing and drove to work at *The Times*.

Now in those days, Philip Howard, the kindly literary editor, used to hold book sales for the staff a couple of times a year when his office became so filled with review copies that he'd lost his desk. These were always exciting occasions because you could acquire stacks of books for practically nothing. He charged something like 25p for hardbacks and 10p for paperbacks, and then passed the proceeds to the Cirrhosis Foundation or some other charity dear to the hearts of journalists. On this particular day, I arrived at work to find a notice by the elevators announcing a book sale at 4 P.M. It was 3:55, so I dumped my coat at my desk and eagerly hastened to his chamber. The place was already full of mingling people. I stepped into the melee and what should be the very first book my eyes fell on but a paperback called *Remarkable True Coincidences*. How's that for a remarkable true coincidence? But here's the uncanny thing. I opened it up and found that the very first coincidence it discussed concerned a man named Bryson.

I've been telling this story for years in pubs and every time I've finished it, the people to whom I've told it have nodded thoughtfully for quite some time, then turned to each other and said, "You know, it occurs to me there's another way to get to Barnsley without going anywhere near the M62. You know the Happy Eater roundabout at Guiseley? Well, if you take the second turning there . . ."

So anyway, I spent three days at home, immersed in the chaos of domestic life, happy as a puppy—romping with the little ones, bestowing affection indiscriminately, following my wife from room to room. I cleaned out my knapsack, attended to the mail, strode pro-prietorially around the garden, savored the bliss of waking up each morning in my own bed.

I couldn't face the prospect of departing again so soon, so I de-cided to stay on a bit longer and make a couple of day trips. Thus it was that on the third morning I picked up my good friend and neighbor, a kindly and gifted artist named David Cook, and went with him for a day's walk through Saltaire and Bingley, his native turf. It was awfully nice to have some company for a change, and interesting to see this little corner of Yorkshire through the eyes of someone who had grown up in it.

I had never properly been to Saltaire before and what a splendid surprise it was to me. Saltaire is a model factory community built by one Titus Salt between 1851 and 1876. It is a little difficult to know what to make of old Titus. On the one hand he was one of that unattractive breed of teetoling, self-righteous, God-fearing in-dustrialists in which the nineteenth century seemed to specialize—a man who didn't want merely to employ his workers but to own them. Workers at his factory were expected to live in his houses, worship in his church, follow his precepts to the letter. He would not allow a pub in the village and so saddled the local park with stern restrictions regarding noise, smoking, the playing of games, and other indecorous activities that there was not much fun to be had in it. Workers were allowed to take boats out on the river—but only, for some reason, so long as there were never more than four out at any one time. Whether they liked it or not, in short, they were compelled to be sober, industrious, and quiet.

On the other hand, Salt showed a rare degree of enlightenment in terms of social welfare, and there is no question that his workers enjoyed cleaner, healthier, more comfortable living conditions than almost any other industrial workers in the world at that time.

Though it has since been swallowed up by the great sprawl that is the Leeds-Bradford conurbation, when it was built Saltaire stood in clean, open countryside—a vast change from the unhealthy stew of central Bradford, where in the 1850s there were more brothels than churches and not a single yard of covered sewers. From bleak and grimy back-to-back houses (so called because every row of houses was mirrored by another row attached to its back, with no open space between), Salt's workers came to airy, spacious cottages, each with little yards front and rear, a private gas supply, and at least two bedrooms. It must have seemed a very Eden.

On a sloping site overlooking the River Aire and Leeds to Liverpool Canal, Salt built a massive textile mill known as the Palace of Industry—in its day the largest factory in Europe—spreading over nine acres and graced with a striking Italianate campanile modeled on that of Santa Maria Gloriosa dei Frari in Venice. He additionally built a park, a church, an institute for "conversation, refreshment and education," a hospital, a school, and 850 trim and tidy stone houses on a formal grid of cobbled streets, most of them named for Salt's wife and eleven children. The institute was perhaps the most remarkable of these undertakings. Built in the hope of distracting workers from the peril of drink, it contained a gymnasium, a laboratory, a billiard room, a library, a reading room, and a lecture and concert hall. Never before had manual workers been given a more lavish opportunity to better themselves, an opportunity that many scores enthusiastically seized. One James Waddington, an untutored woolsorter, became a world authority on linguistics and a leading light of the Phonetic Society of Great Britain and Ireland.

Today Saltaire remains miraculously intact, though the factory has long since ceased to manufacture cloth and the houses are now privately owned. One floor of the factory houses a permanent exhibition of the works of David Hockney, himself a Bradford lad, and the rest is given over to retail space selling designer clothes, posh and stylish housewares, books, and arty postcards. It was a kind of miracle to find this place—this yuppie heaven—inhabiting a forgotten corner of metropolitan Bradford. And yet it seemed to be doing very well.

David Cook and I had an unhurried look around the gallery—I had never paid much attention to Hockney, but I'll tell you this: The boy can draw—then wandered through the streets of former workers' cottages, all of them snug and trim and lovingly preserved, before striking off through the local park to Shipley Glen, a steep wooded dell leading to a sweep of open common land of the sort where you can usually find people exercising their dogs. It looks as if it has been wild and untended forever, but in fact a century ago this was the site of a hugely successful amusement park—one of the world's first.

Among the many attractions were an aerial gondola ride, an early big dipper, and what was billed as "The Largest, Wildest, Steepest Toboggan Slide Ever Erected on Earth." I've seen pictures of these, filled with ladies with parasols and mustachioed men in stiff collars, and they do actually look pretty exciting, particularly the toboggan ride, which ran for perhaps a quarter of a mile down a formidably steep and perilous hill. One day in 1900, as a carful of smartly dressed tobogganers was being hauled up the hill to be dispatched on another hair-raising descent, the winch cable snapped, sending the passengers hurtling out of control to a messy but exciting death at the bottom, and that was pretty much the end of the Shipley Glen amusement park. Today all that's left of these original thrills is the poky Glen Tramway, which goes up and down a nearby slope in a discreet and sedate fashion, as it has since 1895, but among the tall grass we did find a remnant of old track from the original toboggan ride, which thrilled us mildly.

The whole of this area is a kind of archaeological site of the not-too-distant past. A mile or so away, up an overgrown track, is the site of Milner Field, an ornate palace of stone built by Titus Salt, Jr., in 1870 at a time when the Salt family fortunes seemed boundless and perpetually secure. But weren't they in for a surprise? In 1893, the textile trade went into a sudden slump, leaving the Salts dangerously overextended, and the family abruptly lost control of the firm. In consternation and shame, they had to sell the house, factory, and associated holdings. Then began a strange and sinister series of events. Without apparent exception all the subsequent owners of Milner Field suffered odd and devastating setbacks. One accidentally whacked himself in the foot with a golf club and died when the wound turned gangrenous. Another came home to find his young bride engaged in an unseemly bout of naked bedtop wrestling with a business associate. He shot the associate or possibly both of them—accounts vary—but in any case he certainly made a mess of the bedroom and was taken off to have his neck stretched.

Before long the house developed a reputation as a place where you could reliably expect to come a cropper. People moved in and abruptly moved out again, with ashen faces and terrible wounds. By 1930, when the house went on the market one last time, no buyer could be found. It stayed empty for twenty years, and finally in 1950 it was pulled down. Now the site is overgrown and weedy, and you could walk past it without ever guessing that one of the finest houses in the North had once stood here. But if you poke about in the tall grass, as we did now, you can find one of the old conservatory floors, made of neatly patterned black-and-white tiles. It was strangely reminiscent of the Roman mosaic I had seen at Winchcombe, and scarcely less astonishing.

It seemed remarkable to think that a century ago Titus Salt, Jr., could have stood on this spot, in a splendid house, looking down the Aire Valley to the distant but formidable Salt's Mill, clanging away and filling the air with steamy smoke, and beyond it the sprawl of the richest center of woolen trade in the world, and that now it could all be gone. What would old Titus senior think, I wondered, if you brought him back and showed him that the family fortune was spent and his busy factory was now full of stylish chrome housewares and paintings of naked male swimmers with glistening buttocks?

We stood for a long time on this lonely summit. You can see for miles across Airedale from up there, with its crowded towns and houses climbing up the steep hillsides to the bleak upland fells, and I found myself wondering, as I often do when I stand on a northern hillside, what all those people in all those houses do. There used to be scores of factories all up and down Airedale—ten or more in Bingley alone—and now they are virtually all gone, torn down to make room for supermarkets or converted into heritage centers, apartment buildings, or shopping complexes. French's Mill, Bingley's last surviving textile factory, had closed a year or two before and now sat forlorn with broken windows.

One of the great surprises to me upon moving north was discovering the extent to which it felt like another country. Partly it was from the look and feel of the North—the high, open moors and big skies, the wandering drystone walls, the grimy mill towns, the snug stone villages of the Dales and Lakes—and partly, of course, it was to do with the accents, the different words, the refreshing if sometimes startling frankness of speech. Partly it was also to do with the way southerners and northerners were so extraordinarily, sometimes defiantly, ignorant of the geography of the other end of the country. It used to astonish me, working on newspapers in London, how often you could call out a question like "Is Halifax in West Yorkshire or South Yorkshire?" and be met with a tableful of blank frowns. And when I moved north and told people that I'd previously lived in Surrey near Windsor, I often got the same look— a kind of nervous uncertainty, as if they were afraid I was going to say, "Now you show me on the map just where that is."

Mostly what differentiated the North from the South, however, was the exceptional sense of economic loss, of greatness passed, when you drove through places like Preston or Blackburn or stood on a hillside like this. If you draw an angled line between Bristol and The Wash, you divide the country into two halves with roughly 27 million people on each side. Between 1980 and 1985, the southern half lost 103,600 jobs. The northern half in the same period lost 1,032,000 jobs, almost exactly ten times as many. And still the factories are shutting. Turn on the local television news in the North on any evening and at least half of it will be devoted to factory closures. So I ask again: What do all those people in all those houses do—and what, more to the point, will their children do?

We walked out of the grounds along another track toward Eldwick, past a large and flamboyant gatehouse, and David made a crestfallen noise. "I used to have a friend who lived there," he said. Now it was crumbling, its windows and doorways bricked up, a sad waste of a fine structure. Beside it, an old walled garden was neglected and overgrown.

Across the road, David pointed out the house where the famous astronomer Fred Hoyle had grown up. In his autobiography, Hoyle recalls how he used to see servants in white gloves going in and out of the gate of Milner Field, but is mysteriously silent on all the scandal and tragedy that was happening beyond the high wall. I had spent £3 on his autobiography in a secondhand bookshop in the certain expectation that the early chapters would be full of accounts of gunfire and midnight screams, so you can imagine my disappointment. A bit farther on, we passed three large blocks of council flats, which were not only ugly and remote but positioned in such an odd and careless way that, although they stood on an open hillside, the tenants didn't actually get a view. They had, David told me, won many architectural awards.

As we ambled into Bingley down a curving slope, David told me about his childhood there in the forties and fifties. He painted an attractive picture of happy times spent going to the pictures ("Wednesdays to the Hippodrome, Fridays to the Myrtle"), eating fish and chips out of newspapers, listening to *Dick Barton* and *Top of the Form* on the radio—a magic lost world of half-day closings, second posts, people on bicycles, endless summers. The Bingley he described was a confident, prosperous cog at the heart of a proud and mighty empire, with busy factories and a lively center full of cinemas, tearooms, and interesting shops, which was strikingly at odds with the dowdy, traffic-frazzled, knocked-about place we were passing into now. The Myrtle and Hippodrome cinemas had shut years before. The Hippodrome had been taken over by a Woolworth, but that, too, was now long gone. Today there isn't a movie theater in Bingley or much of anything else to make you want to go there. The center of the town is towered over by the forbidding presence of the Bradford and Bingley Building Society—not a particularly awful building as these things go, but hopelessly out of scale with the town around it. Between it and a truly squalid 1960s brick shopping precinct, the center of Bingley has had its character destroyed beyond repair. So it came as a pleasant surprise to find that beyond its central core Bingley remains a delightful spot.

We walked past a school and a golf course to a place called Beck-foot Farm, a pretty stone cottage in a dell beside a burbling beck. The main Bradford road was only a few hundred yards away, but it was another, premotorized century back here. We followed a meandering riverside path, which was exceedingly fetching in the mild sunshine. There used to be a factory here that rendered fat, David told me. It had the most awful smell, and the water always had a horrible rusty-creamy color with a skin of frothy grunge, and it was reliably rumored that if you dipped your hand into it, all the skin would fall off. Now the river was sparkling green and healthy looking and the spot seemed totally untouched by either time or industry. The old factory had been scrubbed up and gutted and turned into a block of stylish flats. We walked up to a place called Five-Rise Locks, where the Leeds to Liverpool Canal climbs a hundred feet or so in five quick stages, and had a look at the broken windows beyond the razor-wire perimeter of French's Mill. Then, feeling as if we had exhausted pretty much all that Bingley had to offer, we went to a convivial pub called the Old White Horse and drank a very large amount of beer, which is what we had both had in mind all along.

The next day I went shopping with my wife in Harrogate—or rather I had a look around Harrogate while she went shopping. Shopping is not, in my view, something that men and women should do together since all men want to do is buy something noisy like a drill and get it home so they can play with it, whereas women aren't happy until they've seen more or less everything in town and felt at least fifteen hundred different textures. Am I alone in being mystified by this strange compulsion on the part of women to finger things in shops? I have many times seen my wife go twenty or thirty yards out of her way to feel something—a mohair sweater or a velveteen bed jacket or something.

"Do you like that?" I'll say in surprise since it doesn't seem her type of thing, and she'll look at me as if I'm mad.

"That?" she'll say. "No, it's hideous."

"Then why on earth," I always want to say, "did you walk all the way over there to touch it?" But of course like all long-term husbands I have learned to say nothing when shopping, because no matter what you say—"I'm hungry," "I'm bored," "My feet are tired," "Yes, that one looks nice on you, too," "Well, have them both then," "Oh, for fuck sake," "Can't we just go home?" "Monsoon? *Again?* Oh, for fuck sake," "Then why on earth did you walk all the way over there to touch it?"—it doesn't pay, so I say nothing.

On this day, Mrs. B was in shoe-shopping mode, which means hours and hours of making some poor guy in a cheap suit fetch endless boxes of more or less identical footwear and then deciding not to have anything, so I wisely decided to clear off and have a look at the town. To show her I love her, I took her for coffee and cake at Betty's (and at Betty's prices you need to be pretty damn smitten),

where she issued me with her usual precise instructions for a rendezvous. "Three o'clock outside Woolworth's. But listen—stop fiddling with that and listen—if Russell and Bromley don't have the
shoes I want, I'll have to go to Ravel, in which case meet me at
three-fifteen by the frozen foods in Marks. Otherwise I'll be in Hammick's in the cookery books section or possibly the children's
books—unless I'm in Boots feeling toasters. But probably, in fact,
I'll be at Russell and Bromley trying on all the same shoes all over
again, in which case meet me outside Next no later than three
twenty-seven. Have you got that?"

"Yes." No.

"Don't let me down."

"Of course not." In your dreams.

And then with a kiss she was gone. I finished my coffee and savored the elegant, old-fashioned ambience of this fine institution
where the waitresses still wear frilly caps and white aprons over black
dresses. There really ought to be more places like this, if you ask
me. It may cost an arm and a leg for a *cafetière* and a sticky bun,
but it is worth every penny and the management will let you sit there
all day, which I seriously considered doing now as it was so agreeable. But then I thought I really ought to have a look around the
town, so I paid the bill and hauled myself off through the shopping
precinct to have a look at Harrogate's newest feature, the Victoria
Gardens Shopping Centre. The name is a bit rich because the developers built it on *top* of Victoria Gardens, so it really ought to be
called the Nice Little Public Gardens Destroyed by This Shopping
Centre.

I wouldn't mind this so much, but they also demolished the last
great public toilets in Britain—a little subterranean treasure house
of polished tiles and gleaming brass in the aforementioned gardens.
The Gents was simply wonderful and I've had good reports about
the Ladies as well. I might not even mind this so much either, but
the new shopping center is just heartbreakingly awful, the worst kind

of pastiche architecture—a sort of Bath Crescent meets Crystal Palace with a roof by McDonald's. For reasons I couldn't begin to guess at, a balustrade along the roofline had been adorned with life-sized statues of ordinary men, women, and children. Goodness knows what this is meant to suggest—I suppose that this is some sort of Hall of the People—but the effect is that it looks as if two dozen citizens of various ages are about to commit mass suicide.

On the Station Parade side of the building, where the pleasant little Victoria Gardens and its pleasant little public toilets formerly existed, there is now a kind of open-air amphitheater of steps, where I suppose it is intended for people to sit on those two or three days a year when Yorkshire is sunny, and high above the road there has been built a truly preposterous covered footbridge in the same Georgian/Italianate/Fuck Knows style connecting the shopping center to a parking garage across the way.

Now, on the basis of my earlier remarks about Britain's treatment of its architectural heritage, you may foolishly have supposed that I would be something of an enthusiast for this sort of thing. Alas, no. If by *pastiche* you mean a building that takes some note of its surroundings and perhaps endeavors to match adjoining rooflines and echo the size and position of its neighbors' windows and door openings and that sort of thing, then yes, I am in favor of it. But if by *pastiche* you mean a kind of Disneyland version of Jolly Olde England like this laughable heap before me, then thank you but no.

You could argue, I suppose—and I daresay Victoria Gardens' architect would—that at least it shows some effort to inject traditional architectural values into the townscape and that it is less jarring to the sensibilities than the nearby glass-and-plastic box in which the Co-op department store is happy to reside (which is, let me say here, a building of consummate ugliness), but in fact it seems to me that it is just as bad as, and in its way even more uninspired and unimaginative than, the wretched Co-op building. (But let me also say that neither is even remotely as bad as the Maples building, a sixties block that rises, like some kind of halfwitted practical joke, a dozen or so stories into the air in the middle of a long street of innocuous Victorian structures. Now how did *that* happen?)

So what are we to do with Britain's poor battered towns if I won't let them have Mies van der Rohe *or* Walt Disney? I wish I knew. More than this, I wish the architects knew. Surely there must be *some* way to create buildings that are stylish and forward looking without destroying the overall ambience of their setting. Most other European nations manage it (with the notable and curious exception of the French). So why not here?

But enough of this tedious bleating. Harrogate is basically a very fine town, and far less scarred by careless development than many other communities. It has in the Stray, a 215-acre sweep of parklike common land overlooked by solid, prosperous homes, one of the largest and most agreeable open spaces in the country. It has some nice old hotels, a pleasant shopping area, and, withal, a genteel and well-ordered air. It is, in short, as nice a town as you will find anywhere. It reminds me, in a pleasantly English way, a little of Baden-Baden, which is of course not surprising since it was likewise a spa town in its day—and a very successful one, too. According to a leaflet I picked up at the Royal Pump Room Museum, as late as 1926 the spa was still dispensing as many as twenty-six thousand glasses of sulfurous water in a single day. You can still drink the water if you want. According to a notice by the tap, it is reputedly very good for flatulence, which seemed an intriguing promise, and I very nearly drank some until I realized the notice meant it *prevented* it. What an odd notion.

I had a look around the museum and walked past the Old Swan Hotel, where Agatha Christie famously went and hid after she found out that her husband was a philanderer, the beastly cad, then wandered up Montpellier Parade, a very pretty street filled with awesomely expensive antique shops. I examined the seventy-five-foot-high War Memorial, and went for a long, pleasantly directionless amble through the Stray, thinking how nice it must be to live in one of the big houses overlooking the park and be able to stroll to the shops from your own front door.

You would never guess that a place as prosperous and decorous as Harrogate could inhabit the same zone of the country as Bradford or Bolton, but of course that is the other thing about the North—that it has these pockets of immense prosperity, like Harrogate and Ilkley, that are even more decorous and flush with visible wealth than their counterparts in the South. Makes it a much more interesting place, if you ask me.

Eventually, with the afternoon fading, I took myself back into the heart of the shopping area, where I scratched my head and, with a kind of panicky terror, realized I didn't have the faintest idea where or when I had agreed to meet my dear missus. I was standing there wearing an expression like Stan Laurel when he turns around to find that the piano he was looking after is rolling down a steep hill with Ollie aboard, legs wriggling, when by a kind of miracle my wife walked up.

"Hello, dear!" she said brightly. "I must say, I never expected to find you here waiting for me."

"Oh, for goodness' sake, give me a bit of credit, please. I've been here ages."

And arm in arm we strode off into the wintry sunset.

chapter
19

I took a train to Leeds and then another to Manchester—a long,
slow, but not unpleasant ride through steep-sided dales that looked
uncannily like the one I lived in except that these were thickly strewn
with old mills and huddled, soot-blackened villages. The old mills
seemed to come in three types: (1) derelict, with broken windows
and TO LET signs; (2) gone—just grassless open spaces; (3) converted to something nonmanufacturing, like a depot for a courier
service or a plumbing supply business or similar. I must have passed
a hundred of these old factories, but not until we were well into the
outskirts of Manchester did I see a single one that appeared to be
engaged in the manufacture of anything.

I had left home late, so it was four o'clock and getting on for dark
by the time I emerged from Piccadilly Station in Manchester. The
streets were shiny with rain, and busy with traffic and hurrying pedestrians, which gave Manchester an attractive big-city feel. For
some totally insane reason, I had booked a room in an expensive
hotel, the Piccadilly. My room was on the eleventh floor, but it
seemed like about the eighty-sixth, such were the views. If my wife
had had a flare and an inclination to get up on the roof of our house,

I could just about have seen her. Manchester seemed enormous—a boundless sprawl of yellow streetlights and streets filled with slow-moving traffic.

I played with the TV, confiscated the stationery and spare tablet of soap, and put a pair of trousers into the trouser press—at these prices I was determined to extract full value from the experience—even though I knew that the trousers would come out with permanent pleats in the oddest places. (Is it me or are these things totally counterproductive?) That done, I went out for a walk and to find a place to eat.

There seems to be a kind of inverse ratio where British dinner establishments and I are concerned—namely that the more of them there are, the harder it is for me to find one that looks even remotely adequate to my modest needs. What I really wanted was a little Italian place on a side street—the kind with checked tablecloths and Chianti bottles with candles and a nice 1950s feel about it. British cities used to abound in these places, but they are deucedly hard to find now. I walked for some distance, but the only restaurants I could find were either the kind of national chain with big plastic menus and dismal food or hotel dining rooms where you had to pay £17.95 for three courses of pompous description and overcooked disappointment. Eventually I ended up in Chinatown, which announces itself to the world with a big colorful arch and then almost immediately loses heart. There was a scattering of restaurants among big office buildings, but I can't say I felt as if I had wandered into a little corner of the Orient. The bigger, better-looking restaurants were packed, so I ended up going to some upstairs place, where the decor was tatty, the food barely OK, and the service totally indifferent.

Afterward, I went on a long, purposeless walk through Manchester's dank and strangely ill lit streets. (I can't remember a darker city.) I couldn't say where I went exactly, because Manchester's streets always seem curiously indistinguishable to me. I felt as if I was never getting nearer to or farther from anything in particular, but just wandering around in a kind of urban limbo.

Eventually I ended up beside the great dark bulk of the Arndale shopping center (there's that name again). What a monumental mistake that was. I suppose it must be nice, in a place as perennially rainy as Manchester, to be able to shop undercover, and if you are going to have these things at all, much better to have them *in* the city than outside it. But after 6 P.M. it is just twenty-five acres of deadness, a massive impediment to anyone trying to walk through the heart of the city since the doors are locked at night. I could see through the windows that the inside had been tarted up since the last time I had been there—and very nice it appeared now, too—but outside it was still covered in those awful tiles that make it look like the world's largest Gents lavatory, and indeed as I passed up Cannon Street three young men with close-cropped heads and abundantly tattooed arms were using an outside wall for that very purpose. They paid me scant heed, but it suddenly occurred to me that it was getting late and the streets were awfully empty of respectable-looking fellows like me, so I decided to get back to my hotel before some other late-night carousers put me to similar use.

I awoke early and hit the drizzly streets determined to form some fixed impression of the city. My problem with Manchester, you see, is that I have no image of it, none at all. Every other great British city has something about it, some central motif, that fixes it in my mind: Newcastle has its bridge, Liverpool the Liver Building and docks, Edinburgh its castle, Glasgow the great sprawl of Kelvingrove Park and the buildings of Charles Rennie Mackintosh; even Birmingham has the Bull Ring, a famously ugly roundabout. But Manchester to me is a perennial blank—an airport with a city attached. Mention Manchester to me and all that swims into my mind is a vague and unfocused impression of Manchester United, the artist L. S. Lowry, some plan to introduce trams because they have them in Zurich or someplace and they seem to work pretty

well there, the Hallé Orchestra, the old *Manchester Guardian* newspaper (which hasn't in fact been in Manchester for years), and these
rather touching attempts every four years or so to win the bid for the
next summer Olympics, usually illustrated with ambitious plans to
build a £400 million velodrome or a £250 million table tennis complex or some other edifice vital to the future of a declining industrial
city.

Apart from L. S. Lowry, I couldn't name a single great Mancu-
nian, as Manchester natives are known (something to do with the
city's Roman name). It's clear from the abundance of statues outside
the town hall that Manchester has produced its share of worthies in
its time, though it is equally clear from all the frock coats and muttonchops that it has either stopped producing worthies or stopped
producing statues. I had a look around them now and didn't recognize a single name.

If I haven't got a very clear image of the city, it's not entirely my
fault. Manchester doesn't appear to have a very fixed image of itself.
"Shaping Tomorrow's City Today" is the official local motto, but
in fact Manchester seems decidedly of two minds about its place in
the world. In the Castlefield district, workmen were busy creating
yesterday's city today, cleaning up the old brick viaducts and warehouses, recobbling the quaysides, putting fresh coats of glossy paint
on the old arched footbridges, and scattering about a generous assortment of old-fashioned benches, bollards, and lampposts. By the
time they have finished, you will be able to see exactly what life was
like in nineteenth-century Manchester—or at least what it would
have been like if it had had wine bars and cast-iron litter bins and
directional signs for heritage trails and the G-Mex exhibition center.
At Salford Quays, on the other hand, planners have taken the opposite tack and done everything they can to obliterate the past, creating a kind of mini-Dallas on the site of the once-booming docks
of the Manchester Ship Canal. It's the most extraordinary place—a
huddle of glassy modern office buildings and executive flats in the

middle of a vast urban nowhere, all of them seemingly quite empty.

The one thing you have a job to find in Manchester is the one thing you might reasonably expect to see—row after row of huddled Coronation Streets. *Coronation Street,* I should perhaps explain, is a long-running TV soap opera, adored by anyone with any sense, that depicts life on a typical working-class street of brick terrace houses somewhere in greater Manchester. These streets used to exist in abundance, I'm told, but now you could walk miles without seeing a single brick terrace anywhere, thanks to the city's tireless efforts at urban renewal. But that doesn't matter because you can always go and see the real Coronation Street on the Granada Studios Tour, which was what I did now. Granada, one of the main independent television networks, borrowed the idea from Universal Studios in Hollywood of turning itself into a tourist attraction, and I had been wanting for years to see it because, frankly, it seemed a ridiculous notion.

I was astounded to see that the place was extremely popular. For some distance along the road to the studios there were massive parking lots, and even at 9:45 in the morning they were filling up. Buses from all over the North—from Workington, Darlington, Middlesbrough, Doncaster, Wakefield—were decanting streams of sprightly white-haired people, while from the cars issued throngs of families, everyone looking happy and good-natured.

I joined a queue that was a good 150 yards long and three or four people wide and wondered if this wasn't a mistake, but when the turnstiles opened at 10 A.M. sharp the line advanced pretty smartishly and within minutes I was inside. To my deep and lasting surprise, it was actually quite wonderful. I had expected it to consist of a stroll up the *Coronation Street* set and a perfunctory guided tour of the studios, but Granada has made it into a kind of amusement park and done it exceedingly well. It had one of those Motionmaster cinemas, where the seats tilt and jerk, so that you actually felt as if you were being hurled through space or thrown off the edge of a mountain, and another theater where you put on plastic glasses and watched a 3-D comedy involving a crew of inept painters and decorators. There was an entertaining demonstration of sound effects, an adorably gruesome show about special-effects makeup, and a lively, hugely amusing debate in an ersatz House of Commons, presided over by a troupe of youthful actors. And the thing was, all of these were done not just with considerable polish but with great and genuine wit.

Even after twenty years in Britain, I remain constantly amazed and impressed by the quality of humor you find in the most unlikely places—places where it would simply not exist in other countries. You find it in the patter of stallholders in open-air markets and in the routines of street performers—the sort of people who juggle flaming clubs or do tricks on unicycles and keep up a steady stream of jokes about themselves and selected members of the audience—and in Christmas pantomimes and pub conversations and encounters with strangers in lonely places.

I remember once years ago arriving at Waterloo Station to find the place in chaos. A fire up the line at Clapham Junction had disrupted service. For an hour or so, hundreds of people stood with incredible patience and implacable calm watching a blank departure board. Occasionally a rumor would rustle through the crowd that a train was about to leave from Platform 7, and everyone would traipse off there, only to be met at the gate by a new rumor that the train was in fact departing from Platform 16 or possibly Platform 2. Eventually, after visiting most of the station's platforms and sitting on a series of trains that went nowhere, I found myself in the guards' van of an express reputed to be departing for Richmond shortly. The van had one other occupant: a man in a suit sitting on a pile of mailbags. He had an enormous red beard—you could have stuffed a mattress with it—and the sort of world-weary look of someone who has long since abandoned hope of reaching home.

"Have you been here long?" I asked.

He exhaled thoughtfully and said, "Put it this way. I was clean-shaven when I got here." I just love that.

Not too many months before this, I had been with my family to Euro Disneyland. Technologically, it had been stunning. The amount of money invested by Disney in a single ride would make any part of the Granada Studios Tour look like amateur night in a village hall. But it occurred to me now, as I sat in the immense conviviality of Granada's mock House of Commons debate, that not once at Disneyland had there been a single laugh. Wit, and particularly the dry, ironic, understated sort of wit in which the British specialize, was completely beyond Disney's wholesome and drearily serious Imagineers, as I believe they are unfortunately known. If Disney had had a House of Commons debate, it would have been earnest, hokey, frighteningly competitive, and over in three minutes. The people on the two sides of the chamber would have cared deeply, if briefly, about *winning*. Here, the debate went on for half an hour and things were so contrived that there wasn't the remotest possibility of anyone's winning. It was all about having a good time, and it was done so well, so cheerfully and cleverly, that I could hardly stand it. And I knew that this above all else was the one thing from Britain I would miss.

The one place you don't find any humor on the Granada Studios Tour is on the *Coronation Street* set, but that is because for millions of us it is a near-religious experience. I have a great fondness for *Coronation Street* because it was one of the first programs I watched on British television. I had no idea what was going on, of course, but I found myself strangely absorbed by it. Where I came from, soap operas were always about rich, ruthless, enormously successful people with $1,500 suits and offices high up in angular skyscrapers, and the main characters were always played by the sort of actors and actresses who, given a choice between being able to act and having really great hair, would always go for the hair. And here was this amazing program about ordinary people living on an anonymous

northern street, talking a language I could barely understand, and
never doing much of anything. By the time the first adverts came on,
I was a helpless devotee.

Then I was cruelly forced into working nights on Fleet Street and
fell out of the habit. Now I am not even permitted in the room when
Coronation Street is on because I have lost touch with the manifold
plot lines and spend the whole time saying, "Where's Ernie Bishop?
So who's that then? I thought Deirdre was with Ray Langton.
Where's Len? Stan Ogden is *dead*?" and after a minute I find myself
shooed away. But, as I discovered now, you can go years without
watching *Coronation Street* and still enjoy walking along the open-
air set because it's so obviously the street from the TV series. It's
the real set, by the way—Granada closes the park on most Mondays
to film on it—and it feels like a real street. The houses are solid and
made of real bricks; though, like everyone else, I was disappointed
to peer into the windows and find through gaps in the curtains that
they were empty shells with nothing but electrical cables and car-
penters' sawhorses inside. (The interior scenes are all shot in the
studio building behind.) I was a bit confused to encounter a pair of
modern houses at one end of the street, and the newsagent's, to my
clear distress, was much smarter and better ordered than it used to
be, but I still felt uncannily on familiar and hallowed turf. Throngs
of people walked up and down the street in a kind of reverential
hush, identifying front doors and peering through lace curtains. I
latched onto a friendly little lady with blue-rinsed hair under a transparent rain hat she seemed to have made from a bread wrapper, and
she not only informed me who lived in which houses now, but who
had lived in which houses way back when, so that I was pretty well
brought up to speed. Pretty soon I found myself surrounded by a
whole flock of little blue-haired ladies answering my shocked questions ("Deirdre with a toy boy? Never!") and assuring me with solemn nods that it was so. It is a profoundly thrilling experience to
walk up and down this famous street, and it comes as something of

a shock to round the corner at the far end and find yourself abruptly—I might almost say mercilessly—on a nineteenth-century London street, the set for *Sherlock Holmes*, and realize that it is all just an elaborate fantasy.

I had intended to stay only an hour or so at the park, and hadn't gotten anywhere near the guided studio tour or the *Coronation Street* gift shop, when I glanced at my watch and discovered with a snort of alarm that it was nearly one o'clock. In a mild panic, I hastened from the park and back to my distant hotel, fearful that I would be charged for another day or, at the very least, that my trousers would be overcooked.

In consequence I found myself, three quarters of an hour later, standing on the edge of Piccadilly Gardens with a heavy knapsack and a pretty near total uncertainty about where to go next. I had it vaguely in mind to head for the Midlands, since I had given this noble if challenging region of the country pretty short shrift on my previous foragings, but as I was standing there a faded red double-decker bus announcing WIGAN in its little destination window pulled up beside me and the matter was out of my hands. It happened that at this very moment I had a copy of George Orwell's *The Road to Wigan Pier* sticking out of my back pocket, so unhesitatingly I took this for a sign.

I bought a one-way ticket to Wigan and found my way to a seat midway along the back upstairs. Wigan can't be more than fifteen or sixteen miles from Manchester, but it took most of the afternoon to get there. We lurched and reeled through endless streets that never seemed to change character or gain any. They were all lined with tiny terraced houses, of which every fourth one seemed to be a hairdresser's, and dotted with filling stations and brick shopping precincts with an unvarying array of supermarkets, banks, video take-outs, pie and pea shops, and betting establishments. We went through Eccles and Worsely, then through a surprisingly posh bit, and on to Boothstown and Tyldesley and Atherton and Hindley and other such places of which I had never heard. The bus stopped frequently—every twenty feet in places, it seemed—and at nearly every stop there was a large exchange of people. They nearly all looked poor and worn out and twenty years older than I suspect they actually were. Apart from a sprinkling of old men in flat caps and dun-colored, tightly zippered Marks & Spencer jackets, the passengers were nearly all middle-aged women with unlikely hairdos and the loose, phlegmy laughter of hardened smokers, but they were unfailingly friendly and cheerful and seemed happy enough with their lot. They all called each other "darlin' " and "love."

The most remarkable thing—or perhaps the least remarkable thing, depending on how you look at it—was how neat and well looked after were the endless terraces of little houses we passed. Everything about them bespoke an air of modesty and make-do, but every stoop shone, every window gleamed, every sill had a fresh, glossy coat of paint. I took out my copy of *The Road to Wigan Pier* and lost myself for a bit in another world, one that occupied the same space as these little communities we were passing through but was impossibly at odds with what my eyes were telling me when I glanced up from the pages.

Orwell—and let us never forget that he spent his formative years at Eton—regarded the laboring classes the way we might regard Yap Islanders, as a strange but interesting anthropological phenomenon. In *Wigan Pier* he records how one of the great panic moments of his boyhood years was when he found himself in the company of a group of workingmen and thought he would have to drink from a bottle they were passing around. Ever since I read this, I've had my doubts about old George, frankly. Certainly he makes the working class of the 1930s seem disgustingly filthy, but in fact almost every piece of evidence I've ever seen shows that most of them were almost obsessively dedicated to cleanliness. My own father-in-law grew up in an environment of starkest poverty and used to tell the most appalling stories of deprivation—you know the kind of thing: father

killed in a factory accident, thirty-seven brothers and sisters, nothing
for tea but lichen broth and a piece of roofing slate, except on Sundays when they might trade in a child for a penny's worth of rotten
parsnips, and all that sort of thing—and *his* father-in-law, a York-
shireman, used to tell even more appalling stories of hopping forty-
seven miles to school because he only had one boot and subsisting
on a diet of stale buns and snot butties. "But," they would both
invariably conclude, "we were always clean and the house was spotless." And it must be said they *were* the most fastidiously scrubbed
persons imaginable, as were all their countless brothers and sisters
and friends and relatives.

It also happened that not long before this I had met Willis Hall,
the author and playwright (and a very nice man into the bargain),
and somehow we got to talking about this very matter. Hall had
grown up poor in Leeds, and he unhesitatingly confirmed that
though the houses were barren and conditions hard, there was never
the tiniest hint of dirtiness. "When my mother was to be rehoused
after the war," he told me, "she spent her last day at home scrubbing
it from top to bottom until it shone, even though she knew it was
going to be torn down the next day. She just couldn't bear the
thought of leaving it dirty—and I promise you that that wouldn't
have been thought peculiar by anyone from that neighborhood."

For all his professed sympathy for the masses, you would never
guess from reading Orwell that they were capable of any higher mental talents, and yet one Leeds neighborhood alone produced in a
single generation Willis Hall, the writer Keith Waterhouse, and the
actor Peter O'Toole, while a similarly impoverished district of Salford that I know of produced Alistair Cooke (hard to believe he grew
up in an impoverished environment, isn't it?) and the artist Harold
Riley, and I am sure there were many similar cases all up and down
the country.

Such was the picture of appalling squalor Orwell painted that
even now I was startled to find how neat and well maintained Wigan

appeared to be as we entered it by means of a long hill. I got off at the bottom, pleased to return to the fresh air, and set off in search of the famous pier. Wigan Pier is an arresting landmark, yet—and here's another reason to be a bit cautious with regard to old George's reporting skills—after spending some days in the town, he concluded that the pier had been demolished. (So, too, for that matter, did Paul Theroux in *The Kingdom by the Sea*.) Now correct me if I'm wrong, but don't you think it a bit odd to write a book called *The Road to Wigan Pier* and to spend some days in the town and never once think to ask anybody whether the pier was still there or not?

In any case, you could hardly miss it now since there are cast-iron signposts pointing the way to it on almost every corner. The pier—it is really just an old coal shed on the side of the Leeds to Liverpool Canal—has (inevitably) been refurbished as a tourist attraction and incorporates a museum, gift shop, snack bar, and a pub called, without evident irony, The Orwell. Alas for me, it was shut on Fridays, so I had to content myself with walking around it and peering into the windows at the museum displays, which looked reasonably diverting. Across the street was something nearly as arresting as the pier—a real working factory, a mountain of red bricks with the name TRENCHERFIELD MILL emblazoned across an upper story. It's now part of Courtauld's, the textile company, and is a sufficient rarity these days that it is something of a tourist attraction, too. There were signs out front telling you which way to go for the guided tours, the factory shop, and the snack bar. It seemed a bit of an odd notion to me, the idea of joining a queue to watch people making towels or whatever it is they do in there, but in any case it, too, appeared to be closed to the public on Fridays. The snack bar door was padlocked. So I walked into the center, a fair hike but a not unrewarding one. Such is Wigan's perennially poor reputation that I was truly astounded to find it has a handsome and well-maintained town center. The shops seemed prosperous and busy and there were lots of public benches to sit on for the many people unable to take an active

part in all the economic activity around them. Some talented architect had managed to incorporate a new shopping arcade into the
existing fabric of the buildings in a simple but deceptively clever
and effective way, by making the glass canopy of the entrance match
the line of the gables of the surrounding structures. The result was
an entrance that was bright and modern but pleasantly harmoni-
ous—precisely the sort of thing I've been going on about for all these
many pages—and I was delighted to think that if this sort of thing
is going to happen just once in Britain, it should be in poor belea-
guered Wigan.

To celebrate, I went off to have a cup of tea and a sticky bun at
a place called the Corinthia Coffee Lounge, which boasted, among
its many other advertised features, a "Georgian Potato Oven." I
asked the girl at the counter what that was and she looked at me as
if I were very strange.

"It's for cooking potatoes and tha'," she said.

But of course. I took my tea and sticky bun to a table, where I
spent a little time going, "Ooh, lovely," and smiling inanely at some
nice ladies at the next table, and afterward, feeling strangely pleased
with my day, went off to find the station.

chapter
20

I took a train to Liverpool. They were having a festival of litter when I arrived. Citizens had taken time off from their busy activities to add ice cream wrappers, empty cigarette boxes, and plastic carrier bags to the otherwise bland and neglected landscape. They fluttered gaily in the bushes and brought color and texture to pavements and gutters. And to think that elsewhere we stick these objects in trashbags.

In another bout of extravagant madness, I had booked a room in the Adelphi Hotel. I had seen it from the street on earlier visits and it appeared to have an old-fashioned grandeur about it that I was keen to investigate. On the other hand, it looked expensive and I wasn't sure my trousers could stand another session in the trouser press. So I was most agreeably surprised when I checked in to discover that I was entitled to a special weekend rate and that there would be money spare for a nice meal and a parade of beer in any of the many wonderful pubs in which Liverpool specializes.

And so, soon afterward, I found myself, like all fresh arrivals in Liverpool, in the grand and splendorous surroundings of the Philharmonic public house, clutching a pint glass and rubbing shoulders with a happy Friday evening throng. The Phil (you can call it this if you have been there twice) was in fact a bit too crowded for my liking. There was nowhere to sit and scarcely any room to stand, so I drank two pints, just enough at my time of life to need a pee—for there is no place in the world finer for a pee than the fabulously ornate Gents room of the Philharmonic—then went off to find someplace a little quieter.

I ended up in a place called The Vines, which was nearly as ornate as the Philharmonic but infinitely quieter. There were only three other customers, which was a mystery to me because it was a very fine pub with wood paneling by some Grinling Gibbons wannabe and a plaster ceiling even more ornate than the paneling. As I was sitting there drinking my beer and savoring my plush surroundings, some guy came in with a plastic collecting container from which the original label had been roughly scratched, and asked me for a donation for handicapped children.

"Which handicapped children?" I asked.

"Ones in wheelchairs like."

"I mean which organization do you represent?"

"It's, er, the, er, Handicapped Children's Organization like."

"Well, as long as it's totally legitimate," I said and gave him 20p. And that is what I like so much about Liverpool. The factories may be gone, there may be no work, the city may be pathetically dependent on soccer for its sense of destiny, but the Liverpudlians still have character and initiative, and they don't bother you with preposterous ambitions to win the bid for the next Olympics.

So nice was The Vines that I drank two more pints and then realized that I really ought to get something in my stomach lest I grow giddy and end up staggering into street furniture and singing "Mother McCree." Outside, the hill on which the pub stood seemed suddenly and unaccountably steep and taxing, until it dawned on me, in my mildly addled state, that I had come down it before whereas now I was going up it, which seemed to put everything in a new light. I found myself, after no great distance, standing outside a Greek restaurant and surveying the menu with a hint of a sway. I'm not much of one for Greek food—no disrespect to a fine cuisine, you understand, but I always feel as if I could boil my own leaves if I had a taste for that sort of thing—but the restaurant was so forlornly empty and the proprietress accosted me with such imploring eyes that I found myself wandering in. Well, the meal was wonderful. I have no idea what I ate, but it was abundant and delicious and they treated me like a prince. Foolishly I washed it all down with many additional drafts of beer. By the time I finished and settled the bill, leaving a tip of such lavishness as to bring the whole family to the kitchen door, and began the long process of stabbing an arm at a mysteriously disappearing jacket sleeve, I was, I fear, pretty nearly intoxicated. I staggered out into the fresh air, feeling suddenly queasy and largely incapable.

Now the second rule of excessive drinking (the first, of course, is don't take a sudden shine to a woman larger than Hoss Cartwright) is never to drink in a place on a steep slope. I walked down the hill on unfamiliar legs that seemed to snap out in front of me like whipped lengths of rope. The Adelphi, glowing beckoningly at the foot of the hill, managed the interesting trick of being both nearby and astonishingly distant. It was like looking at it through the wrong end of a telescope—a sensation somewhat enhanced by the fact that my head was a good seven or eight yards behind my manically flopping feet. I followed them helplessly, and by a kind of miracle they hurtled me down the hill, safely across the road, and up the steps to the entrance to the Adelphi, where I celebrated my arrival by making a complete circuit in the revolving door so that I emerged into open air once again, before plunging back in and being flung with a startling suddenness into the Adelphi's grand and lofty lobby. I had one of those where-am-I moments, then grew aware that the night staff was silently watching me. Summoning as much dignity as I could and knowing that the lifts would be quite beyond me, I went to the grand staircase and managed—I know not how—to fall up them in a manner uncannily reminiscent of a motion picture run in reverse. All I know is that at the very end I leaped backward to my feet and announced to the craning faces that I was quite all right, and then embarked on a long search for my room among the Adelphi's endless and mysteriously numbered corridors.

Here's a piece of advice for you. Don't go on the Mersey ferry unless you are prepared to have the famous song by Gerry and the Pacemakers running through your head for about eleven days afterward. They play it when you board the ferry and they play it when you get off and for quite a lot of time in between. I went on it the following morning thinking a bit of a sit-down and a cruise on the water would be just the way to ease myself out of a killer hangover, but in fact the inescapable sound of "Ferry Cross the Mersey" only worsened my cranial plight. Apart from that, it must be said that the Mersey ferry is an agreeable, if decidedly breezy, way of passing a morning. It's a bit like the Sydney Harbour cruise, but without Sydney.

When they weren't playing "Ferry Cross the Mersey," they played a soundtrack outlining the famous sights from the deck, but the acoustics were terrible and 80 percent of whatever was said was instantly blown away on the wind. All I could hear was snatches of things like "three million" and "world's biggest," but whether they were talking about oil refinery capacity or number of winos I couldn't say. But the gist of it was that this was once a great city and now it's Liverpool.

Now don't get me wrong. I'm exceedingly fond of Liverpool. It's probably my favorite English city. But it does rather feel like a place with more past than future. Leaning on a deck rail gazing out on miles of motionless waterfront, I found it impossible to believe that until quite recently—and for two hundred proud and prosperous years before that—Liverpool's ten miles of docks and shipyards provided employment for a hundred thousand people, directly or indirectly. Tobacco from Africa and Virginia, palm oil from the South Pacific, copper from Chile, jute from India, and almost any other commodity you could care to name passed through here on its way to being made into something useful. So, too, no less significantly, did some 10 million people bound for a new life in the new world, drawn by stories of streets paved with gold and the possibility of accumulating immense personal wealth, or in the case of my own forebears by the giddy prospect of spending the next century and a half dodging tornadoes and shoveling snow in Iowa.

Liverpool became the third richest city in the empire. Only London and Glasgow had more millionaires. By 1880 it was generating more tax revenue than Birmingham, Bristol, Leeds, and Sheffield together, even though collectively they had twice the population. The Cunard and White Star lines had their headquarters in Liverpool, and there were countless other lines, now mostly forgotten— Blue Funnel, Bank, Coast, Pacific Steam, McAndrews, Elder Dempster, Booth. There were more lines operating out of Liverpool then than there are ships today, or so at least it can seem when there is nothing much along the waterfront but the ghostly warble of Gerry Marsden's voice.

The decline happened in a single generation. In 1966, Liverpool was still the second busiest port in Britain, after London. By 1985, it had fallen so low that it was smaller and quieter than even Tees and Hartlepool, Grimsby and Immingham. But in its heyday it was something special. Maritime commerce brought Liverpool not just wealth and employment, but an air of cosmopolitanism that few cities in the world could rival, and it still has that sense about it. In Liverpool, you still feel like you are someplace.

I walked from the ferry to the Albert Dock. There were plans at one time to drain it and turn it into a parking lot—it seems a miracle sometimes that there is anything at all left in this poor, stumbling country—but now the dock buildings have been scrubbed up and gentrified, the old warehouses turned into offices, flats, and restaurants for the sort of people who carry telephones in their briefcases. The dock also incorporates an outpost of the Tate Gallery and the Merseyside Maritime Museum. It is a model of urban renewal of which Liverpool is justifiably proud.

I love the Merseyside Maritime Museum, not merely because it is well done but because it gives such a potent sense of what Liverpool was like when it was a great port—indeed when the world was full of a productive busyness and majesty of enterprise that it seems utterly to have lost now. How I'd love to have lived in an age when you could walk to a waterfront and see mighty ships loading and unloading great bales of cotton fiber and weighty burlap bags of coffee and spices, and when every sailing involved hundreds of people—sailors and dockers and throngs of excited passengers. Today, you go to a waterfront and all you find is an endless expanse of battered brick-red containers and one lonely guy in an elevated cabin shunting them about.

Once there was infinite romance in the sea, and the Merseyside Maritime Museum captures every bit of it. I was particularly taken with an upstairs room full of outsized ships' models, the sort that must once have decorated executive boardrooms. Gosh, they were wonderful. Even as models they were wonderful. All the great Liverpool ships were there—the *Titanic,* the *Imperator,* the RMS *Majestic* (which began life as the *Bismarck* before being seized as war reparations), and the unutterably lovely TSS *Vauban,* with its broad decks of polished maple and its jaunty funnels. According to its label, it was owned by the Liverpool, Brazil, and River Plate Steam Navigation Company Limited. Just reading those words I was seized with a dull ache at the thought that never again will we see such a beautiful thing. Priestley called these ships the greatest constructions of the modern world, our equivalent of cathedrals, and he was ab-

solutely right. I was appalled to think that never in my life would I
have an opportunity to stride down a gangplank in a Panama hat
and a white suit and go looking for a bar with a revolving ceiling
fan. How crushingly unfair life can sometimes be.

I spent two hours wandering through the museum, looking with
care at all the displays. I would happily have stayed longer, but I
had to check out of the hotel, so I regretfully departed and walked
back through central Liverpool's fine Victorian streets to the hotel,
where I grabbed my things and settled my account.

I had a hankering to go to Port Sunlight, a model community
built in 1888 by William Lever to house his soap workers, as I was
interested to see how it compared with Saltaire. So I went to Liverpool Central and caught a train. At Rock Ferry we were informed
that because of engineering works we would have to complete the
journey by bus. This was OK by me because I was in no hurry and
you can always see more from a bus. We rode along the Wirral Peninsula for some time before the driver announced the stop for Port
Sunlight. I was the only person to get off, and the most striking thing
about it was that it was patently not Port Sunlight. I tapped on the
front doors and waited for them to gasp open.

"Excuse me," I said, "but this doesn't look like Port Sunlight."

"That's because it's Bebington," he said. "It's as close as I can
get to Port Sunlight because of a low bridge."

Oh.

"So where exactly is Port Sunlight then?" I asked but it was to a
cloud of blue smoke. I hooked my rucksack over a shoulder and set
off along a road that I hoped might be the right one—and no doubt
would have been had I taken another. I walked for some distance,
but the road seemed to go nowhere, or at least nowhere that looked
Port Sunlightish. After a time an old man in a flat cap came dod-
dering along and I asked him if he could point me the way to Port
Sunlight.

"*Port Sunlight!*" he replied in the bellow of someone who thinks the world is going deaf with him, and with a hint that that was a bloody daft place to want to go. "You want a *boose!*"

"A bus?" I said in surprise. "How far am I then?"

"I say you want a *boose!*" he repeated, but more vehemently.

"I understand that. But which way is it exactly?"

He jabbed me with a bony finger in a tender spot just below the shoulder. *"It's a boose you're wanting!"*

"I understand that." You tedious deaf old fart. I raised my voice to match his: "I need to know which way to go!"

He looked at me as if I were unsustainably stupid. *"A bloody boose! You want a bloody boose!"* And then he shuffled off, working his jaw wordlessly.

"Thank you. Die soon," I called after him, rubbing my shoulder.

I returned to Bebington where I sought directions in a shop, which I should have done in the first place, of course. Port Sunlight, it turned out, was just down the road, under a railway bridge and over a junction—or perhaps it was the other way around. I don't know because rain was now pelting down and I tucked my head so low into my shoulders that I didn't see much of anything.

I walked for perhaps half a mile, but it was worth every sodden step. Port Sunlight was lovely, a proper little garden community, even cheerier in aspect than the huddled stone cottages of Saltaire. This had open green spaces and a pub and pretty little houses half hidden behind drifts of foliage. There wasn't a soul about and nothing seemed to be open—neither the shops nor the pub nor the heritage center nor the Lady Lever Art Gallery, all of which was a bit of a pisser after the effort I'd taken to get there—but I made the best of things by having a long slog around the rainy streets. I was surprised to see a factory still there, still churning out soap as far as I could tell, and then I realized that I had exhausted all that Port Sunlight had to offer on a rainy Saturday out of season, so I trudged back to the bus stop where I had so recently alighted and waited an hour and a quarter in a driving rain for a bus onward to Hooton, which was even less fun than it sounds.

Hooton offered the world not only a mildly ridiculous name, but the dumpiest British Rail station I ever hope to sneeze in. The shacklike platform waiting rooms were dripping wet, which didn't matter a great deal as I was soaked already. With six others, I waited a small eternity for a train to Chester, where I changed to another for Llandudno.

The Llandudno train was gratifyingly empty, so I took a seat at a table for four, and contented myself with the thought that I would soon be in a nice hotel or guesthouse where I could have a hot bath followed by a generously apportioned dinner. I spent a little time watching the scenery, then pulled out my copy of *The Kingdom by the Sea* to see if Paul Theroux had said anything about the vicinity that I might steal or modify to my own purposes. As always, I was amazed to find that as he rattled along these very tracks he had been immersed in a lively conversation with his fellow passengers. How *does* he do it? Quite apart from the consideration that my carriage was nearly empty, I don't know how you strike up conversations with strangers in Britain. In America, of course, it's easy. You just offer a hand and say, "My name's Bryson. How much money did you make last year?" and the conversation never looks back from there.

But in England—or in this instance Wales—it's so hard, or at least it is for me. I've never had a train conversation that wasn't disastrous or at least regretted. Generally it turns out that the person whose companionship I've encouraged has a serious mental disorder that manifests itself in murmurings and prolonged helpless weeping, or is a sales rep for the Hoze-Blo Stucco Company who mistakes your polite attention for keenness and promises to drop by for an estimate the next time he's in the Dales, or who wants to tell you all about his surgery for rectal cancer and then makes you guess where he keeps his colostomy bag ("Give up? Look, it's here under my arm. Go on, have a squeeze") or is a recruiter for the Branch Davidians or any of ten thousand other things I would sooner be spared. Over a long period of time it gradually dawned on me that the sort of person who will talk to you on a train is almost by definition the sort of person you don't want to talk to on a train, so these days I mostly keep to myself and rely for conversational entertainment on books by more loquacious types like Jan Morris and Paul Theroux.

So there is a certain neat irony that as I was sitting there minding my own business some guy in a rustling anorak came by, spied the book, and cried, "Aha, that Thoreau chap!" I looked up to find him taking a perch on a seat opposite me. He looked to be in his early sixties, with a shock of white hair and festive, lushly overgrown eyebrows that rose in pinnacles, like the tips of whipped meringue. They looked as if somebody had been lifting him up by grabbing hold of them. "Doesn't know his trains, you know," he said.

"Sorry?" I answered warily.

"Thoreau." He nodded at my book. "Doesn't know his trains at all. Or if he does, he keeps it to himself." He laughed heartily at this and enjoyed it so much that he said it again, and then sat with his hands on his knees and smiling as if trying to remember the last time he and I had had this much fun together.

I gave an economical nod of acknowledgment for his quip and returned my attention to my book in a gesture that I hoped he would correctly interpret as an invitation to fuck off. Instead, he reached across and pulled the book down with an invasive finger—an action I find deeply annoying at the best of times. "Do you know that book of his—*Great Railway* whatsit? All across Asia. You know the one?"

I nodded.

"Do you know that in that book he goes from Lahore to Islamabad on the *Delhi Express* and never once mentions the make of engine?"

I could see that I was expected to comment, so I said, "No fooling?"

"Never mentioned it. Can you imagine that? What use is a railway book if you don't talk about the engines?"

"You like trains, then?" I said and immediately wished I hadn't. The next thing I knew the book was open on my lap and I was being regaled by the world's most boring man. I didn't actually much listen to what he said. I found myself riveted by his soaring eyebrows and by the discovery that he had an equally rich crop of nose hairs. He seemed to have bathed them in Miracle-Gro. He wasn't just a train spotter, but a train talker, a far more dangerous condition.

"Now *this* train," he was saying, "is a Metro-Cammel self-sealed unit built at the Swindon works, at a guess I'd say between July 1986 and August, or at the very latest September, of '88. At first I thought it couldn't be a Swindon '86–'88 because of the cross-stitching on the seatbacks, but then I noticed the dimpled rivets on the side panels, and I thought to myself, I thought, What we have here, Cyril my old son, is a hybrid. There aren't many certainties in this world but Metro-Cammel dimpled rivets never lie. So where's your home?"

It took me a moment to realize that I had been asked a question. "Uh, Skipton," I said, only half lying.

"You'll have Fibber McGee cross-cambers up there," he said or something similarly meaningless to me. "Now me, I live in Upton-upon-Severn—"

"The Severn bore," I said reflexively, employing the local name for a tidal wave on the River Severn, but meaning something quite other.

"That's right. Runs right past the house." He looked at me with a hint of annoyance, as if I were trying to distract him from his principal thesis. "Now down there we have Z-46 Whirlpool spin cycles with Abbott and Costello horizontal thrusters. You can always tell a Z-46 because they go *patoosh-patoosh* over seamed points rather than *katoink-katoink*. It's a dead giveaway every time. I bet you didn't know that."

I ended up feeling sorry for him. His wife had died two years before—suicide, I would guess—and he had devoted himself since then to traveling the rail lines of Britain, counting rivets, noting breastplate numbers, and doing whatever else it is these poor people do to pass the time until God takes them away to a merciful repose. I had recently read a newspaper article in which it was reported that a speaker at the British Psychological Society had described train spotting as a form of autism called Asperger's syndrome.

He got off at Prestatyn—something to do with a Faggots & Gravy twelve-ton blender tender that was rumored to be coming through in the morning—and I waved to him from the window as the train pulled out, then luxuriated in the sudden peace. I listened to the train rushing over the tracks—it sounded to me like it was saying *Asperger's syndrome Asperger's syndrome*—and passed the last forty minutes to Llandudno idly counting rivets.

chapter
21

From the train, north Wales looked like holiday hell—endless ranks of prison-camp trailer parks standing in fields in the middle of a lonely, windbeaten nowhere, on the wrong side of the railway line and a merciless dual carriageway, with views over a boundless estuary of moist sand dotted with treacherous-looking sinkholes and, far off, a distant smear of sea. It seemed an odd type of vacation option to me, the idea of sleeping in a tin box in a lonesome field miles from anywhere in a climate like Britain's and emerging each morning with hundreds of other people from identical tin boxes, crossing the railroad tracks and dual carriageway and hiking over a desert of sinkholes in order to dip your toes into a distant sea full of Liverpool turds. I can't put my finger on what exactly, but something about it didn't appeal to me.

Then suddenly the trailer parks thinned, the landscape around Colwyn Bay took on a blush of beauty and grandeur, the train made a sharp jag north, and minutes later we were in Llandudno.

It is truly a fine and handsome place, built on a generously proportioned bay and lined along its broad front with a huddle of prim but gracious nineteenth-century hotels that reminded me in the fading light of a lineup of Victorian nannies. Llandudno was purpose-built as a resort in the mid-1800s, and it cultivates a nice old-fashioned air. I don't suppose that Lewis Carroll, who famously strolled this front with little Alice Liddell in the 1860s, telling her captivating stories of white rabbits and hookah-smoking caterpillars and asking between times if he could borrow her knickers to wipe his fevered brow and possibly take a few innocuous snaps of her in the altogether, would notice a great deal of change today, except of course that the hotels are now lit with electricity and Alice would be—what?—140 years old and perhaps less of a distraction to a poor, perverted mathematician.

To my consternation, the town was packed with weekending pensioners. Buses from all over were parked along the side streets, every hotel I called at was full, and in every dining room I could see crowds—veritable oceans—of nodding white heads spooning soup and conversing happily. Goodness knows what had brought them to the Welsh seaside at this bleak time of year.

Farther on along the front there stood a clutch of guesthouses, large and virtually indistinguishable, and a few of them had vacancy signs perched in their windows. I had eight or ten to choose from, which always puts me in a mild fret because I have an unerring instinct for choosing badly. My wife can survey a row of guesthouses and instantly identify the one run by a white-haired widow with a kindly disposition and a fondness for children, snowy sheets, and sparkling bathroom porcelain, whereas I can generally count on choosing the one run by a guy with a grasping manner, a drooping fag, and the sort of cough that makes you wonder where he puts the phlegm. Such, I felt gloomily certain, would be the case tonight.

All the guesthouses had boards out front listing their many amenities—COLOUR TV, HOSPITALITY TRAYS, FULL CENTRAL HEATING, and the coyly euphemistic EN SUITE ALL ROOMS, meaning private bathrooms. One place offered satellite TV and a trouser press, and another boasted, in special jaunty italics, *CURRENT FIRE CERTIFI-*

CATE—something I had never thought to look for in a B&B. All this
only heightened my sense of unease and doom. How could I possibly
choose intelligently among such a welter of options? It was so much
easier in the days when the most you could hope for—the very
most—was a room with a private sink.

I selected a place that looked reasonable enough from the outside—its board promised a color TV and coffeemaking facilities,
about all I require these days for a lively Saturday night—but from
the moment I set foot in the door and drew in the mildewy aroma
of neglected plaster, I knew it was a bad choice. I was about to turn
and flee when the proprietor emerged from a back room and stayed
my retreat with an unenthusiastic "Yes?" A short conversation revealed that a single room with breakfast could be had for £19.50—
little short of a swindle. It was entirely out of the question that I
would stay the night in such a dismal place at such a larcenous price,
so I said, "That sounds fine," and signed in. Well, it's so hard to
say no.

My room was everything I expected it to be—cold and cheerless,
with laminated furniture, grubbily matted carpet, and those mysterious ceiling stains that bring to mind a neglected corpse in the room
above. Fingers of icy wind slipped through the single ill-fitting sash
window. I drew the curtains and was not surprised that they had to
be yanked violently before they would budge and came nowhere near
meeting in the middle. There was a tray of coffee things but the
cups were—let me be charitable—disgusting, and the spoon was
stuck to the tray. The bathroom, faintly illuminated by a distant light
activated by a length of string, had curling floor tiles and years of
accumulated muck packed into every corner and crevice. I peered
at the yellowy grouting around the bath and sink and realized what
the landlord did with his phlegm. A bath was out of the question,
so I threw some cold water on my face, dried it with a towel that
had the texture of shredded wheat, and gladly took my leave.

I had a long stroll along the promenade to boost my appetite and pass an hour. The air was still and sharp and there wasn't a soul about, though there were still lots of white heads in the hotel lounges and dining rooms, all bobbing merrily. Perhaps they were having a Parkinson's convention. I walked nearly the length of the Parade, enjoying the chill autumn air and the trim handsomeness of the setting: a soft glow of hotels to the left, an inky void of restless sea to my right, and a scattered twinkling of lights on the near and far headlands of Great and Little Ormes.

I couldn't help notice—it seemed so obvious now—that all the other hotels and guesthouses looked markedly superior to mine. Almost without exception they had names that bore homage to other places—Windermere, Stratford, Clovelly, Derby, St. Kilda, even Toronto—as if their owners feared that it would be too much of a shock to the system to remind visitors that they were in Wales. Only one place, with a sign that said GWELY A BRECWAST/BED AND BREAKFAST, gave any hint that I was, at least in a technical sense, abroad.

I dined simply at a small nondescript restaurant off Mostyn Street and afterward, feeling disinclined to return to my dingy room in a state of stark sobriety, went hunting for a pub. Llandudno had surprisingly few of these vital institutions. I walked for some time before I found one that looked even vaguely approachable. It was a typical town pub inside—maroon-velvety, stale smelling, smoky—and it was busy, mostly with young people. I took a seat at the bar, thinking I might be able to eavesdrop on my neighbors and receive more immediate attention when my glass was empty, but neither of these was to be. There was too much music and background noise to discern what my neighbors were saying and too much clamor for service at a spot near the cash register for the single harried server to notice an empty glass and a beggarly face up at my end.

So I sat and drank beer when I could get some and instead watched, as I often do in these circumstances, the interesting process by which customers, upon finishing a pint, would present the barman with an empty glass (still bearing a lining of clinging suds and a residue of golden dribble at the bottom), which would be carefully filled to slightly overflowing, so that the excess froth, charged with an invisible load of bacteria, spittle, and microfragments of loosened food, would run down the side of the glass and into a plastic slop tray, where it would be carefully—I might almost say *scientifically*—conveyed by means of a clear plastic tube back to a barrel in the cellar. There these tiny impurities would drift and float and mingle, like flaky poo in a goldfish bowl, awaiting summons back to someone else's glass. If I am to drink dilute dribble and mouth rinsings, then I do rather wish I could do it in a situation of comfort and cheer, seated in a Windsor chair by a blazing fire, but this appears to be an increasingly elusive dream. As sometimes also happens in these circumstances, I had a sudden urge not to drink any more beer, so instead I hauled myself from my barside perch and returned to my seafront lodgings for an early night.

In the morning, I emerged from the guesthouse into a world drained of color. The sky was low and heavy and the sea along the front vast, lifeless, and gray. As I walked along, rain began to fall, dimpling the water. By the time I reached the station it was coming down steadily. Llandudno Station is closed on Sundays—that the largest resort in Wales has no Sunday rail service is too preposterous and depressing to elaborate on—but there was a bus to Blaenau Ffestiniog from in front of the station at eleven. The bus stop had no bench or shelter, no place to get out of the rain. If you travel much by public transit in Britain these days you soon come to feel like a member of some unwanted sub class, like the handicapped or unemployed, and that everyone essentially wishes you would just go away. I felt a bit like that now—and I am rich and healthy and immensely good-looking. What must it be like to be permanently poor or disabled or otherwise unable to take a full and active part in the nation's headlong rush for the sunny slopes of Mt. Greedy?

It is remarkable to me how these matters have become so thoroughly inverted in the past twenty years. There used to be a kind of unspoken nobility about living in Britain. Just by existing, by going to work and paying your taxes, catching the occasional bus, and being a generally decent if unexceptional soul, you felt as if you were contributing in some small way to the maintenance of a noble enterprise—a generally compassionate and well-meaning society with health care for all, decent public transport, intelligent television, universal social welfare, and all the rest of it. I always felt rather proud to be part of that. But now, no matter what you do, you end up stung with guilt. Go for a ramble in the country and you are reminded that you are inexorably adding to congestion in the national parks and footpath erosion on fragile hills. Try to take a sleeper to the Scottish Highlands or a train on a branch line or a bus from Llandudno to Blaenau on a Sunday, and you begin to feel shifty and aberrant because you know that these services require vast and costly subsidization. Go for a drive in your car, look for work, seek a place to live, and all you are doing is taking up valuable space and time. And as for needing medical care—well, how thoughtless and selfish can you possibly be? ("We *can* treat your ingrown toenails, Mr. Smith, but it will of course mean taking a child off a life-support machine.")

I dread to think how much it cost the state-run Gwynedd Transport to convey me to Blaenau Ffestiniog on this wet Sunday morning since I was the only customer, apart from a young lady who joined us at Betws-y-Coed and left us soon after at the interestingly named Pont-y-Pant. I had been looking forward to the journey for the chance to see a little of Mount Snowdon and its environs, but the rain was soon falling so hard, and the bus windows were so beaded with dirty droplets, that I could see almost nothing—just blurry expanses of skeletal, rust-colored ferns interspersed at intervals with motionless, soaked, seriously discontented looking sheep. Rain pattered against the windows like thrown pebbles and the bus swayed alarmingly under gusts of wind. It was like being on a ship in rough seas. The bus lumbered with grinding reluctance up twisting mountain roads, its wipers flapping wildly, to a plateau in the clouds, and then embarked on a precipitate, seemingly out-of-control descent into Blaenau Ffestiniog through steep defiles covered with numberless slagheaps of broken, rain-shiny slate. This was once the heart of the Welsh slate-mining industry, and the scattered rejects and remnants, which covered virtually every inch of ground, gave the landscape an unearthly and eerie aspect like nothing else I had seen before in Britain. At the epicenter of this unearthliness squatted the village of Blaenau, itself a kind of slate slagheap, or so it seemed in the teeming rain.

The bus dropped me in the center of town near the terminus of the famous Blaenau Ffestiniog Railway, now a private line run by enthusiasts and that I hoped to take through the cloudy mountains to Porthmadog. The station platform was open, but all the doors to waiting rooms, toilets, and ticket halls were padlocked, and there was no one around. I had a look at the winter timetable hanging on the wall and discovered to my dismay that I had just missed—literally just missed—a train. Puzzled, I dragged my crumpled bus timetable from my pocket and discovered with further dismay that the bus was actually scheduled to arrive just in time to miss the one midday train out of Blaenau. Running a finger down the rail timetable, I learned that the next train would not be for another four hours. The next bus would follow that by minutes. How could that be possible and, more to the point, what on earth was I supposed to do with myself in this godforsaken, rain-sodden place for four hours? There was no possibility of staying on the platform. It was cold and the rain was falling at such a treacherous slant that there was no place to escape it even in the furthest corners.

Muttering uncharitable thoughts about Gwynedd Transport, the Blaenau Ffestiniog Railway company, the British climate, and my own mad folly, I set off through the little town. This being Wales and this being Sunday, there was nothing open and no life on the narrow streets. Nor, as far as I could see, were there any hotels or guesthouses. It occurred to me that perhaps the train wasn't running at all in this weather, in which case I would be truly stuck. I was soaked through, cold, and deeply, deeply gloomy. At the far end of town stood a little restaurant called Myfannwy's and by a miracle it was open. I hastened into its beckoning warmth, where I peeled off my sodden jacket and sweater and went with a headful of suddenly enlivened hair to a table by a radiator. I was the only customer. I ordered a coffee and a little something to eat and savored the warmth and dryness. Somewhere in the background Nat King Cole sang a perky tune. I watched the rain beat down on the road outside and told myself that one day this would be twenty years ago.

If I learned just one thing in Blaenau that day it was that no matter how hard you try, you cannot make a cup of coffee and a cheese omelet last four hours. I ate as slowly as I could and ordered a second cup of coffee, but after nearly an hour of delicate eating and sipping, it became obvious that I was either going to have to leave or pay rent, so I reluctantly gathered up my things. At the till, I explained my plight to the kindly couple who ran the place and they both made those sympathetic, oh-dear noises that kindly people make when confronted with someone else's crisis.

"He might go to the slate mine," suggested the woman to the man.

"Yes, he might go to the slate mine," agreed the man and turned to me. "You might go to the slate mine," he said to me as if thinking I might somehow have missed the foregoing exchange.

"Oh, and what's that exactly?" I said, trying not to sound too doubtful.

"The old mine. They do guided tours."

"It's very interesting," said his wife.

"Yes, it's very interesting," said the man. "Mind, it's a fair hike," he added.

"And it may not be open on a Sunday," said his wife. "Out of season," she explained.

"Of course, you could always take a cab up there if you don't fancy the walk in this weather," said the man.

I looked at him. A cab? Did he say "*a cab*"? This seemed too miraculous to be taken in. "You have a cab service in Blaenau?"

"Oh, yes," said the man as if this were one of Blaenau's more celebrated features. "Would you like me to order one to take you to the mine?"

"Well—" I sought for words; I didn't want to sound ungrateful when these people had been so kind, but on the other hand I found the prospect of an afternoon touring a slate mine in damp clothes about as appealing as a visit to the proctologist. "Do you think the cab would take me to Porthmadog?" I wasn't sure how far it was, and I dared not hope.

"Of course," said the man. So he called a cab for me and the next thing I knew I was departing to a volley of good wishes from the proprietors and stepping into a cab, feeling like a shipwreck victim being winched to unexpected safety. I cannot tell you with what joy I beheld the sight of Blaenau disappearing into the distance behind me.

The cab driver was a friendly young man and on the twenty-minute ride to Porthmadog he filled me in on much important economic and sociological data with regard to the Llyen Peninsula. The most striking news was that the peninsula was dry on Sundays. You couldn't get an alcoholic drink to save your life between Porthmadog and Aberdar. I didn't know such pockets of rectitude still existed in Britain, but I was so glad to be getting out of Blaenau that I didn't care.

Porthmadog, squatting beside the sea under a merciless rain, looked a gray and forgettable place, full of wet pebble dash and dark stone. Despite the rain, I examined the meager stock of local hotels with some care—I felt entitled to a spell of comfort and luxury after my night in a cheerless Llandudno guesthouse—and I chose an inn called the Royal Sportsman. My room was adequate and clean, if not exactly outstanding, and suited my purposes. I made a cup of coffee and, while the kettle boiled, changed into dry clothes, then sat on the edge of the bed with a coffee and a rich tea biscuit, and watched a Welsh-language soap opera called *Pobol Y Cwm* on television, which I enjoyed very much. I had no idea what was going on, of course, but I can say with some confidence that it had better acting, and certainly better production values, than any program ever made in, say, Sweden or Norway—or Australia, come to that. At least the walls didn't wobble when someone shut a door. It was an odd experience watching people who existed in a recognizably British milieu—they drank tea and wore Marks & Spencer cardigans—but talked in Martian. Occasionally, I was interested to note, they dropped in English words—"hi ya," "right then," "OK"—presumably because a Welsh equivalent didn't exist, and in one memorable encounter a character said something like *"Wlch ylch aargh ybsy cwm dirty weekend, look you,"* which I just loved. How sweetly endearing of the Welsh not to have their own term for an illicit bonk between Friday and Monday.

By the time I finished my coffee and returned to the streets, the rain had temporarily abated, but the streets were full of vast puddles where the drains were unable to cope with the volume of water. Correct me if I'm wrong, but you would think that if one nation ought by now to have mastered the science of drainage, Britain would be it. In any case, cars aquaplaned daringly through these temporary lakes and threw sheets of water over nearby houses and shops. Mindful of my experience with puddles in Weston, I proceeded up the High Street in a state of some caution.

I nosed around the tourist information center, where I picked up a leaflet that informed me that Porthmadog had been built in the early nineteenth century as a port for Blaenau slate by one Alexander Maddocks, and that by late in the century a thousand ships a year were entering the port to carry off 116,000 tons of Welsh stone. I had a look at the quayside, then followed a back lane through a harborside neighborhood of small boatyards and other marine businesses, and up one side of a residential hill and down the other until I found myself in the tranquil hamlet of Borth-y-Gest, a pretty village of brick villas on a small horseshoe bay with gorgeous views across to Harlech Point and Tremadog Bay beyond. In the middle of the village, overlooking the bay, was a sub–post office with a blue awning announcing on the dangling part SWEETS and ICES and nearby was an establishment called the Sea View Café. This place might have been lifted whole from *Adventures on the Island*. I was charmed at once.

I followed a grassy path out above the sea toward a headland. Even under low cloud, the views across the Glaslyn estuary and Snowdon range beyond were quite majestic. The wind was gusting, and down below the sea battered the rocks in an impressively tempestuous way, but the rain at least held off and the air was sweet and fresh in that way you get only when you are beside the sea. The light was failing and I was afraid of ending up joining the waves on the rocks far below, so I headed back into town. When I got there, I discovered that the few businesses that had been open were now shut. Only one small beacon of half-light loomed from the enclosing darkness. I went up to see what it was and was interested to find that it was the southern terminus and operational HQ for the famous Blaenau Ffestiniog Railway.

Interested to see the nerve center of this organization that had caused me so much distress and discomfort earlier, I went in. Though it was well after five, the station bookshop was still open and liberally sprinkled with silent browsers, so I went in and had a nose around. It was an extraordinary place, densely packed with shelves of books, magazines, and railway paraphernalia. The books all had titles like *Railways of the Wnion Valley and Mawddach Estuary* and *The Complete Encyclopaedia of Signal Boxes*. There was a multivolume series of books called *Trains in Trouble*, each consisting of page after page of photographs of derailments, crashes, and other catastrophes—a sort of train spotter's equivalent of a snuff movie, I suppose. For those seeking more animated thrills, there were scores of videos. I took down one at random, called *The Hunslet and Hundreds Steam Rally 1993*, which bore a bold label promising "50 Minutes of Steam Action!" Under that there was a sticker that said, "Warning: Contains explicit footage of a Sturrock 0-6-0 Heavy Class coupling with a GWR Hopper." Actually, I just made that last part up, but I did notice, with a kind of profound shock, that all the people around me were browsing with precisely the same sort of self-absorbed, quiet-breathing concentration that you would find in a porno parlor, and I suddenly wondered if there was an extra dimension to this train-spotting hobby that had never occurred to me.

According to a plaque on the wall in the ticket hall, the Blaenau Ffestiniog Railway was formed in 1832 and is the oldest still running in the world. I also learned from the plaque that the railway society has six thousand active members, a figure that staggers me from every possible direction. Though the last train of the day had finished its run some time ago, there was still a man in the ticket booth, so I went over and interrogated him quietly about the lack of coordination between the train and bus services in Blaenau. I don't know why, because I was charm itself, but he got distinctly huffy, as if I were being critical of his wife, and said in a petulant tone, "If Gwynedd Transport want people to catch the midday train from Blaenau, then they should have the buses set off earlier."

"But equally," I persisted, "you could have the train leave a few minutes later."

He looked at me as if I were being outrageously presumptuous, and said, "But why should we?"

And there, you see, you have everything that is wrong with these train-enthusiast types. They are irrational, argumentative, dangerously fussy, and often, as here, have an irritating little toothbrush moustache that makes you want to stick out two forked fingers and pop them in the eyes. Moreover, thanks to my journalistic sleuthing in the bookshop, I think we can safely say that there is a prima facie case to presume that they perform unnatural acts with steam videos. For their own good, and for the good of society, they should be taken away and interned behind barbed wire.

I thought about making a citizen's arrest there and then—"I detain you in the name of Her Majesty the Queen for the offense of being irritatingly intractable about timetables, and also for having an annoying and inadequate little moustache"—but I was feeling generous and let him go with a hard look and an implied warning that it would be a cold day in hell before I ventured anywhere near *his* railway again. I think he got the message.

chapter
22

in the morning, I walked to Porthmadog Station—not the Blae-nau Ffestiniog let's-play-at-trains one, but the real British Rail one. There were several people on the platform, all studiously avoiding each other's gazes and standing, I do believe, on the same spot on which they stood every morning. I am pretty certain of this because, as I was standing there minding my own business, a man in a suit arrived and looked at first surprised and then annoyed to find me occupying what was evidently his square yard of platform. He took a position a few feet away and regarded me with an expression not a million miles from hate. How easy it is sometimes, I thought, to make enemies in Britain. All you have to do is stand in the wrong spot or turn your car around in their driveways—this guy had NO TURNING written all over him—or inadvertently take their seats on a train, and they will quietly hate you to the grave. Eventually a two-carriage Sprinter train came in and we all shuffled aboard. Sprinters really are the most comfortless, utilitarian, deeply unlovely trains, with their hard-edged seats, their mystifyingly simultaneous hot and cold drafts, their harsh lighting, and, above all, their noxious interior design based on orange stripes and hopelessly jaunty chevrons. Why

would anyone think that train passengers would like to be surrounded by a lot of orange, particularly first thing in the morning?
I longed for one of those old-style trains that you found when I first
came to Britain, the ones that had no corridors but consisted of just
a series of self-contained compartments, each with a pair of lushly
padded facing banquette seats and a door at either end but no com-
munication with the neighboring compartments. There was always
a frisson of uncertainty and excitement as you boarded—rather like
on those television game shows where the contestants have to say, "I
think I'll try door number three, Barry"—because you never knew
what you would find on the other side. There was something pleas-
ingly intimate and random in sitting in such close proximity with
total strangers. You got to know things about them—their tastes in
reading, their capacity for dealing with tedium, whether they slept
with their mouths open—that perhaps not even their closest ac-
quaintances knew, and then their stops would arrive and they would
get off and you would never see them again.

And sometime there were surprises. I remember once I was on
one of these trains when one of the other passengers, a shy-looking
young man in a trenchcoat, startled everyone including, I think,
himself by being abruptly sick on the floor—it was during a flu
epidemic—and then had the gall to stumble from the train at the
next station, leaving three of us to ride on into the evening in silence,
with pinched faces and tucked-in toes and behaving, in that most
extraordinary British way, as if nothing had happened. On second
thought, perhaps it is just as well that we don't have those trains
anymore. But I'm still not happy with the orange chevrons.

We followed a coastal route past broad estuaries and craggy hills
beside the gray, flat expanse of Cardigan Bay. The towns along the
way all had names that sounded like a cat bringing up a hairball:
Llywyngwril, Morfa Mawddach, Llandecwyn, Dyffryn Ardudwy. At
Penrhyndeudraeth the train filled with children of all ages, all in
school uniforms. I expected shouting and smoking and things to be

flying about, but they were impeccably behaved, every last one of
them. They all departed at Harlech and the interior suddenly felt
empty and quiet—quiet enough that I could hear the couple behind
me conversing in Welsh, which pleased me. At Barmouth we crossed
another broad estuary, on a rickety-looking wooden causeway. I had
read somewhere that this causeway had been closed for some years
and that Barmouth had until recently been the end of the line. It
seemed a kind of miracle in these straitened times that British Rail
had found the funds and energy to repair the causeway and keep the
line open, but I bet that if I were to come back in ten years, this
trundling, half-forgotten line to Porthmadog will be in the hands of
enthusiasts like those of the Blaenau Ffestiniog Railway and that
some twit with a fussy little moustache will be telling me that I can't
make a connection at Shrewsbury because it doesn't suit the society's
timetable.

So I was pleased, three hours and 105 miles after setting off, to
make a connection at Shrewsbury while the chance was still there.
My intention was to turn north and resume my stately progress toward John o'Groats, but as I was making my way through the station,
I heard a platform announcement for a train to Ludlow, and impulsively I boarded it. For years I had heard that Ludlow was a
delightful spot, and it suddenly occurred to me that this might be
my last chance to see it. Thus it was that I found myself, some twenty
minutes later, alighting onto a lonely platform at Ludlow and making
my way up a long hill into the town.

Ludlow was indeed a charming and agreeable place on a hilltop
high above the River Teme. It appeared to have everything you could
want in a community—bookshops, a cinema, some appealing-
looking tearooms and bakeries, a couple of places that styled themselves "family butchers" (I always want to go in and say, "How much
to do mine?"), an old-fashioned Woolworth's, and the usual assortment of chemists, pubs, haberdashers, and the like, all neatly
arrayed and respectful of their surroundings. The Ludlow Civic So-

ciety had thoughtfully put up plaques on many of the buildings announcing who had once lived there. One such hung on the wall of the Angel, an old coaching inn on Broad Street now sadly—and I hoped only temporarily—boarded up. According to the plaque, the famous *Aurora* coach once covered the one hundred or so miles to London in just over twenty-seven hours, which just shows you how much we've progressed. Now British Rail could probably do it in half the time.

Nearby I chanced upon the headquarters of an organization called the Ludlow and District Cats Protection League, which intrigued me. Whatever, I wondered, did the people of Ludlow do to their cats that required the setting up of a special protective agency? Perhaps I'm coming at this from the wrong angle, but short of setting cats alight and actually throwing them at me, I can't think of what you would have to do to drive me to set up a charity to defend their interests. There is almost nothing, apart perhaps from a touching faith in the reliability of weather forecasts and the universal fondness for jokes involving the word *bottom,* that makes me feel more like an outsider in Britain than the nation's attitude to animals. Did you know that the National Society for the Protection of Children was formed sixty years *after* the founding of the Royal Society for the Protection of Animals, and as an offshoot of it? (That's right. The monarchy is happy to be associated with the protection of animals, but not apparently with the protection of children.) Did you know also that in 1994 Britain voted for a European Union directive requiring statutory rest periods for transported animals, but against similar statutory rest periods for factory workers?

But even against this curious background, it seemed extraordinary to me that there could be a whole, clearly well-funded office dedicated just to the safety and well-being of Ludlow and district cats. I was no less intrigued by the curiously specific limits of the society's self-imposed remit—the idea that it was interested only in the safety and well-being of Ludlow and district cats. What would happen, I wondered, if the members of the league found you teasing a cat just outside the district boundaries? Would they shrug resignedly and say, "Out of our jurisdiction"? Who can say? Certainly not I, because when I approached the office with a view to making inquiries, I found that it was shut, its members evidently—and I wish you to read nothing into this—out to lunch.

Which is where I decided to be. I went across the road to a pleasant little salad-bar restaurant called the Olive Branch, where I quickly made myself into a pariah by taking a table for four. The place was practically empty when I arrived, and as I was struggling with a knapsack and a tippy tray, I took the first empty table. But immediately after I sat down people poured in from all quarters, and for the rest of my brief lunch period I could feel eyes burrowing into me from patrons who turned from the till to find me occupying a space obviously not designed for a solitary diner, requiring them to take their trays to the unpopular MORE SEATING UPSTAIRS section, evidently a disagreeable option. As I sat there, trying to eat quickly and be obscure, a man from two tables away came and asked in a pointed tone if I was using one of the chairs, and took it without awaiting my reply. I finished my food and slunk from the place in shame.

I returned to the station and bought a ticket for the next train to Shrewsbury and Manchester Piccadilly. Because of a mechanical breakdown somewhere along the line, the train was forty minutes late arriving. It was packed and the passengers were testy. I found a seat by disturbing a tableful of people who gave up their space grudgingly and glared at me with disdain—more enemies! what a day I was having—and sat crammed into a tiny space in my overcoat in an overheated carriage with my knapsack on my lap. I had vague hopes of getting to Blackpool, but I couldn't move a muscle and so couldn't get at my rail timetable to see where I needed to change trains, so I just sat and trusted that I could catch an onward train at Manchester.

British Rail was having a bad day. We crept a mile or so out of the station, then sat for a long time for no evident reason. Eventually, a voice announced that because of faults farther up the line this train would terminate at Stockport, which elicited a general groan. Finally, after about twenty minutes, the train falteringly started forward and limped across the green countryside. At each station the voice apologized for the delay and announced anew that the train would terminate at Stockport. When at last we reached Stockport, ninety minutes late, I expected everyone to get off, but no one moved, so neither did I. Only one passenger, a Japanese fellow, dutifully disembarked, then watched in dismay as the train proceeded on, without explanation and without him, to Manchester.

At Manchester I discovered that I needed a train to Preston, so I had a look at a television screen, but these gave only the final destination and not the stations in between. So I went off and joined a queue of travelers asking a BR employee for directions to various places. It was unfortunate for him that there were no stations in Britain called Fuck Off because that was clearly what he wanted to tell people. He told me to go to Platform 13, so I set off for it, but the platforms ended at 11. So I went back to the guy and informed him that I couldn't find a Platform 13. It turned out that Platform 13 was up some secret stairs and over a footbridge. It appeared to be the platform for missing trains. There was a whole crowd of travelers standing there looking lost and doleful, like the people in that Monty Python milkman sketch. Eventually we were sent back to Platform 3. The train, when it arrived, was of course a two-carriage Sprinter. The usual seven hundred people squeezed on to it.

Thus it was, fourteen hours after setting off from Porthmadog that morning, that I arrived tired, disheveled, hungry, and full of woe, in Blackpool, a place that I didn't particularly want to be in anyway.

chapter

23

blackpool attracts more visitors every year than Greece and has more holiday beds than the whole of Portugal. It consumes more fish and chips per capita than anywhere else on the planet. (Of potatoes alone, it gets through forty acres' worth a day.) It has the largest concentration of roller coasters in Europe. It has the continent's second most popular tourist attraction, the forty-two-acre Pleasure Beach, whose 6.5 million annual visitors are exceeded in number only by those going to the Vatican. And on Friday and Saturday nights it has more public toilets than anywhere else in the world; elsewhere they call them doorways.

Whatever you may think of the place, it does what it does very well—or if not very well, at least very successfully. In the past twenty years, during a period in which the number of Britons taking traditional seaside holidays has declined by a fifth, Blackpool has increased its visitor numbers by 7 percent and built tourism into a £250 million-a-year industry—no small achievement when you consider the British climate, the fact that Blackpool is ugly, dirty, and a long way from anywhere, that its sea is an open toilet, and that its attractions are nearly all cheap, provincial, and dire.

I had come for the Illuminations, the famous (well, famous in Britain) open-air light shows the town puts on in the fall as a way of extending the tourist season. I had been hearing and reading about them for so long that I was genuinely keen to see them. So, after securing a room in a modest guesthouse on a back street, I hastened to the front in a sense of some expectation. Well, all I can say is that Blackpool's Illuminations are nothing if not splendid, and they are not splendid. There is, of course, always a danger of disappointment when you finally encounter something you have wanted to see for a long time, but in terms of letdown it would be hard to exceed Blackpool's light show. I thought there would be lasers sweeping the sky, strobe lights tattooing the clouds, and other gasp-making dazzlements. Instead there was just a rumbling procession of old trams decorated as rocket ships or Christmas crackers, and several miles of paltry Christmas-style decorations on lampposts. I suppose if you had never seen electricity in action, it would be pretty breathtaking, but I'm not even sure of that. It all just seemed tacky and inadequate on rather a grand scale, like Blackpool itself.

What was no less amazing than the meagerness of the Illuminations was the crowds of people who had come to witness the spectacle. Traffic along the front was bumper to bumper, with childish faces pressed to the windows of every creeping car, and there were masses of people ambling happily along the spacious promenade. At frequent intervals hawkers sold luminous necklaces and bracelets or other short-lived diversions, and were doing a roaring trade. I read somewhere once that half of all visitors to Blackpool have been there at least ten times. Goodness knows what they find in the place. I walked for a mile or so along the prom, and couldn't understand the appeal of it at all—and I, as you may have realized by now, am an enthusiast for tackiness. Perhaps I was just weary after my long journey from Porthmadog, but I couldn't work up any enthusiasm for it at all. I wandered through brightly lit arcades and peered into bingo halls, but the festive atmosphere that seemed to seize everyone failed to rub off on me. Eventually, feeling very tired and very foreign, I retired to a fish restaurant on a side street, where I had a plate of haddock, chips, and peas, and was looked at like I was some kind of London pansy when I asked for tartar sauce, and afterward took yet another early night.

In the morning, I got up early to give Blackpool another chance. I liked it considerably better by daylight. The promenade had some nice bits of cast iron and elaborate huts with onion domes selling nougat, candied rock, and other sticky things, which had escaped me in the darkness the night before, and the beach was vast and empty and unexpectedly agreeable. Blackpool's beach is seven miles long and the curious thing about it is that it doesn't officially exist. I am not making this up. In the late 1980s, when the European Community issued a directive about standards of ocean-borne sewage, it turned out that nearly every British seaside town failed to come anywhere near even the minimum compliance levels. Most of the bigger resorts like Blackpool went right off the edge of the turdometer, or whatever it is they measure these things with. This presented an obvious problem to Mrs. Thatcher's government, which was loath to spend money on British beaches when there were perfectly good beaches for wealthy people in Mustique and Barbados, so it drew up a policy under which it officially decreed—this is so bizarre I can hardly stand it, but I swear it is true—that Brighton, Blackpool, Scarborough, and many other leading resorts did not have, strictly speaking, beaches. Christ knows what it then termed these expanses of sand—intermediate sewage buffers, I suppose—but in any case it disposed of the problem without either solving it or costing the treasury a penny, which is of course the main thing, or, in the case of the present government, the only thing.

But enough of political satire! Let us away in haste to Morecambe, another resort up the Lancashire coast. I went there next, on a series of rattling Sprinters, partly to make poignant comparisons with Blackpool, but mostly because I like Morecambe. I'm not at all sure why, but I do.

Looking at it now, it is hard to believe that not so very long ago Morecambe rivaled Blackpool. In fact, starting in about 1880 and for many decades afterward, Morecambe was *the* northern English seaside resort. It had Britain's first seaside illuminations. It was the birthplace of bingo, lettered rock (that is, a stick of candy with the resort's name running through it; I don't know how they do it), and the traditional seaside ride known as the helter-skelter. During the celebrated Wakes Weeks, when whole northern factory towns went on holiday together (they called Morecambe "Bradford-by-Sea"), up to a hundred thousand visitors at a time flocked to its boarding-houses and hotels. At its peak it had two main-line railway stations, eight music halls, eight cinemas, an aquarium, a fun fair, a menagerie, a revolving tower, a boating garden, a Summer Pavilion, a Winter Gardens, the largest swimming pool in Britain, and two piers. One of these, the Central Pier, was one of the most beautiful and elaborate in Britain, with fabulous towers and domed roofs—an Arabian palace afloat on Morecambe Bay.

It had over a thousand boardinghouses catering for the masses, but also classier diversions for those with more extravagant ambitions. The Old Vic and Sadler's Wells, theater and opera companies respectively, spent whole seasons there. Edward Elgar conducted orchestras in the Winter Gardens and Nellie Melba sang. And it was the home of many hotels that were the equal of any in Europe, like the Grand and the Broadway, where in the early 1900s well-heeled patrons could choose among a dozen types of hydro bath, including "Needle, Brine, Foam, Plombiere and Scotch Douche."

I know all this because I had been reading a book called *Lost Resort: The Flow and Ebb of Morecambe,* by a local vicar named Roger K. Bingham, which was not only exceptionally well written (and it is quite extraordinary, let me say here, how much good local history there is in Britain) but full of photos of Morecambe from its heyday that were just staggeringly at variance with the scene I found before me now as I stepped from the train, one of only three passengers to alight, and ambled out into the sunny but breathtakingly faded charms of Marine Road.

It is hard to say when or why Morecambe's decline started. It remained popular well into the 1950s—as late as 1956 it had thirteen hundred hotels and guesthouses, ten times the number it has today—but its descent from greatness had begun long before. The famous Central Pier was extensively damaged by a fire in the 1930s, then gradually sank into an embarrassing wreck. By 1990 the town officials had removed it from the local map—simply pretended that the derelict heap projecting into the sea, dominating the front, wasn't there. The West End Pier, meanwhile, was swept away by a winter storm in 1974. The magnificent Alhambra music hall burned down in 1970 and the Royalty Theatre was razed to make way for a shopping center two years later.

By the early 1970s Morecambe's decline was precipitate. One by one the local landmarks vanished—the venerable swimming pool in 1978, the Winter Gardens in 1982, the truly sumptuous Grand Hotel in 1989—as people abandoned Morecambe for Blackpool and the Spanish *costas.* By the late 1980s, according to Bingham, you could buy a large, once-proud seafront hotel like the five-story Grosvenor for the same price as a semidetached house in London.

Today Morecambe's tattered front consists largely of little-used bingo halls and amusement arcades, everything-for-£1 shops, and the kind of cut-price boutiques where the clothes are so cheap and undesirable that they can be safely put outside on racks and left unattended. Many of the shops are empty, and most of the rest look temporary. It has become once again—irony of ironies—Bradford-by-Sea. So low had Morecambe's fortunes sunk that the previous summer the town couldn't even find someone to take on the deck chair concession. When a seaside resort can't find anyone willing to set up deck chairs, you know that business is bad.

And yet it has its charms. Its seafront promenade is handsome and well maintained and its vast bay (174 square miles, if you're taking notes) is easily one of the most beautiful in the world, with unforgettable views across to the green-and-blue hills of the Lake District.

Today almost all that remains of Morecambe's golden age is the Midland Hotel, a jaunty, cheery, radiant white art deco edifice with a sweeping, streamlined frontage erected on the seafront in 1933. Concrete structures were all the rage in 1933, but concrete apparently was beyond the capabilities of local builders, so it was built of Accrington brick and rendered in plaster so that it *looked* like concrete, which I find very endearing. Today the hotel is gently crumbling around the edges and streaked here and there with rust stains. Most of the original interior fittings were lost during periodic and careless refurbishments over the years, and several large Eric Gill statues that once graced the entranceway and public rooms simply disappeared, but it still has an imperishable 1930s charm.

I couldn't begin to guess where the Midland gets its custom these days. There didn't seem to be any custom of any sort when I went in now and had a cup of coffee in an empty sun lounge overlooking the bay. One of the small endearments of modern Morecambe is that wherever you go they are grateful for your patronage. I enjoyed superb service and a nice view, two things wholly unobtainable in Blackpool as far as I can tell. As I was departing, my eye was caught by a large white plaster statue by Gill of a mermaid in the empty dining room. I went and had a look at it and found that the tail of the statue, which I presume is worth a small fortune, was held on with a mass of Scotch tape. It seemed a not inappropriate symbol for the town.

I took a room in a modest seafront guesthouse, where I was received with a kind of startled gratitude, as if the owners had forgotten that all those empty rooms upstairs were to let, and spent the afternoon strolling around with Roger Bingham's book looking at the sights, trying to imagine the town in its prime, and occasionally bestowing my patronage on pathetically grateful tearooms.

It was a mild day and there were a number of people, mostly elderly, walking along the promenade, but little sign of anyone spending money. With nothing better to do, I took a long walk along the front nearly to the nearby village of Carnforth, and then walked back along the sands since the tide was out. The surprising thing about Morecambe, it occurred to me, isn't that it declined, but that it ever prospered. It would be hard to imagine a less likely place for a resort. Its beaches consist of horrible gooey mud and its vast bay spends large periods almost totally devoid of water thanks to the vagaries of the tides. You can walk six miles across the bay to Cumbria when the tide is out, but they say it is dangerous to do so without a guide, or sand pilot, as they are known hereabouts. I once spent some time with one of these pilots, who told alarming stories about coaches and horses that tried to cross the bay at low tide and disappeared into the treacherous quicksands, never to be seen again. Even now people sometimes stroll out too far and then get cut off when the tide comes in, about as disagreeable way to finish an afternoon as I could imagine.

Feeling daring, I walked a few hundred yards out onto the sands now, studying worm casts and the interesting corrugated imprints left by the receding waters, and keeping an eye out for quicksand—which isn't really sand at all, but silty mud and it really does suck you up if you blunder into it. The tides at Morecambe don't rush in and out, as you might expect, but creep in from various angles, which is all the more menacing since you can easily find, if you are the sort to get lost in thought, that you are suddenly stranded on a large but insidiously shrinking sandbar in the middle of a great wet bay, so I kept an eye out and didn't venture too far.

It was quite wonderful—certainly better than anything Blackpool could offer. It is an odd sensation to be walking about on a seabed and to think that anytime now this could be under thirty feet of water. I especially liked the solitude. One of the hardest things to adjust to, if you come from a large country, is that you are seldom really alone out of doors in England—that there is scarcely an open space where you could, say, safely stand and have a pee without fear of appearing in some birdwatcher's binoculars or having some matronly ambler bound around the nearest bend—so the sense of aloneness on the open sands was rather luxurious.

From a few hundred yards out, Morecambe looked quite fetching in the late-afternoon sun, and even up close, as I left the sands and clambered up some mossy concrete steps to the prom, it didn't look half bad away from the desolate bingo parlors and novelty shops. The line of guesthouses along the eastern length of Marine Road looked neat and trim and sweetly hopeful. I felt sorry for the owners who had invested their hopes and found themselves now in a dying resort. The decline that began in the fifties and accelerated out of control in the seventies must have seemed bewildering and inexplicable to these poor people as they watched Blackpool, just twenty miles to the south, going from strength to strength.

Foolishly, but not unnaturally, Morecambe responded by trying to compete with Blackpool. It built an expensive dolphinarium and a new outdoor swimming pool, and recently there had been some half-assed plan to open an amusement park modeled on a TV character named Mr. Blobby. But really its charm, and certainly its hope, lies in being *not* Blackpool. That is what I like about it—that it is quiet and friendly and well behaved, that there is plenty of room in the pubs and cafés, that you aren't bowled off the curb by swaggering youths and don't go sidewalk surfing on abandoned plastic chip platters and vomit slicks.

One day, I would like to think, English people will rediscover the charms of a quiet break at the seaside, the simple pleasures of strolling along a well-kept front, leaning on railings, drinking in views, sitting in a café with a book, just pottering about. Then perhaps Morecambe can thrive again. How nice it would be if the government actually erected a policy to this end, took steps to restore fading places like Morecambe—rebuilt the pier to its original plans, gave a grant for a new Winter Gardens, insisted on the restoration of seafront buildings, perhaps moved a government department to the town to give it a bit of year-round life.

With a little priming and a thoughtful long-term plan, I am sure you could attract the sort of people who would want to open bookshops, little restaurants, antique shops, galleries, maybe even *tapas* bars and the odd boutique hotel. Well, why not? Morecambe could become a little northern English equivalent of Sausalito or St. Ives. People could come for weekends to eat in stylish new seafront restaurants overlooking the bay and perhaps take in a play or concert at the Winter Gardens. Yuppie hill walkers could spend the night there and thus ease pressure on the nearby Lake District. It would all make eminent sense. But of course it will never happen.

chapter
24

I have a small, tattered clipping that I sometimes carry with me and pull out for purposes of private amusement. It's a weather forecast from the *Western Daily Mail* and it says, in toto, "Outlook: Dry and warm, but cooler with some rain."

There you have in a single pithy sentence the English weather captured to perfection: dry but rainy with some warm/cool spells. The *Western Daily Mail* could run that forecast every day—for all I know, it may—and scarcely ever be wrong.

To an outsider the most striking thing about the English weather is that there isn't very much of it. All those phenomena that elsewhere give nature an edge of excitement, unpredictability, and danger—tornadoes, monsoons, raging blizzards, run-for-your-life hailstorms—are almost wholly unknown in the British Isles, and this is just fine by me. I like wearing the same type of clothing every day of the year. I appreciate not needing air conditioning or screens on the windows to keep out the kinds of insects and flying animals that drain your blood or feast on your extremities while you are sleeping. I like knowing that so long as I do not go walking up Mount Snowdon in carpet slippers in February, I will almost certainly never perish from the elements in this soft and gentle country.

I mention this because as I sat eating my breakfast in the dining
room of the Old England Hotel in Bowness-on-Windermere, two
days after leaving Morecambe, I was reading an article in *The Times*
about an unseasonable snowstorm—a "blizzard," *The Times* called
it—that had "gripped" parts of East Anglia. According to the *Times*
report, the storm had covered parts of the region with "more than
two inches of snow" and created "drifts up to six inches high." In
response to this, I did something I had never done before: I pulled
out my notebook and drafted a letter to the editor in which I pointed
out, in a kindly, helpful way, that two inches of snow cannot possibly
constitute a blizzard and that six inches of snow is not a drift. A
blizzard, I explained, is when you can't get your front door open.
Drifts are things that make you lose your car till spring. Cold weather
is when you leave part of your flesh on doorknobs, mailbox handles,
and other metal objects. And then I crumpled the letter up because
I realized I was in serious danger of turning into one of the Colonel
Blimp types who sat around me in considerable numbers, eating
cornflakes or porridge with their blimpish wives, and without whom
hotels like the Old England would not be able to survive.

I was in Bowness because I had two days to kill until I was to be
joined by two friends from London with whom I was going to spend
the weekend walking. I was looking forward to that very much, but
rather less to the prospect of another long, purposeless day in Bowness, pottering about trying to fill the empty hours till tea. There
are, I find, only so many windowsful of tea towels, Peter Rabbit
dinnerware, and patterned sweaters I can look at before my interest
in shopping palls, and I wasn't at all sure that I could face another
day of poking about in this most challenging of resorts.

I had come to Bowness more or less by default since it is the only
place in the Lake District with a rail station. Besides, the idea of
spending a couple of quiet days beside the tranquil beauty of Lake
Windermere, and wallowing in the plump comforts of a gracious (if

costly) old hotel, had seemed distinctly appealing from the vantage of Morecambe Bay. But now, with one day down and another to go, I was beginning to feel stranded and fidgety, like someone at the end of a long period of convalescence. At least, I reflected optimistically, the unseasonable two inches of snow that had brutally lashed East Anglia, causing chaos on the roads and forcing people to battle their way through perilous snowdrifts, some of them as high as their ankletops, had mercifully passed this corner of England by. Here the elements were benign and the world outside the dining room window sparkled weakly under a pale wintry sun.

I decided to take the lake steamer to Ambleside. This would not only kill an hour and let me see the lake, but deliver me to a place rather more like a real town and less like a misplaced seaside resort than Bowness. In Bowness, I had noted the day before, there are no fewer than eighteen shops where you can buy sweaters and tea towels and at least twelve selling Peter Rabbit stuff, but just one butcher's. Ambleside, on the other hand, though hardly unfamiliar with the manifold possibilities for enrichment presented by hordes of passing tourists, did at least have an excellent bookshop and any number of outdoor shops, which I find hugely if inexplicably diverting—I can spend hours looking at knapsacks, knee socks, compasses, and survival rations, then go to another store and look at precisely the same things all over again. So it was with a certain animated keenness that I made my way to the steamer pier shortly after breakfast. Alas, there I discovered that the steamers run only in the summer months, which seemed shortsighted on this mild morning because even now Bowness gently teemed with trippers. So I was forced, as a fallback, to pick my way through the scattered, shuffling throngs to the little ferry that shunts back and forth between Bowness and the old ferry house on the opposite shore, three or four hundred yards away. It may not travel far, but at least it runs all year.

A modest lineup of cars was patiently idling on the ferry approach, and there were eight or ten walkers as well, all with fleece-lined jackets, rucksacks, and sturdy boots. One fellow was even wearing shorts—always a sign of advanced dementia in a British walker. Walking—walking, that is, in the British sense—was something that I had come to only relatively recently. I was not yet at the point where I would wear shorts with many pockets, but I had taken to tucking my pants into my socks (though I have yet to find anyone who can explain to me what benefits this actually confers, other than making one look serious and committed).

I remember, when I first came to Britain, wandering into a bookstore and being surprised to find a whole section dedicated to "Walking Guides." This struck me as faintly bizarre and comical— where I came from, people did not as a rule require written instructions to achieve locomotion—but then gradually I learned that there are in fact two kinds of walking in Britain, namely the everyday kind that gets you to the pub and, all being well, back home again, and the more earnest type that involves stout boots, Ordnance Survey maps in plastic pouches, knapsacks with sandwiches and flasks of tea, and, in its terminal phase, the wearing of khaki shorts in inappropriate weather.

For years, I watched these walker types toiling up immense, cloud-hidden hills in wet and savage weather and presumed they were genuinely insane. And then my old friend John Price, who had grown up in the North of England and spent his youth doing foolish things on sheer-faced crags in the Lakes, encouraged me to join him and a couple of his friends for an amble—that was the word he used—up Haystacks one weekend. I think it was the combination of those two untaxing-sounding words *amble* and *Haystacks*, and the promise of lots of drink afterward, that lulled me from my natural caution.

"Are you sure it's not too hard?" I asked.

"Nah, just an amble," John insisted.

Well, of course, it was anything but an amble. We clambered for hours up vast, perpendicular slopes, over clattering scree and lumpy tussocks of grass, around towering citadels of rock, and emerged at length into a cold, bleak, lofty netherworld so remote and forbidding that even the sheep were startled to see us. Beyond it lay even greater and remoter summits that had been quite invisible from the ribbon of black highway thousands of feet below. John and his chums toyed with my will to live in the cruelest possible way; seeing me falling behind, they would lounge around on boulders, smoking and chatting and resting, but the instant I caught up with them with a view to falling at their feet, they would bound up refreshed and, with a few encouraging words, set off anew with large, manly strides, so that I had to stumble after and never got a rest. I gasped and ached and sputtered, and realized that I had never done anything remotely this unnatural before and vowed never to attempt such folly again.

And then, just as I was about to lie down and call for a stretcher, we crested a final rise and found ourselves abruptly, magically, on top of the earth, on a platform in the sky, amid an ocean of swelling summits. I had never seen anything half so beautiful before. "Bugger me," I said in a moment of special eloquence and realized I was hooked. Ever since then I had come back whenever they would have me, never complained, and even started tucking my trousers into my socks. I couldn't wait for the morrow.

The ferry docked and I shuffled on board with the others. Windermere looked serene and exceedingly fetching in the gentle sunshine. Unusually there wasn't a single pleasure boat disturbing its glassy calmness. To say that Windermere is popular with boaters is to flirt recklessly with understatement. Some fourteen thousand powerboats—let me repeat that number: *fourteen thousand*—are registered to use the lake. On a busy summer's day, as many as sixteen hundred powerboats may be out on the water at any one time, a good many of them zipping along at up to forty miles an hour with waterskiers in tow. This is in addition to all the thousands of other types of floating objects that may be out on the water and don't need to register—dinghies, sailboats, sailboards, canoes, kayaks, inflatables, various excursion steamers, and the old chugging ferry I was on now—all of them searching for a boat-sized piece of water. It is all but impossible to stand on a lakeside bank on an August Sunday watching waterskiers slicing through packed shoals of dinghies and other floating detritus and not end up with your mouth open and your hands on your head.

I had spent some weeks in the Lakes a year or so before, working on an assignment for *National Geographic,* and one of the passing thrills of the experience was being taken out for a morning on the lake on a national park launch. To show me just how dangerous it could be to let high-powered craft race around in this kind of crowded environment, the park warden pootled the launch out into the middle of the lake, told me to hang on—I smiled at this: Listen, I do ninety on the motorways—then opened the throttle. Well, let me say this: Forty miles an hour in a boat is nothing like forty miles an hour on a road. We took off with a velocity that snapped me back in the seat and had me clutching on for dear life with both hands, and bounced across the water like a flat stone fired from a gun. I have seldom been so petrified. Even on a quiet morning out of season, Windermere was clogged with impediments. We shot between little islands and skittered sideways past headlands that loomed up with alarming suddenness, like frights on a fun fair ride. Imagine sharing this space with sixteen hundred other similarly dashing craft, most of them in the control of some potbellied urban halfwit with next to no experience of powered craft, plus all the floating jetsam of rowboats, kayaks, and the like, and it is a wonder that there aren't bodies all over the water.

The experience taught me two things—first, that vomit vaporizes at forty miles an hour in an open boat, and second, that Windermere is an exceedingly compact body of water. And here we come to the point of all this. Britain is, for all its topographical diversity and timeless majesty, an exceedingly small-scale place. There isn't a single natural feature in the country that ranks anywhere in world terms—no Alp-like mountains, no stunning gorges, not even a single great river. The British may think of the Thames as a substantial artery, but in world terms it is little more than an ambitious stream. Put it down in North America and it wouldn't even make the top 100. It would come in at number 108, to be precise, outclassed by such relative obscurities as the Skunk, the Kuskokwim, and even the little Milk. At ten miles long by half a mile wide, Windermere may have pride of place among English lakes, but for each twelve square inches of Windermere's surface, Lake Superior offers over three quarters of a square *mile* of water. There is in Iowa a body of water called Dan Green Slough, which even most Iowans have never heard of, but even it is bigger than Windermere. The Lake District itself takes up less space than the Twin Cities.

I think that's just wonderful—not that these features are modest in their dimensions but that they are modest, in the middle of a densely crowded island, and still wonderful. What an achievement that is. Did you know that to achieve the same density of population in America as in England you would have to uproot the entire populations of Illinois, Pennsylvania, Massachusetts, Minnesota, Michigan, Colorado, and Texas and pack them all into Iowa? Twenty million people live within a day trip of the Lake District and 12 million, roughly a quarter of England's population, come to the Lakes each year. No wonder on some summer weekends it can take two hours to get through Ambleside, and that you could almost walk across Windermere by stepping from boat to boat.

Yet even at its worst, the Lake District remains more charming and less rapaciously commercialized than many famed beauty spots in more spacious countries. And away from the crowds—away from Bowness, Hawkshead, and Keswick, with their tea towels, tearooms, teapots, and endless Beatrix Potter paraphernalia—it retains pockets of sheer perfection, as I found now when the ferry nosed into its landing and we tumbled off. For a minute the landing area was a hive of activity as one group of cars got off, another got on, and the eight or ten foot-passengers fanned off in various directions. And then all was abrupt and blissful silence. I followed a pretty, wooded road around the lake's edge, then turned inland and headed for Near Sawrey.

Near Sawrey is the home of Hilltop, the cottage where the inescapable Potter drew her sweet little watercolors and contrived her soppy stories. For most of the year, it is overrun with tourists from far and wide. Much of the village is given over to large but discreetly screened parking lots, and the tearoom even has a sign out front advertising its fare in Japanese, egads. But the approaches to the village—actually, it's just a hamlet (and do you know the difference, by the way, between *village* and *hamlet*? It's quite simple, really: One is a place where people live and the other is a play by Shakespeare)—from every direction are exquisite and unspoiled: a meadowy green Eden laced with wandering slate walls, woodland clumps, and low, white farms against a backdrop of blue, beckoning hills. Even Near Sawrey itself has a beguiling, well-concocted charm that belies the overwhelming hordes who come to shuffle through its most famous residence. Such indeed is Hilltop's alarming popularity that the National Trust doesn't even advertise it anymore. Yet still the visitors come. Two buses were disgorging chattering white-haired occupants when I arrived and the main parking lot was already nearly full.

I had been to Hilltop the year before, so I wandered past it and up a little-known track to a tarn, or wild pond, on some high ground behind it. Old Mrs. Potter used to come up to this tarn regularly to thrash about on it in a rowboat—whether for healthful exercise or as a kind of flagellation I don't know—but it was very lovely and seemingly quite forgotten. I had the distinct feeling that I was the first visitor to venture up there for years. Across the way, a farmer was repairing a stretch of fallen wall and I stood and watched him for a while from a discreet distance, because if there is one thing nearly as soothing to the spirit as repairing a drystone wall (and I speak here with proud experience) it is watching someone else doing

it. What a wonderful feature of the landscape these old walls are. I
remember once, not long after we moved to the North, going for a
stroll and happening on a neighboring farmer rebuilding a wall on
a remote hill. It was a rotten January day full of drifting fog and rain,
and the thing is, there wasn't any discernible point in his rebuilding
the wall. He owned the fields on either side of it, and in any case
there was a gate that stood permanently open between the two, so it
wasn't as if the wall had any real function. I stood and watched him
awhile and finally asked him why he was standing out in a cold rain
rebuilding the wall. He looked at me with that special pained look
Yorkshire farmers save for recent arrivals from the South and other
morons and said, "Because it's fallen *down*, of course." From this I
learned, first of all, never to ask a Yorkshire farmer any question that
can't be answered with "pint of Tetley's if you don't mind," and
that one of the primary reasons so much of the British landscape is
so unutterably lovely and timeless is that most farmers, for whatever
reason, take the trouble to keep it that way.

It certainly has very little to do with money. The government
spends less per person per year on national parks than the cost of a
single daily newspaper; it gives more money to the Royal Opera
House at Covent Garden than it does to all ten national parks together. The annual budget for the Lake District National Park, an
area widely perceived as the most beautiful and environmentally sensitive in England, is £2.4 million, about the same as for a single
large London high school. From that sum the park authorities must
manage the park, run ten information centers, pay 127 full-time staff
and 40 part-time staff in summer, replace and maintain equipment
and vehicles, fund improvements to the landscape, implement educational programs, *and* act as the local planning authority—that is,
assess and rule on all planned developments within the park bounds.
That the Lakes are so generally wonderful, so scrupulously maintained, so seldom troubling to mind and spirit, is a ringing testament
to the people who work in them, the people who live in them, and

the people who use them. I recently read that more than half of Britons surveyed couldn't think of a single thing about their country to be proud of. Well, they can be proud of that.

I spent a happy few hours tramping about through the sumptuous and easygoing landscape between Windermere and Coniston Water, and would gladly have stayed longer except that it began to rain—a steady, dispiriting rain that I foolishly had not allowed for in regard to my walking apparel—and anyway I was growing hungry, so I made my way back to the ferry and Bowness.

Thus it was that I found myself, an hour or so and an overpriced tuna sandwich later, back in the Old England, staring out at the wet lake through a large window and feeling bored and listless in that special way peculiar to wet afternoons spent in plush surroundings. To pass a half hour, I went to the residents' lounge to see if I couldn't scare up a pot of coffee. The room was casually strewn with aging colonels and their wives, sitting amid carelessly folded *Daily Telegraph*s. The colonels were all shortish, round men with tweedy jackets, well-slicked silvery hair, an outwardly gruff manner that concealed within a heart of flint, and, when they walked, a rakish limp. Their wives, lavishly rouged and powdered, looked as if they had just come from a coffin fitting. I felt seriously out of my element, and was surprised to find one of them—a white-haired lady who appeared to have applied her lipstick during an earth tremor—addressing me in a friendly, conversational manner. It always takes me a moment to remember in these circumstances that I am now a reasonably respectable-looking middle-aged man and not a gangly young rube straight off the banana boat.

We began, in the customary fashion, with a few words about the beastliness of the weather, but when the woman discovered I was an American she went off on some elaborate tangent about a trip she and Arthur—Arthur, I gathered, being the shyly smiling clot beside her—had recently taken to visit friends in California, and this gradually turned into what appeared to be a well-worn rant about the shortcomings of Americans. I never understand what people are thinking when they do this. Do they think I'll appreciate their candor, or have they simply forgotten that I am one of the species myself? The same thing often happens when people talk about immigration in front of me.

"They're so forward, don't you think?" the lady sniffed and took a sip of tea. "You've only to chat to a stranger for five minutes and they think you've become *friends*. I had some man in Encino—a retired postal worker or some such thing—asking my address and promising to call *round* next time he's in England. Can you imagine it? I'd never met the man in my life." She took a sip of tea and grew momentarily thoughtful. "He had the most extraordinary belt buckle. All silver and little gemstones."

"It's the food that gets me," said her husband, raising himself a little to embark on a soliloquy, but it quickly became evident that he was one of those men who never get to say anything beyond the first sentence of a story.

"Oh yes, the food!" cried his wife, seizing the point. "They have the most *extraordinary* attitude to food."

"What, because they like it tasty?" I inquired with a thin smile.

"No, my dear, the *portions*. The portions in America are positively *obscene*."

"I had a steak one time—" the man began with a little chortle.

"And the things they do to the language! They simply cannot speak the Queen's English."

Now wait a minute. Say what you will about American portions and friendly guys with colorful belt buckles, but mind what you say about American English. "Why should they speak the Queen's English?" I asked a trifle frostily. "She's not their queen, after all."

"But the words they use. And their accents. What's that word you so dislike, Arthur?"

"*Normalcy*," said Arthur. "I met this one fellow—"

"But *normalcy* isn't an Americanism," I said. "It was coined in Britain."

"Oh, I don't think so, dear," said the woman with the certainty of stupidity, and bestowed a condescending smile. "No, I'm sure not."

"In 1722 . . ." I said, lying through my teeth. Well, I was right in the fundamentals—*normalcy* is an Anglicism. I just couldn't recall the details. ". . . Daniel Defoe in *Moll Flanders* . . ." I added in a flash of inspiration. One of the things you get used to hearing when you are an American living in Britain is that America will be the death of English. It is a sentiment expressed to me surprisingly often, usually at dinner parties, usually by someone who has had a little too much to drink, but sometimes by a semidemented, over-powdered old crone like this one. There comes a time when you lose patience with this sort of thing. So I told her—I told them both, for her husband looked as if he was about to utter another fraction of thought—that whether they appreciated it or not, British speech has been enlivened beyond measure by words created in America, words that they could not do without, and that one of these words was *moron*. I showed them my teeth, drained my coffee, and with a touch of hauteur excused myself. Then I went off to write another letter to the editor of *The Times*.

By eleven the next morning, when John Price and a very nice fellow named David Partridge rolled up at the hotel in Price's car, I was waiting for them by the door. I forbade them a coffee stop in Bowness on the grounds that I could stand it no longer, and made them drive to the hotel near Bassenthwaite where Price had booked us rooms. There we dumped our bags, had a coffee, acquired three packed lunches from the kitchen, accoutred ourselves in stylish hik-

ing apparel, and set off for the valley of Great Langdale. Now this
was more like it.

Despite threatening weather and the lateness of the year, the parking lots and roadsides along the valley were crowded with cars.
Everywhere people delved for equipment in trunks or sat with car
doors open pulling on warm socks and stout boots. We dressed our
feet, then fell in with a straggly army of walkers, all with knapsacks
and knee-high woolly socks, and set off for a long, grassy humpback
hill called the Band. We were headed for the fabled summit of Bow
Fell, at 2,960 feet the sixth highest of the Lakeland hills. Walkers
ahead of us formed well-spaced dots of slow-moving color leading
to a majestically remote summit, lost in cloud. As ever, I was quietly
astounded to find that so many people had been seized with the
notion that struggling up a mountainside on a damp Saturday on
the winter end of October was fun.

We climbed through the grassy lower slopes into ever bleaker terrain, picking our way over boulders and scree, until we were up
among the ragged shreds of cloud that hung above the valley floor
perhaps a thousand feet below. The views were sensational—the
jagged peaks of the Langdale Pikes rising opposite and crowding
against the narrow and gratifyingly remote valley, laced with tiny,
stone-walled fields, and off to the west a swelling sea of hefty brown
hills disappearing in mist and low cloud.

As we pressed on, the weather severely worsened. The air filled
with swirling particles of ice that hit the skin like razor nicks. By the
time we neared Three Tarns, the weather was truly menacing, with
thick fog joining the jagged sleet. Ferocious gusts of wind buffeted
the hillside and reduced our progress to a creeping plod. The fog
cut visibility to a few yards. Once or twice we briefly lost the path,
which alarmed me as I didn't particularly want to die up here—
apart from anything else, I still had 14,700 unspent frequent-flier
miles. Out of the murk ahead of us emerged what looked discon-
certingly like an orange snowman. It proved on closer inspection to

be a high-tech hiker's outfit. Somewhere inside it was a man.

"Bit fresh," the bundle offered understatedly.

John and David asked him if he'd come far.

"Just from Blea Tarn." Blea Tarn was ten miles away over taxing terrain.

"Bad over there?" John asked in what I had come to recognize was the abbreviated speech of walkers.

"Hands and knees job," said the man.

They nodded knowingly.

"Be like that here soon."

They nodded again.

"Well, best be off," announced the man as if he couldn't spend the whole day jabbering, and trundled off into the white soup. I watched him go, then turned to suggest that perhaps we should think about retreating to the valley, to a warm hostelry with hot food and cold beer, only to find Price and Partridge dematerializing into the mists thirty feet ahead of me.

"Hey, wait for me!" I croaked and scrambled after.

We made it to the top without incident. I counted thirty-three people there ahead of us, huddled among the fog-whitened boulders with sandwiches, flasks, and wildly fluttering maps, and tried to imagine how I would explain this to a foreign onlooker—the idea of three dozen English people having a picnic on a mountaintop in an ice storm—and realized there was no way you could explain it. We trudged over to a rock, where a couple kindly moved their ruck-sacks and shrank their picnic space to make room for us. We sat and delved among our brown bags in the piercing wind, cracking open hard-boiled eggs with numbed fingers, sipping warm pop, eating floppy cheese-and-pickle sandwiches, and staring into an impenetrable murk that we had spent three hours climbing through to get here, and I thought, I seriously thought, *God, I love this country*.

chapter
25

I was heading for Newcastle, by way of York, when I did another impetuous thing. I got off at Durham, intending to poke around the cathedral for an hour or so, and fell in love with it instantly in a serious way. Why, it's wonderful—a perfect little city—and I kept thinking, *Why did no one tell me about this?* I knew, of course, that it had a fine Norman cathedral but I had no idea that it was so *splendid*. I couldn't believe that not once in twenty years had anyone said to me, "You've never been to Durham? Good God, man, you must go at once! Please—take my car." I had read countless travel pieces in Sunday papers about weekends away in York, Canterbury, Norwich, Bath, even Lincoln, but I couldn't remember reading a single one about Durham, and when I asked friends about it, I found hardly any who had ever been there. So let me say it now: If you have never been to Durham, go at once. Take my car. It's wonderful.

The cathedral, a mountain of reddish-brown stone standing high above a lazy loop of the River Wear, is of course its glory. Everything about it was perfect—not just its setting and execution but also, no less notably, the way it is run today. For a start there was no nagging for money, no "voluntary" admission fee. Outside, there was simply a discreet sign announcing that it cost £700,000 a year to maintain the cathedral and that it was now engaged on a £400,000 renovation project on the east wing and would very much appreciate any money that visitors might spare. Inside, there were two modest collecting boxes and nothing else—no clutter, no nagging notices, no irksome bulletin boards or stupid Eisenhower flags, nothing at all to detract from the unutterable soaring majesty of the interior. It was a perfect day to see it. Sun slanted lavishly through the stained-glass windows, highlighting the stout pillars with their sumptuously grooved patterns and spattering the floors with motes of floating color. There were even wooden pews.

I'm no judge of these things, but the window at the choir end looked to me at least the equal of the more famous one at York, and this one at least you could see in all its splendor since it wasn't tucked away in a transept. And the stained-glass window at the other end was even finer. Well, I can't talk about this without babbling because it was just so splendid. As I stood there, one of only a dozen or so visitors, a verger passed and issued a cheery hello. I was charmed by this show of friendliness and captivated to find myself amid such perfection, and I unhesitatingly gave Durham my vote for best cathedral in Britain.

When I had drunk my fill, I showered the collection pot with coins and wandered off for the most fleeting of looks at the old quarter of town, which was no less ancient and perfect, and returned to the station feeling simultaneously impressed and desolate at just how much there was to see in this little country and what folly it had been to suppose that I might see anything more than a fraction of it in seven flying weeks.

I took an intercity train to Newcastle and then a local to Pegswood, eighteen miles to the north, where I emerged into more splendid, unseasonal sunshine and hiked a mile or two along an arrow-straight road to Ashington.

Ashington has long called itself the biggest mining village in the world, but there is no mining anymore and, with a population of twenty-three thousand, it is scarcely a village. It is famous as the birthplace of a slew of soccer players—Jackie and Bobby Charlton, Jackie Milbourn, and some forty others good enough to play in the first division, a remarkable outpouring for a modest community—but I was drawn by something else: the once famous and now largely forgotten Pitmen Painters.

In 1934, under the direction of an academic and artist from Durham University named Robert Lyon, the town formed a painting club called the Ashington Group, consisting almost exclusively of miners, or pitmen, who had never painted—in many cases had never seen a real painting—before they started gathering in a wooden hut on Monday evenings. They showed a surprising amount of talent and "carried the name of Ashington over the grey mountains," as a critic for *The Guardian* (who clearly knew nothing of soccer) later put it. In the 1930s and 1940s particularly, they attracted a huge amount of attention and were the frequent focus of articles in national papers and art magazines, as well as exhibitions in London and other leading cities. My friend David Cook had an illustrated book by the *Observer* art critic William Feaver called *Pitmen Painters*, which he had once showed me. The illustrations of the paintings were quite charming, but it was the photographs of burly miners, dressed up in suits and ties and crowded into a little hut, earnestly hunched over easels and drawing boards, that stuck in my mind.

Ashington was nothing at all like I expected it to be. In the old black-and-white photographs from David Cook's book, it appeared to be a straggly, overgrown village, surrounded by filthy waste heaps and layered with smoke from the three local pits, a place of muddy lanes hunched under a perpetual wash of sooty drizzle, but what I found instead was a modern, busy community swimming in clean, clear air. There was even a new business park with fluttering pen-

nants, spindly new trees, and an impressive brick gateway on what
was clearly reclaimed ground. The main street, Station Road, had
been smartly pedestrianized and its many shops appeared to be doing a reasonable trade. It was obvious that there was not a great deal
of money in Ashington—most of the shops were of the Price Busters/
Superdrug/Wotta Loada Crap variety, their windows papered with
strident promises of special offers within—but at least they appeared
to be thriving in a way that those of Bradford, for instance, were not.

I went to the town hall to ask the way to the site of the once-
famous hut, and set off down Woodhorn Road in search of the old
Co-op building behind which the hut had stood. The fame of the
Ashington Group, it must be said, rested on a large measure of well-
meaning but faintly objectionable paternalism. Reading the old accounts of its exhibitions in places like London and Bath, it is hard
to escape the conclusion that the Ashington artists were regarded by
critics and other aesthetes rather like Dr. Johnson's performing dog:
The wonder was not that they did it well but that they did it at all.

Yet the Ashington painters represented only a small fragment of a
greater hunger for betterment in places like Ashington, where most
people were lucky to come away with more than a few years of primary education. It is quite astonishing, seeing it now, to realize just
how rich life was, and how enthusiastically opportunities were
seized, in Ashington in the years before the war. At one time the
town boasted a philosophical society, with a busy year-round program of lectures, concerts, and evening classes; an operatic society;
a dramatic society; a workers' educational association; a miners' welfare institute with workshops and yet more lecture rooms; and gardening clubs, cycling clubs, athletics clubs, and others in a similar
vein almost beyond counting. Even the workingmen's clubs, of
which Ashington boasted twenty-two at its peak, offered libraries and
reading rooms. The town had a thriving theater, a ballroom, five
cinemas, and a concert chamber called the Harmonic Hall. When,
in the 1920s, the Bach Choir from Newcastle came out on a Sunday

afternoon to play at the Harmonic Hall, it attracted an audience of two thousand. This, you understand, in a desolate and chronically poor mining community.

And then, one by one, these wonderful institutions faded away—the thespians, the operatic society, the reading rooms and lecture halls. Even the five cinemas all quietly closed their doors. Today the liveliest diversion in Ashington is a noisy amusement arcade, full of video games and ranks of idle, understimulated young men, which I passed now on my way to the Co-op building. At the back of the Co-op stood a large, unpaved parking lot surrounded by a scattering of low buildings—a builder's merchants, a boy scout hut, a Veterans' Institute building made of wood and painted a dazzling viridian green. I knew from William Feaver's book that the Ashington Group hut had stood beside the Veterans' Institute, but on which side I didn't know and now there was no telling.

The Ashington Group was one of the last local institutions to go. The decline was slow and painful. Throughout the 1950s, its numbers inexorably fell as the older members died off and younger people decided that it was naff to put on a suit and tie and ponce about with paint boxes. For the last several years, only two surviving members, Oliver Kilbourn and Jack Harrison, regularly showed up on Monday nights. In the summer of 1982, they received a notice that the annual rent on the hut was to be raised from 50p a year to £14. "That," as Feaver notes, "plus the £7 standing quarterly charge for electricity seemed too much." In October 1983, just short of its fiftieth anniversary and for want of £42 a year in running costs, the Ashington Group was disbanded and the hut torn down.

Now there is nothing to look at but a parking lot, but the paintings are faithfully preserved in the Woodhorn Colliery Museum another mile or so up Woodhorn Road. I walked there now, past endless ranks of former miners' cottages. The old colliery still looks like a colliery, its brick buildings intact, its old winding wheel hanging in the air like some kind of curious fairground ride. Rusting iron tracks

still curve across the grounds. But all is quiet now and the mar-
shaling yards have been turned to tidy green lawns. I was almost the
only visitor.

The Woodhorn Colliery closed down in 1981, seven years short
of its hundredth anniversary. Once it was one of two hundred pits
in Northumberland, and of some three thousand in the country as
a whole. In the 1920s, at the industry's peak, 1.2 million men
worked in British coal mines. Now, at the time of my visit, there
were just sixteen working pits in the country and the number employed had fallen by 98 percent.

All of which seems a little sad until you step into the museum
and discover how harsh and brutal the work was, and how carefully it systematized generations of poverty. It's no wonder the town
produced so many soccer players; for decades there was no other
way out.

Museums, particularly small, unlikely museums, are something
the British do remarkably well, and this was no exception. It was
full of cleverly engaging displays showing life down the pits and
in the busy village above it. I had no real idea just how hard life had
been in the mines. Well into this century, more than a thousand
men a year died in mines and every pit had at least one fabled disaster. (Woodhorn's was in 1916 when thirty men died in an explo-
sion caused by criminally lax supervision; the mine's owners were
sternly told not to let it happen again or next time they would *really*
get told off.) Until 1847, children as young as four—can you believe
this?—worked in the mines for up to ten hours a day, and until
about 1910 boys of ten were put to work as trapper lads, confined
in total darkness in a small space with nothing to do but open and
shut ventilation trapdoors when a coal cart passed by. One boy's
shift ran from 3 A.M. to 4 P.M., six days a week. And those were the
soft jobs.

Goodness knows how people found the time or strength to haul
themselves off to lectures and concerts and painting clubs, but they

most assuredly did. In a brightly lit room hang thirty or forty paintings executed by members of the Ashington Group. So modest were
the group's resources that many are painted with walpamur, a kind
of primitive emulsion, on paper, card, or fiberboard. Hardly any are
on canvas. It would be cruelly misleading to suggest that the Ashington Group harbored a budding Tintoretto, or even a Hockney,
but the paintings provide a compelling record of life in a mining
community over a period of fifty years. Nearly all depict local
scenes—*Saturday Night at the Club, Whippets*—or scenes down the
pits, and seeing them in the context of a mining museum, rather
than in some gallery in Newcastle or Brighton, adds appreciably to
their luster. For the second time in a day I was impressed and captivated.

As I was leaving, I noticed on a label recording the mine's owners
that one of the principal beneficiaries of all this sweat and toil at
the coal face was none other than our old friend W. J.C. Scott-
Bentinck, fifth Duke of Portland, and it occurred to me, not for the
first time, what a remarkably small world Britain is.

That is its glory, you see—that it manages at once to be intimate
and small scale, and at the same time packed to bursting with incident
and interest. I am constantly filled with admiration at this—at the way
you can wander through a town like Oxford and in the space of a few
hundred yards pass the home of Christopher Wren, the buildings
where Halley found his comet and Boyle his first law, the track where
Roger Bannister ran the first sub-four-minute mile, the meadow
where Lewis Carroll strolled; or how you can stand on Snow's Hill at
Windsor and see, in a single sweep, Windsor Castle, the playing fields
of Eton, the churchyard where Gray wrote his "Elegy," the site where
The Merry Wives of Windsor was first performed. Can there anywhere
on earth be, in such a modest span, a landscape more packed with
centuries of busy, productive attainment?

I returned to Pegswood lost in a small glow of admiration and
caught a train to Newcastle, where I found a hotel and passed an

evening in a state of unaccustomed serenity, walking till late through the echoing streets, surveying the statues and buildings with fondness and respect, and I finished the day with a small thought, which I shall leave you with now. It was this:

How is it possible, in this wondrous land where the relics of genius and enterprise confront you at every step, where every realm of human possibility has been probed and challenged and meticulously extended, where many of the very greatest accomplishments of industry, commerce, and the arts find their seat—how is it possible in such a place that when at length I returned to my hotel and switched on the television, it was *Cagney & Lacey* again?

chapter
26

Can there anywhere be a more beautiful and beguiling city to arrive at by train early on a crisp, dark Novembery evening than Edinburgh? To emerge from the bustling, subterranean bowels of Waverley Station and find yourself in the very heart of such a glorious city is a happy experience indeed. I hadn't been to Edinburgh for years and had forgotten just how captivating it can be. Every monument was lit with golden floodlights—the castle and the Bank of Scotland headquarters on the hill, the Balmoral Hotel and the Sir Walter Scott Monument down below—which gave them a certain eerie grandeur. The city was abustle with end-of-day activity. Buses swept through Princes Street and shop and office workers scurried along the sidewalks, hastening home to have their haggis and cock-a-leekie soup and indulge in a few skirls or whatever it is Scots do when the sun goes doon.

I'd booked a room in the Caledonian Hotel, which was a rash and extravagant thing to do, but it's a terrific building and an Edinburgh institution and I just had to be part of it for one night, so I set off for it down Princes Street, past the Gothic rocket ship that is the Scott Monument, unexpectedly exhilarated to find myself among the hurrying throngs with the sight of the castle on its craggy mount outlined against a pale evening sky.

To a surprising extent, and far more than Wales, Edinburgh felt like a different country. The buildings were thin and tall in an un-English way, the money was different, even the air and light felt different in some ineffable northern way. Every bookshop window was full of books about Scotland or by Scottish authors. And of course the voices were different. I walked along, feeling as if I had left England far behind, and then I would pass something familiar and think in suprise, *Oh, look, they have Marks and Spencer here,* as if I were in Reykjavik or Stavanger and oughtn't to expect to find British things. It was most refreshing.

I checked into the Caledonian, dumped my things in the room, and immediately returned to the streets, eager to be out in the open air and to take in whatever Edinburgh had to offer. I trudged up a long, curving back hill to the castle, but the grounds were shut for the night, so I contented myself with a shuffling amble down the Royal Mile, which was nearly empty of life and very handsome in a dour, Scottish sort of way. I passed the time browsing in the windows of the many tourists shops that stand along it, reflecting on what a lot of things the Scots have given the world—kilts, bagpipes, tam-o'-shanters, tins of oatcakes, bright yellow sweaters with big diamond patterns, sacks of haggis—and how little anyone but a Scot would want them.

Let me say right here, flat out, that I have the greatest fondness and admiration for Scotland and her clever, cherry-cheeked people. Did you know that Scotland produces more university students per capita than any other nation in Europe? And it has churned out a rollcall of worthies far out of proportion to its modest size—Robert Louis Stevenson, James Watt, Robert Burns, Walter Scott, Arthur Conan Doyle, J. M. Barrie, Adam Smith, Alexander Graham Bell, Thomas Telford, Lord Kelvin, John Logie Baird, and Charles Rennie Mackintosh, to name but a few. Among much else we owe the

Scots are whiskey, raincoats, rubber boots, the bicycle pedal, the telephone, Tarmac, penicillin, and an understanding of the active principles of cannabis, and think how insupportable life would be without those. So thank you, Scotland, and never mind that you seem quite unable to qualify for the World Cup soccer championships these days.

At the bottom of the Royal Mile, I came up against the entrance to the Palace of Holyroodhouse, and picked my way back to the center of things along a series of darkened back lanes. Eventually I ended up in an unusual pub on St. Andrew Square called Tiles—an apt name, since every inch of it from floor to ceiling was covered in elaborate, chunky Victorian tiles. It felt a bit like drinking in Prince Albert's loo—a not disagreeable experience, as it happens. In any case, something about it must have appealed to me because I drank a foolish amount of beer and emerged to find that nearly all the restaurants roundabout were closed, so I toddled back to my hotel, where I winked at the night staff and put myself to bed.

In the morning, I awoke feeling famished, perky, and unusually clearheaded. I presented myself in the entrance to the dining room of the Caledonian. Would I like breakfast? asked a man in a black suit.

"Does the Firth have a Forth?" I replied drolly and nudged him in the ribs. I was shown to a table and was so hungry that I dispensed with the menu and told the man to bring me the full whack, whatever it might consist of, then sat back happily and idly glanced at the menu, where I discovered that the full cooked breakfast was listed at £14.50. I snared a passing waiter.

"Excuse me," I said, "but it says here that the breakfast is fourteen pounds fifty."

"That's right, sir."

I could feel a sudden hangover banging on the cranial gates. "Are you telling me," I said, "that on top of the lavish sum I paid for a

room, I must additionally pay fourteen pounds fifty for a fried egg
and an oatcake?"

He allowed that this was, in essence, so. I withdrew my order and
asked instead for a cup of coffee. Well, honestly.

Perhaps it was this sudden early blot on my happiness that put
me in a grumpy mood or perhaps it was the drippy rain I emerged
into, but Edinburgh didn't look half so fine in daylight as it had
appeared the night before. Now people plodded through the streets
with umbrellas, and cars swished through puddles with a noise that
sounded testy and impatient. George Street, the core of the New
Town (as the less old part of central Edinburgh is misleadingly
called), presented an unquestionably fine, if damp, prospect with its
statues and stately squares, but far too many of the Georgian buildings had been clumsily abused by the addition of modern frontages.
Just around the corner from my hotel was an office supply shop with
plate-glass windows that had been grafted onto an eighteenth-
century frontage in a way that was nothing short of criminal, and
there were others in like vein here and there along the surrounding
streets.

I wandered around looking for some place to eat, and ended up
on Princes Street. It, too, seemed to have changed overnight. Then,
with homeward-bound workers scurrying past, it had been beguiling
and vibrant, exciting even, but now in the dull light of day it felt
merely listless and gray. I shuffled along it looking for a café or
bistro, but, with the exception of a couple of truly dumpy discount-
woolens places where the goods seemed to have been drop-kicked
onto display counters, Princes Street appeared to offer nothing but
the usual array of chain stores—Boots, Littlewoods, Virgin Records,
Marks & Spencer, Burger King, McDonald's. What central Edinburgh lacked, it seemed to me, was a venerable and much-loved
institution—a Viennese-style coffeehouse or treasured tearoom,
someplace with newspapers on gripper rods, potted palms, and

perhaps a fat little lady playing a grand piano. In the end, fractious and impatient, I went into a crowded McDonald's, waited ages in a long, shuffling line, which made me even more fractious and impatient, and finally ordered a cup of coffee and an Egg McMuffin.

"Do you want an apple turnover with that?" asked the young man who served me.

I looked at him for a moment. "I'm sorry," I said, "do I appear to be brain-damaged?"

"Pardon?"

"Correct me if I'm wrong, but I didn't ask for an apple turnover, did I?"

"Uh . . . no."

"So do I look as if I have some mental condition that would render me unable to request an apple turnover if I wanted one?"

"No, it's just that we're told to ask everyone, like."

"What, you think everyone in Edinburgh is brain-damaged?"

"We're just told to ask everyone, like."

"Well, I don't want an apple turnover, which is why I didn't ask for one. Is there anything else you'd like to know if I don't want?"

"We're just told to ask everyone."

"Do you remember what I do want?"

He looked in confusion at his cash register. "Uh, an Egg McMuffin and a cup of coffee."

"Do you think I might have it this morning or shall we talk some more?"

"Oh, uh, right, I'll just get it."

"Thank you."

Well, honestly.

Afterward, feeling only fractionally less fractious, I stepped out to find the rain beating down. I sprinted across the road and, on an impulse, ducked into the Royal Scottish Academy, a grand pseudo-Hellenic edifice with banners suspended between the columns, which make it look a little like a lost outpost of the Reichstag. I paid

£1.50 for a ticket and, shaking myself dry like a dog, shuffled in. The academy was having its autumn show, or perhaps it was its winter show or perhaps it was its annual show. I couldn't say because I didn't notice any signs and the pictures were labeled with numbers. You had to pay an extra £2 for a catalog to find out what was what, which frankly annoys me when I have just parted with £1.50. (The National Trust does this, too—puts numbers on the plants and trees in its gardens and so on, so that you have to buy a catalog—which is one reason why I won't be leaving my fortune to the National Trust.) The works in the RSA exhibition extended over many rooms and appeared to fall chiefly into four categories: (1) boats on beaches; (2) lonely Highland cottages; (3) half-clad girlfriends engaged in their toilet; and, for some reason, (4) French street scenes, always with at least one shop front saying BOULAN-GERIE or ÉPICERIE, so that there was no possibility of mistaking the setting for Carnoustie or Troon.

Many of the pictures—indeed most—were outstanding, and when I saw red gummed circles attached to some of them I not only realized that they were for sale but developed a sudden, strange hankering to buy one myself. So I started making trips to the lady at the front desk and saying, "Excuse me, how much is number one twenty-five?" She would look it up in the catalog and state a figure several hundred pounds beyond what I was prepared to pay, so I would wander off again and after a while come back and say, "Excuse me, how much is number forty-seven?" At one point, I saw a picture I particularly liked—a painting of Solway Firth by a fellow named Colin Park—and she looked it up and told me that it was £125. This was a good price and I was prepared to buy it then and there even if I had to carry it all the way to John o'Groats under my arm, but then she discovered that she had read the wrong line, that the £125 picture was a little thing about three inches square and that the Colin Park was very considerably more than that, so I went off again. Eventually, when my legs began to tire, I tried a new tack and asked her what she had for £50 or less, and when it turned out there was nothing, I left, discouraged in my quest but £2 richer in regard to the catalog.

Then I went to the National Gallery of Scotland, which I liked even better and not just because it was free. The National Gallery is tucked away behind the RSA and doesn't look much from outside, but inside it is very grand in an imperial, nineteenth-century sort of way, with red baize walls, outsized pictures in extravagant frames, scattered statues of naked nymphs, and furniture trimmed in gilt, so that it rather brought to mind a stroll through Queen Victoria's boudoir. The pictures were not only outstanding, but they had labels telling you their historical background and what the people in them were doing, which I think is to be highly commended and in fact should be made mandatory everywhere.

I read these instructive notes gratefully, pleased to know, for instance, that the reason Rembrandt looked so glum in his self-portrait was that he had just been declared insolvent; but in one of the salons I noticed that there was a man, accompanied by a boy of about thirteen, who didn't need the labels at all.

They were from what I suspect the Queen Mother would call the lower orders. Everything about them murmured poorness and material want—poor diet, poor income, poor dentistry, poor prospects, even poor laundering—but the man was describing the pictures with a fondness and familiarity that were truly heartwarming and the boy was raptly attentive to his every word. "Now this is a later Goya, you see," he was saying in a quiet voice. "Just look at how controlled those brushstrokes are—a complete change in style from his earlier work. D'ye remember how I told you that Goya didn't paint a single great picture till he was nearly fifty? Well, this is a great picture." He wasn't showing off, you understand; he was sharing.

I have often been struck in Britain by this sort of thing—by how mysteriously well educated people from unprivileged backgrounds so often are, how the most unlikely people will tell you plant names in Latin or turn out to be experts on the politics of ancient Thrace or irrigation techniques at Glanum. This is a country, after all, where the grand finale of a television quiz show like *Mastermind* (which asks very hard questions indeed) is frequently won by cabbies and railway engine drivers and the like. I have never been able to decide whether that is deeply impressive or just appalling—whether this is a country where engine drivers know about Tintoretto and Leibniz or a country where people who know about Tintoretto and Leibniz end up driving engines. All I know is that it exists here more than anywhere else.

Afterward, I climbed up the steep slope to the castle grounds, which seemed oddly, almost spookily, familiar. I hadn't been here before, so I couldn't think why this should be, and then I realized that a regimental tattoo from Edinburgh Castle had been one of the features of *This Is Cinerama* back in Bradford. The castle precinct was just as it had been in the film, apart from a change of weather and a merciful absence of strutting Gordon Highlanders, but one other thing had changed mightily since 1951—the view of Princes Street from the terrace.

In 1951, Princes Street remained one of the world's great streets, a gracious thoroughfare lined along its northern side with solid, weighty Victorian and Edwardian edifices that bespoke confidence, greatness, and empire: the North British Mercantile Insurance Company, the sumptuous, classical New Club building, the old Waverley Hotel. And then, one by one, they were unaccountably torn down, and replaced for the most part with gray concrete bunkers. At the eastern end of the street the whole of St. James's Square, an open green space surrounded by a crowd of eighteenth-century apartment buildings, was bulldozed to make way for one of the squattest, ugliest shopping center/hotel complexes ever to spill from an architect's pen. Now about all that is left of Princes Street's age of confident grandeur is odd fragments like the Balmoral Hotel and the Scott Monument and part of the front of Jenners department store.

Later, when I was back home, I found in my *AA Book of British
Towns* an artist's illustration of central Edinburgh as it might be
seen from the air. It showed Princes Street lined from end to end
with nothing but fine old buildings. The same was true of all the
other artist's impressions of British cities—Norwich and Oxford and
Canterbury and Stratford. You can't do that, you know. You can't
tear down fine old structures and then pretend that they are still
there. But that is exactly what has happened in Britain in the past
thirty years, and not just with buildings.

And on that sour note, I went off to try to find some real food.

chapter
27

So let's talk about something heartening. Let's talk about John Fallows. One day in 1987 Fallows was standing at a window in a London bank waiting to be served, when a would-be robber named Douglas Bath stepped in front of him, brandished a handgun, and demanded money from the cashier. Outraged, Fallows told Bath to "bugger off" to the back of the line and wait his turn, to the presumed approving nods of others in the queue. Unprepared for this turn of events, Bath meekly fled the bank empty-handed and was arrested a short distance away.

I bring this up here to make the point that if there is one golden quality that characterizes the British it is an innate sense of good manners, and you defy it at your peril. Deference and a quiet consideration for others are such a fundamental part of British life that few conversations could even start without them. Almost any encounter with a stranger begins with the words "I'm terribly sorry but," followed by a request of some sort—"could you tell me the way to Brighton?," "help me find a shirt my size?," "get your steamer trunk off my foot?" And when you've fulfilled their request, they invariably offer a hesitant, apologetic smile and say sorry again, begging forgiveness for taking up your time or carelessly leaving their foot where your steamer trunk clearly needed to go.

As if to illustrate my point, when I checked out of the Caledonian late the next morning, I arrived to find a woman ahead of me wearing a helpless look and saying to the receptionist, "I'm terribly sorry but I can't seem to get the television in my room to work." She had come all the way downstairs to apologize to *them* for their TV not working. Where else but Britain?

And it is all done so instinctively. I remember, when I was still new to the country, arriving at a railway station one day to find that just two of the dozen or so ticket windows were open. (I should perhaps explain that as a rule in Britain no matter how many windows there are in a bank, post office, or rail station, only two of them will be open, except at very busy times, when just one will be open.) Both ticket windows were occupied. Now, in other countries one of two things would have happened. Either there would be a crush of customers at each window, all demanding simultaneous attention, or else there would be two slow-moving lines, each full of gloomy people convinced that the other line was moving faster.

Here in Britain, however, the waiting customers had spontaneously come up with a much more sensible and ingenious arrangement. They had formed a single line a few feet back from both windows. When either position became vacant, the customer at the head of the line would step up to it and the rest of the line would shuffle forward a space. It was a wonderfully fair and democratic approach, and the remarkable thing was that no one had commanded it or even suggested it. It just happened.

Much the same sort of thing occurred now, for when the lady with the recalcitrant TV set had finished with her apology (which the receptionist, I must say, accepted with uncommonly good grace, going so far as to hint that if anything else in the woman's room was found to be out of order, she wasn't to blame herself for a minute), the receptionist turned to me and another gentleman who was also waiting and said, "Who's next?" and he and I went through an elaborate after-you, no-after-you, but-I-insist, well-that's-most-gracious-of-you routine, which simply warmed the heart.

And so, on my second morning in Edinburgh, I stepped from the hotel in happy spirits, at one with the world, buoyed by this cheerful and civilized encounter, to find the sun shining and the city transformed yet again. On this day, George Street and Queen Street looked positively ravishing, their stone fronts burnished with sunlight, the damp, brooding darkness that had suffused them the day before banished utterly. The Firth of Forth gleamed in the distance and the little parks and squares seemed alive with green. I trudged up The Mound to the Old Town terraces to take in the view and was astonished to see how different the city looked. Princes Street was still a scar of architectural regrettabilities, but beyond it the hills were thronged with jaunty roofs and thrusting steeples that gave the city a character and graciousness that had entirely escaped me the day before.

I spent the morning doing touristy things—I went to St. Giles's Cathedral and had a look at Holyroodhouse, climbed to the top of Calton Hill—and finally fetched my pack and returned to the station, happy to have made my peace with Edinburgh and pleased to be on the move again.

And what a fine thing a train journey is. I was instantly lulled by the motion of the train as we lumbered out through Edinburgh and its quiet suburbs and over the Forth Bridge. (And, gosh, what a mighty structure it is; suddenly I understood why the Scots are always on about it.) The train was mostly empty and rather splendidly posh. It was done up in restful blues and grays, which provided a sharp contrast to all the Sprinters I had been on in recent days and proved so deeply soothing that soon my eyelids were growing unsustainably heavy and my neck seemed to be turning into a rubbery material. In no time at all, my head was slumped on my chest and I was engaged in the quiet, steady manufacture of several gallons of saliva—all of them, alas, spare.

Some people simply should not be allowed to fall asleep on a train, or, having fallen asleep, should be discreetly covered with a tarpaulin, and I'm afraid I am one of them. I awoke, some indeterminate time later, with a rutting snort and a brief, wild flail and lifted my head from my chest to find myself mired in a cobweb of drool from beard to belt buckle, and with three people gazing at me in a curiously dispassionate manner. At least I was spared the usual experience of waking to find myself stared at open-mouthed by a group of small children who would flee with shrieks at the discovery that the dribbling hulk was alive.

Shrinking from my audience and dabbing myself discreetly with the sleeve of my jacket, I attended to the view. We were rattling through an open landscape that was pleasant rather than dramatic— arable farmland running off to big round hills—under a sky that seemed ready to collapse under its own weight of gray. From time to time we stopped in some inert little town with a dead little station—Ladybank, Cupar, Leuchars—before eventually entering a larger, fractionally more active world at Dundee, Arbroath, and Montrose. And then, some three hours after leaving Edinburgh, we were sliding into Aberdeen in a thin and fast-fading light.

I pressed my face to the glass keenly. I had never been to Aberdeen before and didn't know anyone who had. I knew almost nothing about it, other than that it was dominated by the North Sea oil industry and proudly called itself "the Granite City." It had always seemed to me exotically remote, a place I was unlikely ever to get to, so I was eager to see it.

I had booked into a hotel that was warmly described in my guidebook (a tome that later went for kindling) but turned out to be a dreary, overpriced back-street block. My room was small and ill lit, with battered furniture, a narrow prison-cell bed with a thin blanket and a single grudging pillow, and wallpaper doing its best to flee a damp wall. Once, in a moment of ambition, the management had installed a bedside console that operated lights, radio, and TV, and incorporated an alarm clock, but none of these appeared to work. The alarm clock knob came off in my hand. With a sigh, I dumped my stuff on the bed and returned to the dark streets of Aberdeen looking for food, drink, and granite splendor.

One thing I have learned over the years is that your impressions of a place are necessarily, and often unshakably, colored by the route you take into it. Enter London by way of the leafy suburbs of Richmond, Barnes, and Putney and alight at, say, Kensington Gardens or Green Park, and you would think that you were in the midst of some vast, well-tended arcadia. Enter it by way of Southend, Romford, and Liverpool Street Station, and you would perceive it in another way altogether. So perhaps it was simply the route I took from my hotel. All I know is that I walked for nearly three hours up streets and down, and I couldn't find anything remotely adorable about Aberdeen. There were some briefly diverting vignettes—an open pedestrianized space around an ancient landmark called the Mercat Cross, an interesting-looking little museum called John Dun's House, some imposing university buildings—but no matter how many times I crisscrossed its heart, all I seemed to encounter was a vast, glossy new shopping center that was a damnable nuisance to circumnavigate (I kept ending up, muttering and lost, in dead-end delivery bays and collecting compounds for cardboard boxes) and a single broad, endless street lined with precisely the same stores I had seen in every other city for the last six weeks. It was like anywhere and nowhere—like a small Manchester or a random fragment of Leeds. In vain I sought a single place where I could stand with hands on hips and say, "Aha, so *this* is Aberdeen." Perhaps, too, it was the dreary time of year. I had read somewhere that Aberdeen had won the Britain in Bloom competition nine times, but I saw hardly any gardens or green spaces. Above all, I had scant sense of being in the midst of a rich, proud city built of granite.

On top of that, I couldn't settle on a place to eat. I hankered for something different, something I hadn't encountered a hundred times already on this trip—Thai or Mexican, perhaps, or maybe Indonesian or even Scottish—but there seemed nothing but the usual scattering of Chinese and Indian establishments, usually on a side street, usually up a flight of stairs that looked as if they had been recently used for a motorcycle rally, and I couldn't bring myself to make that terrible climb into the unknown. In any case, I knew exactly what would be up there—low lighting, a reception area with a padded bar, twangy Asian music, tables covered with glasses of lager and stainless-steel plate warmers. I couldn't face it. In the end, I engaged in a desperate session of eenie meenie minie mo on a street corner and opted for an Indian. It was, in every degree, exactly like every other Indian meal I had had in the previous weeks. Even the postdinner burp tasted exactly the same. I returned to my hotel in a dim and restless frame of mind.

In the morning, I went for a walk around the town sincerely hoping that I would like it better, but alas, alas. It wasn't that there was anything wrong with Aberdeen exactly, more that it suffered from a surfeit of innocuousness. I had a shuffle around the new shopping center and ranged some distance out into the surrounding streets, but they all seemed equally colorless and forgettable. And then I realized that the problem really wasn't with Aberdeen so much as with the nature of modern Britain. British towns are like a deck of cards that have been shuffled and endlessly redealt—same cards, different order. If I had come to Aberdeen fresh from another country, it would probably have seemed vibrant and exceptional. It was prosperous and clean. It had bookshops and cinemas and a university and pretty much everything else you could want in a community. It is, I've no doubt, a nice place to live. It's just that it was so much like everywhere else. It was a British city. How could it be otherwise?

Once I had packed this small thought into my head I liked Aberdeen much better. I can't say I ached to up sticks and move there—but then why should I, when I could get exactly the same things, the same shops, libraries, and leisure centers, the same pubs and television programs, the same phone boxes, post offices, traffic lights, park benches, zebra crossings, marine air, and post-Indian-dinner burps, anywhere else? In an odd way the very things that had made Aberdeen seem so dull and predictable the night before now made it feel comfortable and homey. But I still never had the slightest sense that I was in the midst of a lot of granite, and it was without regret that I fetched my things from the hotel and returned to the station to resume my stately progress north.

The train was again very clean and nearly empty, with more soothing blues and grays. It was just two carriages, but it had a trolley service, which impressed me. The difficulty was that the young chap in charge of this mobile commissary was uncommonly devoted to his task—I gathered from his spanking new uniform that he had just started the job and was probably still at the point where it was fun to dispense teas and chocolate biscuits and make change—but as there were only two other passengers and just sixty yards of train to patrol, he came by about once every three minutes. Still, the constant metallic ruckus of the passing trolley kept me from nodding off and falling into a state of embarrassing hypersalivation.

We rode through a pleasant but unexciting landscape. All my previous experience of the Highlands was up the more exciting and dramatic west coast, and this was decidedly muted in comparison—rounded hills, flat farms, occasional glimpses of an empty, steel-gray sea—but by no means disagreeable. Nothing of incident happened except that at Nairn a big plane took off and did all kinds of astonishing things in the sky, climbing vertically for hundreds of feet, then slowly tipping over and plunging toward earth before pulling out in a steep bank at nearly the last moment. I supposed it was from some sort of a test base for RAF planes, but it was more exciting to imagine that it had been hijacked by a suicidal madman. And then an arresting thing happened. The plane began coming toward the train, really bearing down on it, as if the pilot had spotted us and thought that it would be amusing to take us with him. It got larger and larger and nearer and nearer—I looked around uneasily but there was no one to share the experience with—until it nearly filled the window, and then, quite abruptly, the train went into a cutting and the plane disappeared from view. I bought a cup of coffee and a packet of biscuits from the trolley to steady my nerves and waited for Inverness to appear.

I liked Inverness immediately. It is never going to win any beauty contests, but it has some likable features—an old-fashioned little cinema called La Scala, a well-preserved market arcade, a large and adorably overembellished nineteenth-century sandstone castle on a hill, some splendid riverside walks. I was particularly taken with the dim-lit market arcade, an undercover thoroughfare apparently locked in a perpetual 1953. It had a barbershop with a revolving pole out front and pictures inside of people who looked like they had modeled their hairstyles on *Thunderbirds* characters. There was even a joke shop selling useful and interesting items that I hadn't seen for years: sneezing powder and plastic vomit (very handy for saving seats on trains) and chewing gum that turns the teeth black. It was shut, but I made a mental note to return in the morning to stock up.

Above all, Inverness has an especially fine river, the Ness, which is green and sedate and charmingly overhung with trees, lined on one side with big houses, trim little parks, and the old sandstone castle (now the home of regional courts) and on the other with old hotels with steep-pitched roofs, more big houses, and the stolid, Notre Dame–like grandeur of the cathedral, standing on a broad lawn beside the river. I checked into a hotel at random and immediately set off for a walk through the milky twilight. The river was

lined on both sides with gracious promenades thoughtfully punc-
tuated with benches, which made it very agreeable for an evening
stroll.

Nearly all the houses on both sides of the river were rambling
places built for an age of servants. What, I wondered, had brought
all this late-Victorian wealth to Inverness, and who supported these
handsome heaps today? Not far from the castle, on spacious grounds
in what I suppose a developer would call a prime location, stood a
particularly grand and elaborate mansion, with a wandering roofline
and an abundance of turrets and towers. It was a wonderful, spacious
house, the kind you could imagine riding a bicycle around in, and
it was boarded, derelict, and up for sale. I couldn't imagine how
such a likable place could have ended up in such a neglected state.
As I walked along, I lost myself in a reverie of buying it for a song,
doing it up, and living happily ever after on these large grounds
beside this deeply fetching river, until I realized what my family
would say if I told them we weren't after all going to the land of
shopping malls, one-hundred-channel television, and hamburgers
the size of a baby's head, but instead to the damp north of Scotland.

And anyway, I regret to say that I could never live in Inverness
because of two sensationally ugly modern office buildings that stand
by the central bridge and blot the business district beyond any hope
of redemption. I came upon them now as I returned to the town
center and was positively riveted with astonishment to realize that an
entire town could be ruined by two inanimate structures. Everything
about them—scale, materials, shape, design—was madly inappropriate to the surrounding scene. They weren't just ugly and large
but so ill-planned that you could actually walk around them at least
twice without ever identifying the main entrance. In the larger of the
two, on the river side where there might have been a restaurant or
terrace or at least shops or offices with a view, much of the road
frontage had been given over to a huge delivery bay with overhead
metal doors. This in a building that overlooked one of the hand-

somest rivers in Britain. It was awful, awful beyond words.

I had recently been to Hobart in Tasmania, where the Sheraton chain had built a hotel of simply stunning plainness on its lovely waterfront. I had been told that the architect hadn't actually visited the site and in consequence had sited the hotel restaurant at the back of the building, where diners couldn't see the harbor. Since then, I had thought that was the most brainless thing I had ever heard of architecturally. I don't suppose this pair of buildings in Inverness could possibly have been designed by the same architect— it was terrifying to think that there could be two architects in the world this bad—but he could certainly have worked for the same firm.

Of all the buildings that I would deeply love to blow up in Britain—the Maples building in Harrogate, the Hilton Hotel in London, the post office building in Leeds, a random selection among almost any of the structures owned by British Telecom—I have no hesitation in saying that my first choice would be either of these two.

And here is the cruncher. Guess who inhabits these two piles of heartbreak? The larger is the regional headquarters of the Highland Enterprise Board and the other is home of the Inverness and Nairn Enterprise Board, the two bodies entrusted with maintaining and enhancing the attractiveness and well-being of this lovely and vital corner of the country.

chapter
28

I had big plans for the morning: I was going to go to the bank, buy some plastic vomit, have a look at the local art gallery, perhaps take another stroll along the lovely River Ness, but I woke late and had no time to do anything but fumble my way into clothes, check out of the hotel, and waddle in a sweat to the station. Beyond Inverness trains run infrequently—just three times a day to Thurso and Wick—so I couldn't afford to be late.

As it happened, the train was waiting, humming quietly, and left right on time. We slid out of Inverness against a backdrop of round mountains and the cold flatness of the Beauly Firth. The train was soon rattling along at a fair old clip. There were more passengers this time, and there was a trolley service again—all credit to BR—but no one wanted anything from it because the other passengers were almost all pensioners and they had brought their own provisions.

I bought a tandoori chicken sandwich and a coffee. How far things have come. I can remember when you couldn't buy a British Rail sandwich without wondering if this was your last act before a long period on a life-support machine. And anyway you couldn't buy one because the buffet car was nearly always closed. And now here I was sitting eating a tandoori chicken sandwich and drinking a creditable cup of coffee brought to me in my seat by a friendly and presentable young man on a two-carriage train across the Highlands.

Here's an interesting statistic for you, which is kind of boring but must be taken in. Rail infrastructure spending per person per year in Europe is $30 in Belgium and Germany, $46 in France, more than $75 in Switzerland, and in Britain a slightly less than munificent $7.50. Britain spends less per capita on rail improvements than any other country in the European Union except Greece and Ireland. Even Portugal spends more. And the thing is, despite this paucity of support you actually have an excellent train service in this country, all things considered. Trains are now much cleaner than they used to be and staff generally more patient and helpful. Ticket people always say please and thank you, bless them, and you can eat the food.

So I ate my tandoori chicken sandwich and drank my cup of coffee with pleasure and gratification, and passed the time between nibbles watching a white-haired couple at a table across the way delving among their traveling fare, setting out little plastic boxes of pork pies and hard-boiled eggs, lifting out thermoses, unscrewing lids, finding little salt and pepper shakers. It's amazing, isn't it, how you can give a couple of old people a canvas holdall, an assortment of Tupperware containers, and a thermos flask and they can amuse themselves for hours. They worked away with well-ordered precision and total silence, as if they had been preparing for this event for years. When the food was laid out, they ate for four minutes with great delicacy, then spent most of the rest of the morning quietly packing everything away. They looked very happy.

They reminded me in an odd but heartwarming way of my mother, since she is something of a Tupperware devotee herself. She doesn't picnic on trains, since there are no passenger trains in her part of the country anymore, but she does like to put stray items of food in plastic containers of various sizes and file them away in the fridge. It's an odd thing about mothers generally, I believe. As soon as you leave home they merrily throw away everything that you cherished through childhood and adolescence—your valuable collection of baseball cards, a complete set of *Playboys* from 1966–75, your high school yearbooks—but give them half a peach or a spoonful of leftover peas and they will put it in a Tupperware container at the back of the fridge and treasure it more or less forever.

And so the long ride to Thurso passed. We rattled on through an increasingly remote and barren landscape, treeless and cold, with heather clinging to the hillsides like lichen on rock and thinly scattered with sheep that took fright and scampered off when the train passed. Now and then we passed through winding valleys speckled with farms that looked romantic and pretty from a distance, but bleak and comfortless up close. Mostly they were small holdings with lots of rusted tin everywhere—tin sheds, tin hen huts, tin fences—looking rickety and weather battered. We were entering one of those weird zones, always a sign of remoteness from the known world, where nothing is ever thrown away. Every farmyard was cluttered with piles of castoffs, as if the owner thought that one day he might need 132 half-rotted fenceposts, a ton of broken bricks, and the shell of a 1964 Ford Zodiac.

Two hours after leaving Inverness, we came to a place called Golspie. It was a good-sized town with big council estates and winding streets of those gray pebble-dash bungalows that seem to have been modeled on public toilets and for which they have a strange fondness in Scotland, but no sign of factories or workplaces. What, I wondered, do all the people in all those houses do for a living in a place like Golspie? Then came Brora, another good-sized community, with a seafront but no harbor as far as I could see, and no factories. What *do* they *do* in these little places in the middle of nowhere?

After that, the landscape became quite empty, with neither farmhouses nor field animals. We rode for a seeming eternity through a

great Scottish void, full of miles of nothingness, until, in the middle
of this great emptiness, we came to a place called Forsinard, with
two houses, a railway station, and an inexplicably large hotel. What
a strange lost world this was. And then at long last we arrived in
Thurso, the northernmost town on the British mainland, the end of
the line in every sense of the word. I stepped from the little station
on slightly unsteady legs and set off down the long main street toward the center.

I had no idea what to expect, but my initial impressions were
favorable. It seemed a tidy, well-ordered place, comfortable rather
than showy, considerably larger than I had expected, and with several small hotels. I took a room in the Pentland Hotel, which seemed
a nice enough place in a deathly quiet, end-of-the-world sort of way.
I accepted a key from the pleasant receptionist, conveyed my things
to a distant room reached through spooky, winding corridors, then
went out to have a look around.

The big event in Thurso, according to civic records, was in 1834
when Sir John Sinclair, a local worthy, coined the term *statistics* in
the town, though things have calmed down pretty considerably since.
When he wasn't contriving neologisms, Sinclair also extensively rebuilt the town, endowing it with a splendid library in a cautiously
baroque style and a small square with a little park in the middle.
Around the square today stands a modest district of small, useful,
friendly looking shops—chemists and butchers, a wine merchant, a
ladies' boutique or two, a scattering of banks, lots of hair salons (why
is there always an abundance of hair salons in little out-of-the-way
communities?)—pretty well everything, in short, you would hope to
find in a model community. There was a small old-fashioned Woolworth's, but apart from that and the banks, nearly everything else
appeared to be locally owned, which gave Thurso a nice, homey feel.
It had the air of a real, self-contained community. I liked it very
much.

I pottered about for a bit among the shopping streets, then followed some back lanes down to the waterfront, where there was a lonely fish warehouse marooned in an acre of empty parking lot and a vast empty beach with thunderous crashing waves. The air was fresh and vigorously abundant in the blowy way of the seaside, and the world was bathed in an ethereal northern light that gave the sea a curious luminescence—indeed, gave everything an odd, faint bluish cast—that intensified my sense of being a long way from home.

At the far end of the beach there stood a spectral tower, a fragment of old castle, and I set off to investigate. A rocky stream stood between me and it, so I had to backtrack to a footbridge some distance from the beach, then pick my way along a muddy path liberally strewn with litter. The castle tower was derelict, its lower windows and door openings bricked over. A notice beside it announced that the coastal path was closed because of soil erosion. I stood for a long time by this little headland gazing out to sea, then turned to face the town and wondered what to do next.

Thurso was to be my home for the next three days and I wasn't at all sure how I was going to fill such an expanse of empty time. Between the smell of sea air and the sense of utter remoteness, I had a moment of quiet panic at finding myself alone here at the top of the earth, where there was no one to talk to and the most exciting diversion was an old bricked-up tower. I wandered back into town the way I had come and, for want of anything better to do, had another pottering look in the shop windows, And then, outside a greengrocer's, it happened—something that sooner or later always happens to me on a long trip away from home. It is a moment I dread.

I started asking myself unanswerable questions.

Prolonged solitary travel, you see, affects people in different ways. It is an unnatural business to find yourself in a strange place with an underutilized brain and no particular reason for being there, and eventually it makes you go a little crazy. I've seen it in others often. Some solitary travelers start talking to themselves: little silently murmured conversations that they think no one else notices. Some desperately seek the company of strangers, striking up small talk at shop counters and hotel reception desks and then lingering awkwardly after it has become clear that the conversation has finished. Some become ravenous, obsessive sightseers, tramping from sight to sight with a guidebook in a lonely quest to see everything. Me, I get a sort of interrogative diarrhea. I ask private questions for which I cannot supply an answer. And so as I stood by a greengrocer's in Thurso, looking at its darkened interior with pursed lips and a more or less empty head, from out of nowhere I thought, *Why do they call it a grapefruit?* and I knew that the process had started.

It's not a bad question, as these things go. I mean to say, why *do* they call it a grapefruit? I don't know about you, but if someone presented me with an unfamiliar fruit that was yellow, was the size of a cannonball, and tasted sour I don't believe I would think, *Well, you know, it rather puts me in mind of a grape.*

The trouble is that once these things start, there is no stopping them. A couple of doors away was a shop that sold sweaters and I thought, *Why do the British call them jumpers?* I've actually been wondering this for years, off and on, usually in lonely places like Thurso, and I would sincerely like to know. If you are British, do they make you want to jump? Do Britons think to themselves when they put one on in the morning, *Now not only shall I be warm all day, no small consideration in a nation where central heating still cannot be assumed, but if I should be required to do some jumping I shall be suitably attired*?

And so it went on. I proceeded through the streets under a meteor shower of interrogations. Why do they call milk trucks *milk floats*? They don't float at all. Why do we *foot* a bill rather than, say, head it? Why do we say that our nose is *running*? (Mine slides.) Who ate the first oyster, and how on earth did anyone ever figure out that ambergris would make an excellent fixative for perfumes?

When this happens, I know from years of experience, it takes a special distraction to shock the mind from this solitary torment, and fortunately Thurso had one. On a side street, I happened on an extraordinary little establishment called the Fountain Restaurant, which offered three complete but different menus—a Chinese menu, an Indian menu, and a "European" menu. Thurso evidently couldn't maintain three separate restaurants, so it had one restaurant offering three kinds of cuisine. Immediately taken with this concept, I went in and was shown to a table by a pretty young lady who left me with a menu that ran to many pages. It was apparent from the title page that all three kinds of meals were cooked by a single Scottish chef, so I pored through the entries hoping to find "sweet and sour oatcakes" or "haggis vindaloo," but the dishes were strictly conventional. I opted for Chinese, then sat back and enjoyed a state of blissful mindlessness.

When it came, the food tasted, I have to say, like a Chinese meal cooked by a Scottish chef—which is not to say that it wasn't good. It was just curiously unlike any other Chinese meal I had ever had. The more I ate it, the more I liked it. At least it was different, and that, by this stage of the trip, was all I craved.

When I emerged, I felt much better. Lacking anything better to do, I strolled back down to the vicinity of the fish warehouse to take the evening air. As I stood there in the darkness, listening to the pounding surf and gazing contentedly at the great starry dome of sky above me, I thought, *Why when we are happy do we say that we are head over heels, when in fact our head normally is over our heels?* and I knew then that it was time for bed.

In the morning, I was roused early by my alarm clock and rose reluctantly, for I was having my favorite dream—the one where I own a large, remote island, not unlike those off this section of Scottish coast, to which I invite carefully selected people (like the person who invented those strings of Christmas tree lights that go out when one bulb blows, the person in charge of escalator maintenance at Heathrow Airport, nearly anyone who has ever written a user's manual for a personal computer), let them loose with a *very* small amount of survival rations, and then go out with baying dogs and mercilessly hunt them down—but then I remembered that I had a big, exciting day in front of me. I was going to John o'Groats.

I had been hearing about John o'Groats for years, but I had not the faintest idea of what it would be like. It seemed exotic beyond words and I ached to see it. So I breakfasted in a spirit of keenness at the Pentland Hotel, the only person in the dining room, and then repaired at the stroke of nine to William Dunnet's, the local Ford dealer's, where I had arranged by phone some days earlier to hire a car for the day, since there was no other way to get to John o'Groats at this time of year.

It took the man in the showroom a moment to recall the arrangement. "Ah, you're the chap from down south," he said, remembering, which threw me a little. It isn't often you hear Yorkshire referred to as down south.

"Isn't every place down south from here?" I asked.

"Yes. Why, yes, I suppose it is," he said as if I had stumbled on a rare profundity.

He was a friendly fellow—everyone in Thurso is friendly—and while he scratched away at the voluminous paperwork that would put me in charge of one of his vehicles, we chatted amiably about life in this remote outpost of civilization. He told me it took sixteen hours to drive to London, not that anyone much ever did. For most people, Inverness, four hours to the south by car, was the southern limit of the known world.

It seemed like months since I had had a conversation, and I babbled away at him with questions. What did people in Thurso do for a living? How did the castle come to be derelict? Where did they go if they wanted to buy a sofa, see a movie, have a Chinese meal not cooked by a Scotsman, or otherwise experience something beyond the modest range of pleasures available locally?

Thus I learned that the local economy was underpinned by the Dounreay nuclear reactor down the road, that the castle had once been a thing of well-maintained beauty but had been allowed to fall into decrepitude by an eccentric owner, that Inverness was the seat of all forms of excitement. I must have betrayed a flutter of astonishment at this because he smiled and said dryly, "Well, it has a Marks and Spencer's."

Then he took me outside, sat me in the driver's seat of a Ford Thesaurus (or something; I'm not very good at car names), gave me a quick rundown on all the many movable stalks and dashboard buttons, and then stood by with a kind of nervous frozen smile while I activated controls that made the seatback jettison away from me, the trunk pop open, and the windshield wipers go into monsoon mode. And then, with a worrisome grinding of gears and several jerky movements, I blazed a trail from the car lot by a novel and lavishly bumpy route and took to the road.

Moments later, for such is Thurso's diminutive size, I was out on the open highway and cruising with a light heart toward John o'Groats. It was an arrestingly empty landscape, with nothing much but fields of billowy winter-bleached grass running down to a choppy sea and the hazy lumps of the Orkney Islands beyond, but the feeling of spaciousness was exhilarating and for the first time in years I felt comparatively safe behind a wheel. There was absolutely nothing to crash into.

You really are on the edge of a great deal of emptiness when you reach the far north of Scotland. Only twenty-seven thousand people live in the whole of Caithness, an area considerably larger than most English counties. More than half of that population is accounted for by just two towns, Thurso and Wick, and none of it by John o'Groats, since John o'Groats isn't a community at all but just a place to stop and buy postcards and ice cream.

It is named for Jan de Groot, a Dutchman who ran a ferry service from there to somewhere else (Amsterdam if he had any sense) in the fifteenth century. He charged fourpence a trip apparently, and they will tell you in these parts that that sum became known ever after as a groat, but alas it is a pathetic fiction. It is more probable that Groot was named Groat after the money rather than it for he. But anyway who gives a shit?

Today John o'Groats consists of a capacious parking lot, a little harbor, a lonely white hotel, a couple of ice cream kiosks, and three or four shops selling postcards, sweaters, and videos by a singer named Tommy Scott. I thought there was supposed to be a famous finger-sign telling you how far it is to Sydney and Los Angeles, but I couldn't find it; perhaps they take it in out of season so that people like me don't carry it off as a souvenir. Only one of the shops was open. I went in and was surprised to find that there were three middle-aged ladies working there, which seemed a bit excessive as I was obviously the only tourist for four hundred miles. The ladies were exceedingly cheerful and chipper and greeted me warmly with those wonderful Highland accents—so clinically precise and yet so dulcet. I unfolded some sweaters so that they would have something to do after I left, watched open-mouthed a demo video for Tommy Scott singing perky Scottish tunes on various blowy headlands, bought some postcards, chatted with the ladies about the weather, and lingered for an awkwardly long period after it was clear that the conversation was over. Then I stepped back out into the gusty parking lot and realized that I had about exhausted the possibilities presented by John o'Groats.

I wandered around above the harbor; peered with hooded hands into the windows of the little museum, which was closed till spring; looked appreciatively at the view across the Pentland Firth to Stroma and the Old Man of Hoy; and then wandered back to the car. John o'Groats exists in the popular consciousness as the northernmost point of the British mainland, but in fact it isn't. That distinction belongs to a spot called Dunnet Head, five or six miles away down a nearby single-lane road, so I went there now. Dunnet Head offers even less to the world in the way of diversions than John o'Groats, but it has a handsome unmanned lighthouse and sensational sea views, and a nice sense of being a long way from anywhere.

I stood on the gusty eminence gazing at the view for a long time, waiting for some profundity to steal over me, since this was the end of the line, as far as I was going. Part of me longed to catch a ferry to the outward islands, to follow the scattered outcrops of stone all the way up to distant Shetland, but I was out of time and anyway there didn't seem a great deal of need. Whatever its bleak and airy charms, Shetland would still be just another piece of Britain, with the same shops, the same television programs, the same people in the same Marks & Spencer cardigans. I didn't find this depressing at all—rather the contrary—but I didn't feel any pressing need to see it just now. It would still be there next time.

I had one more port of call in my rented Ford. Six or seven miles south of Thurso lies the village of Halkirk, now forgotten but famous during World War II as a deeply, *deeply* unpopular posting for British soldiers on account of its remoteness and the reputed unfriendliness of the locals. The soldiers sang a charming little refrain that went:

> This fucking town's a fucking cuss;
> No fucking trams, no fucking bus;

> Nobody cares for fucking us
> In fucking Halkirk.
>
> No fucking sport, no fucking games,
> No fucking fun. The fucking dames
> Won't even give their fucking names
> In fucking Halkirk.

and carried on in a similarly affectionate spirit for another ten stanzas. (In answer to the obvious question, I'd looked earlier and no, it wasn't one of Tommy Scott's standards.) So I went to Halkirk now, along the lonely B874. Well, there was nothing much to Halkirk—just a couple of streets on a road to nowhere, with a butcher's, a builder's merchant, two pubs, a little grocery, and a village hall with a war memorial. There was no sign that Halkirk had ever been more than a dreary little interruption to the general emptiness around it, but the memorial contained the names of sixty-three dead from World War I (nine of them named Sinclair and five named Sutherland) and eighteen from World War II.

You could see for miles across grassy plains from the edges of the village, but there was no sign anywhere of tumbledown army barracks. In fact, there was no sign that there had ever been anything in this district but endless grassy plains. I went into the grocery in investigative mood. It was the strangest grocery—a large shedlike room, barely lit and nearly empty except for a couple of racks of metal shelves near the door. These, too, were nearly empty but for a few scattered packets of porridge oats, detergent, and other odds and ends. There was a man on the till and an old guy ahead of me making some small purchase, so I asked them about the army camp.

"Oh, aye," said the proprietor. "Big POW camp. We had fourteen thousand Germans here at the end of the war. There's a book here all about it." To my small astonishment, given the meagerness of the other stocks, he had a stack of picture books by the till called

Caithness in the War or something like that, and he handed me one to examine. It was full of the usual pictures of bombed-out houses and pubs with people standing around scratching their heads in consternation or looking at the camera with those idiot grins that people in disaster pictures always wear, as if they're thinking, *Well, at least we'll be in* Picture Post. I didn't find any pictures of soldiers looking bored in Halkirk, and there wasn't any mention of the village in the index. The book was ambitiously priced at £15.95.

"Lovely book," said the proprietor encouragingly. "Good value."

"We had fourteen thousand Germans here during the war," said the old boy in a deaf bellow.

I couldn't think of a tactful way of asking about Halkirk's dire reputation. "It must have been pretty lonely for the British soldiers, I bet," I suggested speculatively.

"Oh, no, I don't think so," disagreed the man. "There's Thurso just down the road, you see, and Wick if you fancy a change. There was dancing back then," he added a trifle ambiguously, then nodded at the book in my hands. "Good value, that."

"Is there anything left of the old base?"

"Well, the buildings are gone, of course, but if you go out the back way"—he gestured in the appropriate direction—"you can still see the foundations." He was silent for a moment and then he said, "So will you be having the book?"

"Oh—well, I might come back for it," I lied and handed it back.

"It's good value," said the man.

"Fourteen thousand Germans there was," called the older man as I left.

I had another look around the surrounding countryside on foot, and then drove around for a bit in the car, but I couldn't find any sign of a prison camp, and gradually it dawned on me that it hardly mattered, so in the end I drove back to Thurso and returned the car to the Ford dealer, to the frank surprise of the friendly fellow since it was only a little after two in the afternoon.

"Are you sure there isn't anywhere else you want to go?" he said. "It seems a shame when you've hired the car for the day."

"Where else could I go?" I asked.

He thought for a minute. "Well, nowhere really." He looked a little embarrassed.

"It's all right," I said, "I've seen plenty," and I meant it in the broadest sense.

chapter
29

now here is why I will always stay at the Pentland Hotel when I am in Thurso. The night before I left I asked the kindly lady at the checkout desk for a wakeup call at 5 A.M., as I had to catch an early train south. And she said to me—perhaps you should sit down if you are not sitting already—she said, "Would you like a cooked breakfast?"

I thought she must be a bit dim, frankly, so I said, "I'm sorry, I meant five A.M. I'll be leaving at half-past five, you see. Half-past five A.M. In the morning."

"Yes, dear. Would you like a cooked breakfast?"

"At five A.M.?"

"It's included in the room rate."

And damn me if this wonderful little establishment didn't fix me up with a handsome plate of fried food and a pot of hot coffee at 5:15 the following predawn. And so I left the hotel a happy and fractionally fatter man, and waddled up the road in darkness to the station and there met my second surprise of the morning. The place was packed with women, all standing around on the platform in festive spirits, filling the chill, dark air with clouds of breath and happy Highland chatter, and waiting patiently for the guard to finish his fag and open the train doors.

I asked a lady what was up and she told me they were all off to Inverness to do their shopping. It was like this every Saturday. They would ride for the best part of four hours, stock up on Marks & Spencer knickers and plastic vomit and whatever else Inverness had that Thurso hadn't, which was quite a lot, then catch the 6 P.M. train home, arriving back in time for bed.

And so we rode through the misty early morning, a great crowd of us, crammed snugly together on a two-carriage train, in happy, expectant mood. At Inverness the train terminated and we all piled off, the ladies to do their shopping, I to catch the 10:35 to Glasgow. As I watched them go, I found to my small surprise that I rather envied them. It seemed an extraordinary business, the idea of rising before dawn to do a little shopping in a place like Inverness and then not getting home till after ten, but on the other hand I don't think I had ever seen such a happy band of shoppers.

The little train to Glasgow was nearly empty and the countryside lushly scenic. We went through a succession of pretty places—Aviemore, Pitlochry, Perth, and Gleneagles, home of the famous golf course and with a trim little station, now sadly boarded. And then at last, some eight hours after rising from my bed that morning, we were in Glasgow. It seemed odd after so many long hours of traveling to step from Queen Street Station and find myself still in Scotland.

At least it wasn't a shock to the system. I remember when I first came to Glasgow in 1973 stepping from this very station and being profoundly stunned at how suffocatingly dark and soot-blackened the city was. I had never seen a place so choked and grubby. Everything in it seemed black and cheerless. Even the local accent seemed born of clinkers and grit. St. Mungo's Cathedral was so dark that even from across the road it looked like a two-dimensional cutout. And there were no tourists—none at all. My *Let's Go* guide to Europe didn't even mention it.

In the subsequent years Glasgow has gone through a glittering and celebrated transformation. Scores of old buildings in the city center have been sand-blasted and lovingly buffed, so that their granite surfaces gleam anew, and dozens more were vigorously erected in the heady boom years of the 1980s—more than £1 billion of new offices in the previous decade alone. The city acquired one of the finest museums in the world in the Burrell Collection and one of the most intelligent pieces of urban renewal in the Princes Square shopping center—a compact but light and airy inner-city mall squeezed into what was once a derelict courtyard. Suddenly the world began cautiously to come to Glasgow and thereupon discovered to its delight that this was a city densely endowed with splendid museums, lively pubs, world-class orchestras, and no fewer than seventy parks, more than any other city of its size in Europe. In 1990, Glasgow was named European City of Culture, and no one laughed. Never before had a city's reputation undergone a more dramatic and sudden transformation—and none, as far as I am concerned, deserves it more.

Among the city's many treasures, none shines brighter, in my view, than the incomparable Burrell Collection, and after checking into my hotel, I hastened there now by taxi, for it is a long way out.

"D'ye nae a lang roon?" said the driver as we sped along a motorway toward Pollok Park.

"I'm sorry," I said for I don't speak Glaswegian.

"D'ye dack ma fanny?"

I hate it when this happens—when a person from Glasgow speaks to me. "I'm so sorry," I said and floundered for an excuse. "My ears are very bad."

"Aye, ye nae hae doon a lang roon," he said, which I gathered meant, "I'm going to take you a very long way around and look at you frequently in the mirror with these menacing eyes so that you'll begin to wonder if perhaps I'm taking you to a disused wharf where I will beat you up and take your money," but he said nothing further and delivered me at the Burrell without incident.

The Burrell Collection is named for Sir William Burrell, a local shipping magnate who in 1944 left the city his art collection on the understanding that it be placed in a country setting within the city boundaries. He was worried—not unreasonably—about air pollution damaging his art works. Unable to decide what to do with this sumptuous windfall, the city council did, astonishingly, nothing. For the next thirty-nine years, some truly exceptional works of art lay crated away in warehouses, all but forgotten. Finally in the late 1970s, after nearly four decades of dithering, the city engaged a gifted architect named Barry Gasson, who designed a trim and restrained building noted for its airy rooms set against a woodland backdrop, and for the ingenious way architectural features from Burrell's collection—medieval doorways and lintels and the like—were incorporated into the fabric of the building. It opened in 1983 to widespread acclaim.

Burrell was not an especially rich man, but goodness me, he could select. The gallery contains only eight thousand items but they come from all over—from Mesopotamia, Egypt, Greece, and Rome—and nearly every one of them (with the exception of some glazed porcelain figurines of flower girls, which he must have picked up during a fever) is stunning. I spent a long, happy afternoon wandering through the many rooms, pretending, as I sometimes do in these circumstances, that I had been invited to take any one object home with me as a gift from the Scottish people in recognition of my fineness as a person. In the end, after much agonizing, I settled on a head of Persephone from fifth-century-B.C. Sicily, which was not only as stunningly flawless as if it had been made yesterday, but would have looked just perfect on top of the TV. And thus late in the afternoon, I emerged from the Burrell and into the leafy agreeability of Pollok Park in a happy frame of mind.

It was a mild day, so I decided to walk back to town even though I had no map and only the vaguest idea of where the distant center of Glasgow lay. I don't know if Glasgow is truly a wonderful city for walking or whether I have just been lucky there, but I have never wandered through it without encountering some memorable surprise—the green allure of Kelvingrove Park, the Botanic Gardens, the fabulous Necropolis cemetery with its endless avenues of ornate tombs—and so it was now. I set off hopefully down a broad thoroughfare called St. Andrew's Drive and found myself adrift in a handsome district of houses of substance and privilege built around a beguiling park with a little lake. At length I passed the Scotland Street Public School, a wonderful building with distinctive stairwells that I presumed was one of Charles Rennie Mackintosh's, and soon after found myself in a seamier but no less interesting district, which I eventually concluded must be the once-notorious Gorbals. And then I got lost.

I could see the River Clyde from time to time, but I couldn't figure out how to get to it or, more crucially, over it. I wandered along a series of back lanes and soon found myself in one of those dead districts that consist of windowless warehouses and garage doors that say NO PARKING—GARAGE IN CONSTANT USE. I took a series of turns that seemed to lead ever farther away from society before finally bumbling into a short street that had a pub on the corner. Fancying a drink and a sit-down, I wandered inside. It was a dark place, and battered, and there were only two other customers, a pair of men sitting side by side at the bar drinking in silence. There was no one behind the bar. I took a stance at the far end of the counter and waited for a bit, but no one came. I drummed my fingers on the counter and puffed my cheeks and made assorted puckery shapes with my lips the way you do when you are waiting. I cleaned my nails with a thumbnail and puffed my cheeks some more, but still no one came. Eventually I noticed one of the men at the bar eyeing me.

"Hae ya nae hook ma dooky?" he said.

"I'm sorry?" I replied.

"He'll nay be doon a mooning." He hoicked his head in the direction of a back room.

"Oh, ah," I said and nodded sagely, as if that explained it.

I noticed that they were both still looking at me.

"D'ye hae a hoo and a poo?" said the first man to me.

"I'm sorry?" I said.

"D'ye hae a hoo and a poo?" he repeated. It appeared that he was a trifle intoxicated.

I gave a small, apologetic smile and explained that I came from the English-speaking world.

"D'ye nae hae in May?" the man went on. "If ye dinna dock ma donny."

"Doon in Troon they croon in June," said his mate, then added, "Wi' a spoon."

"Oh, ah." I nodded thoughtfully again, pushing my lower lip out slightly, as if it were all very nearly clear to me now. Just then, to my small relief, the barman appeared, looking unhappy and wiping his hands on a tea towel.

"Fuckin' muckle fucket in the fuckin' muckle," he said to the two men, and then to me in a weary voice, "Ah hae the noo." I couldn't tell if it was a question or a statement.

"A pint of Tennent's, please," I said hopefully.

He made an impatient noise, as if I were avoiding his question. "Hae ya nae hook ma dooky?"

"I'm sorry?"

"Ah hae the noo," said the first customer, who apparently saw himself as my interpreter.

I stood for some moments with my mouth open, trying to imagine what they were saying to me, wondering what mad impulse had bidden me to enter a pub in a district like this, and said in a quiet voice, "Just a pint of Tennent's, I think."

The barman sighed heavily and got me a pint. A minute later, I realized that what they were saying to me was that this was the worst pub in the world in which to order lager, since all I would get was a glass of warm soapsuds, dispensed from a gasping, reluctant tap, and that really I should flee with my life while I could. I drank two sips of this interesting concoction, and, making as if I were going to the Gents, slipped out a side door.

And so I returned to the twilit streets along the south bank of the Clyde and tried to find my way back to the known world. It's nearly impossible to imagine what the Gorbals must have been like before they started tarting it up and inviting daring yuppies to move into stylish new blocks of flats around its fringes. After the war, Glasgow did the most extraordinary thing. It built vast estates of shiny tower blocks out in the countryside and decanted tens of thousands of people from inner-city slums like the Gorbals into them, but it forgot to provide any infrastructure. Forty thousand people were moved to the Easterhouse estate alone, and when they got there they found smart new flats with indoor plumbing but no cinemas, no shops, no banks, no pubs, no schools, no jobs, no health centers, no doctors. So every time they wanted anything, like a drink or work or medical attention, they had to climb aboard a bus and ride for miles back into the city. In consequence of this and other considerations like lifts that were forever breaking down (and why, incidentally, does Britain alone among nations have so much difficulty with moving conveyances like escalators and lifts? I think some heads should roll, frankly), they grew peevish and turned them into new slums. The result is that Glasgow has some of the worst housing problems in the developed world. Glasgow Council is the largest landlord in Europe. Its 160,000 houses and flats represent half the city's total housing stock. By its own estimates the council needs to spend £3 billion to bring the housing up to standard. That doesn't include provisions for new housing, but simply making existing housing habitable. At the moment its entire housing budget is about £100 million a year.

At length, I found my way over the river and back into the gleaming center. I had a look at George Square, which is to my mind the

handsomest in Britain with its ornate city hall and stolid Victorian
buildings, and then trudged uphill to Sauchiehall Street, where I
remembered my favorite Glasgow joke (also my only Glasgow joke).
It's not a very good one, but I like it. A policeman collars a thief at
the corner of Sauchiehall and Dalhousie, then drags him by the hair
for a hundred yards to Rose Street to book him.

"Oi, why'd ye do *tha'*?" asks the aggrieved culprit, rubbing his
head.

"Because I can spell Rose Street, ye thieving cunt," says the policeman.

That's the thing about Glasgow. It has all this newfound prosperity and polish, but right at the very edge of things there is always
this sense of grit and menace, which I find oddly exhilarating. You
can wander through the streets on a weekend night, as I did now,
and never know when you turn a corner whether you are going to
bump into a group of tony revelers in dinner jackets or a passel of
idle young yobbos who might decide to fall upon you and carve their
initials in your forehead for purposes of passing amusement. Gives
the place a certain tang.

chapter
30

I spent another day in Glasgow, not so much because I wanted
to be there, but because it was a Sunday and I couldn't get a train
home beyond Carlisle. (The Settle-to-Carlisle service doesn't run
on Sundays in winter because there is no demand for its services.
That there is no demand for its services because it doesn't run appears not to have occurred to British Rail.) So I wandered far and
wide through the wintry streets, and had a respectful look around
the museums, Botanic Gardens, and Necropolis, but really all I
wanted to do was go home.

And so the following morning, in a state of giddy excitement, I
boarded the 8:10 from Glasgow Central to Carlisle and there, after
a refreshing cup of coffee in the station buffet, caught the 11:40
train to Settle.

The Settle-to-Carlisle line is perhaps the most celebrated obscure
line in the world. British Rail has been wanting to close it down for
years on the grounds that it doesn't pay its way. This preposterous
idea, that things must pay their way or be dispensed with, is perhaps
the most intractable legacy of the Thatcher years, so much so that
it has become received wisdom even among many liberals. But when

you think about it for even a nanosecond, it is perfectly obvious that most worthwhile things don't begin to pay for themselves. If you followed this absurd logic any distance at all, you would have to get rid of traffic lights, schools, drains, national parks, museums, universities, old people, and much else besides. So why on earth should something as useful as a railway line, which is generally much more agreeable than old people, and certainly less inclined to bitch and twitter, have to be economically viable to ensure its continued existence? This is a line of thinking that must be abandoned at once.

Having said that, it can't be denied that the Settle-to-Carlisle line has always been something of a monumental folly. In 1870, when James Allport, general manager of the Midland Railway, took it into his head to build a main line through northern England, there already existed an east coast line and a west coast line, so he decided to drive one up the middle, even though it went from nowhere much to nowhere much by way of nothing at all. The whole thing cost £3.5 million, which doesn't sound like much now, but translates to some fantastic sum like £487 trillion billion in current pounds sterling. Anyway, it was enough to convince everyone who knew anything about railways that Allport was totally off his head, as in fact he was.

Because the line went through an insanely bleak and forbidding stretch of the Pennine Hills, Allport's engineers had to come up with all kinds of costly contrivances to make it feasible, including twenty viaducts and fourteen tunnels. This wasn't some eccentric, pootling narrow-gauge line, you understand; this was the nineteenth century's bullet train, something that would allow passengers to fly across the Yorkshire Dales—if, that is, anyone had wanted to, and hardly anyone did.

So from the very beginning it lost money. But who cares? It is a wonderful line, gorgeous in every respect and a wonder of nineteenth-century railway engineering, and I intended to enjoy every minute of my one-hour-and-forty-minute, 71¾-mile journey. Even when you live near Settle, it isn't often you find a reason to use the line, so I sat with my face close to the glass and waited eagerly for the famous landmarks—Blea Moor Tunnel, almost 2,300 yards long; Dent Station, the highest in the country; the glorious Ribblehead Viaduct, a quarter of a mile long, 104 feet high, and with twenty-four graceful arches—and in between I enjoyed the scenery, which is not just spectacular and unrivaled but speaks to me with a particular siren voice.

I suppose we all have a piece of landscape somewhere that we find captivating beyond words and mine is the Yorkshire Dales. There is something about those hills, the shape and heft of them, that just paralyzes me with admiration. I once remarked in my village pub that you had to spend the first twenty years of your life in a flat place like Iowa to truly appreciate the landscape of the Dales. (To which someone replied that in that case it was a shame I hadn't spent the first twenty years of my life in a broom cupboard, because then I would really enjoy it.) But I think there is something in that. I love the constant contrast between the high fells, with their long views and austere beauty, and the bucolic lushness of the valley floors, with their wandering brooks, trim villages, and scattered farms. To drive almost anywhere in the Dales is to make a constant transition between these two hypnotic zones.

Because historically there was little interconnection between the Dales—most of them are long winding dead ends between steep hills—they retain a snug air of self-containment, which I like very much. I remember when we first moved to our little valley, Malhamdale, a car overturned one morning in the road outside our gate with a frightful bang and a noise of scraping metal. The driver, it turned out, had clipped a grass bank and run up against a field wall, which had flipped the car onto its roof. I rushed out to find a neighboring farmer's wife hanging upside down by her seatbelt, bleeding gently from a scalp wound, and muttering dazed sentiments along the lines of having to get to the dentist and that this wouldn't do at all. While I was hopping around and making hyperventilating noises, two farm-

---

ers arrived in Land Rovers and unhurriedly climbed out. As if they had been practicing for this moment for years, they gently hauled the lady from the car and sat her down on a rock. Then they righted the crumpled car and maneuvered it out of the way. Then, while one of them took the lady off to his house to have a cup of tea and get her head seen to by his missus, the other scattered sawdust on an oil slick, directed traffic for a minute till the road was clear, then winked at me and climbed into his Land Rover and drove off. The whole thing was over in less than five minutes and never involved the police or ambulance services or even a doctor. An hour or so later another farmer came along with a tractor and hauled the car away, and it was as if it had never happened. It's another world, you see.

And they do things differently in the Dales. For one thing, people come right into your house. Sometimes they knock once and shout "Hullo!" before sticking their heads in, but often they don't even do that. It's an unusual experience to be standing at the kitchen sink talking to yourself and doing emphatic raised-leg farts and then turning around to find a fresh pile of mail lying on the kitchen table. And I can't tell you the number of times I've had to dart half-clad into the pantry at the sound of someone's approach and stood in breathless silence while they've shouted, "Hullo! Hullo! Anyone t'home?" For a couple of minutes you can hear them moving about in the kitchen, reading the messages on the fridge, and holding the mail to the light. Then they come over to the pantry door and in a quiet voice they say, "Just taking six eggs, Bill. All right?"

When we announced to friends and colleagues in London that we were moving to a farming village in Yorkshire, a surprising number betrayed astonishment and said, "Yorkshire? What, with Yorkshire people? How . . . interesting." Or words to that effect.

I've never understood why Yorkshire people have this terrible reputation for being meanspirited and uncharitable. I've always found them to be decent and open, and if you want to know your short-comings, you won't find more helpful people anywhere. It's true that they don't exactly smother you with affection, which takes a little getting used to if you hail from a more gregarious part of the world, like anywhere else. Where I come from in the American Midwest, if you move into a village or little town everybody comes to your house to welcome you like this is the happiest day in the history of the community—and everyone brings you a pie. You get apple pies and cherry pies and chocolate cream pies. There are people in the Mid-west who move house every six months just to get the pies.

In Yorkshire, that would never happen. But gradually, little by little, they find a little corner for you in their hearts, and begin to acknowledge you when they drive past with what I call the Malham-dale wave. This is an exciting day in the life of any new arrival. To make the Malhamdale wave, imagine you are holding a steering wheel. Now take the index finger of your right hand and very slowly extend it, as if you were having a small involuntary spasm. That's the Malhamdale wave. It doesn't look like much, but it speaks vol-umes, believe me, and I shall miss it very much.

I lost myself in a little reverie along these lines and then, with a start, I realized the train was pulling into Settle Station and my wife was waving to me from the platform. Suddenly my trip was over. I hastened from the train in a state of confusion, like someone wak-ened in the middle of the night by an emergency, and felt as if this was somehow not the right termination at all. This was all too abrupt.

We drove home over the tops, as the local argot has it, a six-mile journey of unutterable gorgeousness, up onto the blowy, treeless Wuthering Heights–like expanses around Kirkby Fell where you can see for miles, and then down into the serene, cupped majesty of Malhamdale, the little lost world that had been my home for seven years. Halfway down the descent, I had my wife stop the car by a

field gate. My favorite view in the world is there, and I got out to
have a look. You can see almost the whole of Malhamdale from there,
green and sheltered and snug beneath imposing hills, with its arrow-
straight drystone walls climbing up impossibly ambitious slopes, its
three clustered villages, its wonderful little two-room schoolhouse,
the old church (built in 1490, two years before Columbus sailed for
America, as I always remind our American visitors, who never fail to
be impressed), the roof of my local pub, and in the center of it all,
obscured by trees, our wonderful old stone house, which itself is far
older than my native land.

It looked so peaceful and wonderful that I could almost have
cried, and yet it was only a tiny part of this small, enchanted island.
Suddenly, in the space of a moment, I realized what it was that I
loved about Britain—which is to say, all of it. Every last bit of it,
good and bad—old churches, country lanes, people saying "Mustn't
grumble" and "I'm terribly sorry but," people apologizing to *me*
when I conk them with a careless elbow, milk in bottles, beans on
toast, haymaking in June, seaside piers, Ordnance Survey maps, tea
and crumpets, summer showers and foggy winter evenings—every
bit of it.

What a wondrous place this was—crazy as all get-out, of course,
but adorable to the tiniest degree. What other country, after all,
could possibly have come up with place names like Tooting Bec and
Farleigh Wallop, or a game like cricket? Who else would have a
constitutional form of government but no written constitution, call
private schools public schools, think it not the least bit odd to make
their judges wear little mops on their heads, seat the chief officer of
the House of Lords on something called the Woolsack, or take pride
in a military hero whose dying wish was to be kissed by a fellow
named Hardy? ("Please, Hardy, full on the lips, with just a bit of
tongue.") Who else could possibly have given us William Shakespeare, pork pies, Christopher Wren, Windsor Great Park, Salisbury
Cathedral, double-decker buses, and the chocolate digestive biscuit?

Wherever else would I find a view like this? Nowhere, of course.

All of this came to me in the space of a lingering moment. I've said it before and I'll say it again. I like it here. I like it more than I can tell you. And then I turned from the gate and got into the car and knew without doubt that I would be back.

Glossary

bank holiday Official public holiday, originally so called because banks closed on such days. There are eight bank holidays in England and Wales (Scotland's vary slightly): New Year's Day, Good Friday, Easter Monday, the first and last Mondays of May, the last Monday in August, Christmas, and Boxing Day.

Belisha beacon Warning light, consisting of a black-and-white-striped pole surmounted by a yellow globe, erected at pedestrian crossings. Named for Leslie Hore-Belisha, who introduced it while Minister of Transport in the 1930s. Pronounced "buh-*lee*-sha." *See also* zebra crossing.

berk Broad term of derogation, roughly equivalent to the American *jerk* or *moron*. A driver who pulls into your path from a side road or gas station is a berk. It's from Cockney rhyming slang (*which see*): Berkshire hunt = cunt.

biscuit Cookie.

B-road Back highway. Main highways, except motorways (*see* motorway), are called *A-roads*.

builder's merchant Business selling building materials.

bum Buttocks.

bus/coach For reasons that are largely unfathomable, the British make a careful distinction between large passenger vehicles used primarily for local journeys and large passenger vehicles used for longer or more specialized trips, such as days out to the seaside. The former are called *buses* and the latter *coaches*, even though the vehicles used may be identical.

butty Northern English term for a sandwich.

Christmas cracker Cylindrical Christmas novelty, festively decorated, which when yanked is supposed to make a small banging noise like a firecracker, but generally doesn't. Each Christmas cracker traditionally contains a riddle, a paper party hat, and a small plastic toy or trinket, which will eventually find its way to a vulnerable part of the family washing machine.

clot Useful variant term for berk (*which see*). The British have a curious but commendable wealth of terms for irritating people. *See also* prat.

Cockney rhyming slang Age-old practice of describing objects or conditions by a rhyming alternative. Thus *apples and pears = stairs*, and *raspberry tart = fart* (which is why, incidentally, when you blow a raspberry you make a farting noise). Often the final element of the rhyming portion is dropped, so that *titfer* (short for *tit-for-tat*) = *hat*, *plates* (short for *plates of meat*) = *feet*, and *bread* (short for *bread and honey*) = *money*.

contraflow blackspot A contraflow is a stretch of highway in which one or more of the outside lanes is temporarily given over to traffic moving in the "wrong" direction, usually to facilitate repairs. If, for example, a motorway is to be rebuilt, the southbound lanes may be closed for some months and the traffic diverted onto what would normally be northbound lanes. This nearly always causes extensive delays. When these delays become persistent or notorious you have a contraflow blackspot.

cooker Stove.

council house House built by a local government council and let at a subsidized rent. Usually built in large clusters, called *council estates*.

Denbighshire Former Welsh county; disappeared in the 1974 boundary reorganization, which created several new counties (Avon, Cleveland, Humberside) and obliterated several others (Rutland, Perthshire).

dirty weekend Weekend, generally away from home, involving illicit or otherwise notable sex.

doner kebab Sandwich-type snack, concocted from a sort of pita bread and a processed meat distantly related to lamb, which becomes mysteriously appealing after seven or eight pints of beer.

dual carriageway Divided highway with two lanes in each direction.

en suite In the context of guesthouses, a room with a private bath.

fag Cigarette, of course.

Fields, Gracie (1898–1979), comedian and singer famous for her attitude of indefatigability in the face of economic depression and war. Often called "Our Gracie."

flubba-wubba Overweight person, particularly one's father; coinage of Sam Bryson, aged five.

Formby, George (1905–61), ukulele-playing comedian noted for his broad Lancashire accent.

garage Gas station as well as a place to park a car. Rhymes with *carriage*.

greengrocer Shop selling fruit and vegetables.

high tea Light evening meal; now seldom heard.

ices Ice cream. An ice cream cone is a *cornet*.

jam roly-poly Dessert made with pastry and jam.

jumper Sweater.

knickers Panties.

kursaal In Germany, a salon at a health resort offering massages, mineral baths, and other such therapies.

Ladybird books   Line of children's books. A ladybird in Britain, in-cidentally, is the insect that most Americans call a ladybug.

lay-by   Parking area beside a highway, often used as a depository for unwanted mattresses and other household rubbish.

lemonade   Kind of warm, fizzy drink that has never seen a lemon in its life and that, with the best will in the world, only a Briton could find refreshing.

loo   Toilet, bathroom. Origin obscure.

lorry   Truck. *The Oxford English Dictionary* suggests (without trou-bling itself over anything as tiresome as actual evidence) that it might be named for an inventor named Laurie. A big lorry is a *juggernaut*.

L-plate   Small rectangular metal plate bearing a red L that must by law be hung on the back of a car when a learner is at the wheel.

Marks & Spencer   Department store chain and a central institution of British life. Often referred to just as *Marks* and sometimes, jocularly, as *Marks and Sparks*.

milk float   Electrically powered milk truck. Milk is still delivered to homes in Britain, in pint bottles.

Morecambe and Wise   Eric Morecambe (1926–84) and Ernie Wise (1925–   ), famous, universally adored comedy duo.

Morris Minor   Much loved British car, last produced in the 1970s. *See jacket for illustration*.

motorway   Express highway. Named M1, M25, M62, and so on.

naff   Slang term denoting items or matters of dubious stylishness; of uncertain origin.

Number Six   Once-popular brand of cigarette, manufactured by Play-er's.

pasty   Pastry filled with substance curiously similar in appearance and texture to cat food, but quite tasty even so. There are two kinds, Cornish and flaky. Rhymes with *rhinoplasty* and possibly some shorter words that don't occur to me at the moment.

pavement   Sidewalk.

Perthshire Former Scottish county. *See* Denbighshire.

pint In pub parlance, the standard serving of a glass of beer. A British pint is twenty ounces, as compared with an American pint of sixteen ounces.

Poppy Day Popular name for Remembrance Sunday (the Sunday nearest to November 11), so called because nearly everyone wears an artificial poppy on the lapel to commemorate the fallen of the two world wars.

pork pie Small pie consisting of processed meat in a pastry casing; very tasty so long as it is not looked at.

Portakabin Type of portable prefabricated hut or shed commonly used as an office on construction sites and the like.

Porton Down Secretive government research center in Wiltshire.

prat Fool or idiot. The word was originally equivalent to *arse* and survives in American English in *pratfall*.

public school Private school. What Americans would call public schools are known in Britain as state schools.

pudding Any kind of dessert (in Britain, ice cream is pudding) or, confusingly, any of several kinds of meat pie, such as steak and kidney pudding.

railway cutting Embankment where a rail line has been cut through a hillside or other obstacle.

relief road Highway designed to divert traffic from congested areas, such as town centers, by bypassing them. When a relief road encircles a town it is called a *ring road*.

scone Kind of sweet biscuit; generally pronounced "skon."

Scotch egg Hard-boiled egg inside a bread-crumb casing. Not as bad as it sounds.

seaside rock Hyper-sweet candy stick, generally made with the name of a seaside resort running laterally through it.

semidetached house House that shares a common wall with one neighbor; a duplex. Most British houses are semis. *See also* terraced house.

serviette Napkin.

shirt-lifter Homosexual male.

short back and sides Style of haircut involving close cropping.

sixth form Final stage of British high school.

Slough Town in Berkshire; rhymes with *cow*.

streaky bacon Bacon with a lot of fat in it.

television There are four networks in Britain, BBC1, BBC2, ITV, and Channel 4, plus BSkyB, a satellite network. The BBC as an institution is often referred to as "the Beeb."

terraced house Row house.

Tesco's Prominent supermarket chain.

Towcester Town in Northamptonshire; pronounced "toaster."

transport café Eating establishment that caters especially to lorry drivers; a truck stop. Often pronounced "caff."

trunk call Long-distance call.

twee Cute, precious—often unbearably so.

VAT Value Added Tax, a sales tax (currently 17.5 percent in Britain) imposed on nearly everything.

yob/yobbo Person of thuggish tendencies. *Yob* is *boy* spelled backward, and is a lone relic of a nineteenth-century fashion for creating slang terms from backward-spelled words.

zebra crossing Pedestrian crossing, so named for the black and white stripes painted on the road surface. Pronounced like "Deborah." When a pedestrian crossing incorporates traffic lights that respond to a pedestrian's pushing a button, it is called a *pelican crossing*—a mild pun created from a shortening of *"pe*destrian-*li*ght-*con*trolled crossing."

Bill Bryson's many books include, most recently, *In a Sunburned Country*, as well as *I'm a Stranger Here Myself*, *A Walk in the Woods*, *The Lost Continent*, *Notes from a Small Island*, *Neither Here Nor There*, *Made in America*, and *The Mother Tongue*. He edited *The Best American Travel Writing 2000*. Born in Des Moines, Iowa, in 1951, he lived in England for almost two decades. He now lives in Hanover, New Hampshire, with his wife and four children.

▦ Perennial

Books by Bill Bryson:

THE LOST CONTINENT
Travels in Small Town America
ISBN 0-06-092008-4 (paperback)

Following an urge to rediscover his youth, Bill Bryson left his native Des Moines, Iowa to journey across 38 states in search for the perfect American small town. With razor wit and a kind heart, Bryson serves up a colorful tale of boredom, kitsch, and 'beauty when you least expect it' that takes us straight into the heart and soul of America.

NEITHER HERE NOR THERE
Travels in Europe
ISBN 0-380-71380-2 (paperback)

Bryson retraces his backpacking journey across Europe, twenty years after his initial voyage—accompanied by his inimitable Pal Katz, of *Walk In The Woods* fame. The result is *Neither Here Nor There*, an affectionate and riotously funny pilgrimage from the frozen wastes of Scandinavia to the chaotic tumult of Istanbul, with stops along the way in Europe's most diverting and historic locales.

NOTES FROM A SMALL ISLAND
ISBN 0-380-72750-1 (paperback)

After spending two-decades on British soil, Bill Bryson set out on a grand farewell tour of the island. Veering from the ludicrous to the endearing and back again, he takes us on a delightfully irreverent and hilarious jaunt around the unparalleled floating nation. The result is an uproarious social commentary that conveys the true glory of Britain.

MADE IN AMERICA
An Informal History of the English Language in the United States
ISBN 0-380-71381-0 (paperback)

Bill Bryson celebrates the magnificent offspring of the American language in a book that reveals once and for all how a dusty western hamlet with neither woods nor holly came to be known as Hollywood...and exactly why Mr. Yankee Doodle call his befeathered cap "Macaroni."

MOTHER TONGUE
English & How It Got That Way
ISBN 0-380-71543-0 (paperback)

With dazzling wit and astonishing insight, Bryson explores the remarkable history, eccentricities, resilience and sheer fun of the English language. From the first descent of the larynx into the throat to the fine lost art of swearing, he tells the fascinating, often uproarious story of an inadequate, second-rate tongue of peasants that developed into one of the world's largest growth industries.

Available wherever books are sold, or call 1-800-331-3761 to order.